Whitehead and Continental Philosophy in the Twenty-First Century

Contemporary Whitehead Studies

Edited by Roland Faber, Claremont Lincoln University,
and Brian G. Henning, Gonzaga University

Contemporary Whitehead Studies, co-sponsored by the Whitehead Research Project, is an interdisciplinary book series that publishes manuscripts from scholars with contemporary and innovative approaches to Whitehead studies by giving special focus to projects that: explore the connections between Whitehead and contemporary Continental philosophy, especially sources, like Heidegger, or contemporary streams like poststructuralism; reconnect Whitehead to pragmatism, analytical philosophy and philosophy of language; explore creative East/West dialogues facilitated by Whitehead's work; explore the interconnections of the mathematician with the philosopher and the contemporary importance of these parts of Whitehead's work for the dialogue between sciences and humanities; reconnect Whitehead to the wider field of philosophy, the humanities, the sciences and academic research with Whitehead's pluralistic impulses in the context of a pluralistic world; address Whitehead's philosophy in the midst of contemporary problems facing humanity, such as climate change, war and peace, race, and the future development of civilization.

Titles in This Series

Whitehead and Continental Philosophy in the Twenty-First Century: Dislocations, edited by Jeremy D. Fackenthal

Beyond Whitehead: Recent Advances in Process Thought, edited by Jakub Dziadkowiec and Lukasz Lamza

Tragic Beauty in Whitehead and Japanese Aesthetics, by Steve Odin

Creaturely Cosmologies: Why Metaphysics Matters for Animal and Planetary Liberation, by Brianne Donaldson

Thinking with Whitehead and the American Pragmatists: Experience and Reality, edited by Brian G. Henning, William T. Myers, and Joseph D. John

The Divine Manifold, by Ronald Faber

Foundations of Relational Realism: A Topological Approach to Quantum Mechanics and the Philosophy of Nature, by Michael Epperson and Elias Zafiris

Butler on Whitehead: On the Occasion, edited by Roland Faber, Michael Halewood, and Deena Lin

Whitehead and Continental Philosophy in the Twenty-First Century

Dislocations

Edited by
Jeremy D. Fackenthal

LEXINGTON BOOKS
Lanham • Boulder • New York • London

Published by Lexington Books
An imprint of The Rowman & Littlefield Publishing Group, Inc.
4501 Forbes Boulevard, Suite 200, Lanham, Maryland 20706
www.rowman.com

6 Tinworth Street, London SE11 5AL, United Kingdom

Copyright © 2019 by The Rowman & Littlefield Publishing Group, Inc.

All rights reserved. No part of this book may be reproduced in any form or by any electronic or mechanical means, including information storage and retrieval systems, without written permission from the publisher, except by a reviewer who may quote passages in a review.

British Library Cataloguing in Publication Information Available

The hardback edition of this book was previously catalogued by the Library of Congress as follows:
Names: Fackenthal, Jeremy, editor.
Title: Whitehead and Continental philosophy in the twenty-first century : dislocations / edited by Jeremy D. Fackenthal.
Description: Lanham : Lexington Books, 2019. | Series: Contemporary Whitehead studies | Includes bibliographical references and index.
Identifiers: LCCN 2019005701 (print) | LCCN 2019007439 (ebook) | ISBN 9781498595117 (electronic) | ISBN 9781498595100 (cloth) | ISBN 9781498595124 (pbk.)
Subjects: LCSH: Continental philosophy. | Philosophy, Modern—21st century. | Whitehead, Alfred North, 1861–1947.
Classification: LCC B805 (ebook) | LCC B805 .W45 2019 (print) | DDC 190—dc23
LC record available at https://lccn.loc.gov/2019005701

Contents

Introduction ... 1
    Jeremy D. Fackenthal

Part I: Technological and Systematic Dislocations ... 9

1. Creativity and Adversity: Building an Ecological Civilization ... 11
William S. Hamrick

2. Interrogating the Quantified Self: The Technological Reinterpretation of Causal Efficacy ... 27
Bo Eberle

3. Can Whitehead Save the World?: Complex Systems and the Limits of Activism ... 41
J. R. Hustwit and Carl Dyke

Part II: Human/Nonhuman Dislocations ... 59

4. Process Philosophy and Neo-Materialism: Nomadic Subjectivity and Evanescing toward Sustainability ... 61
Jeremy D. Fackenthal

5. Welcoming Syrian Life: Recognitions of Immanent Vulnerability ... 77
Deena M. Lin

6. Conceptual Prehensions, Worlds of Experience: Whitehead and Uexküll on the Nonhuman Subject ... 99
Tano Posteraro

Part III: Time, the World, and Abstraction   **119**

7   Philosophy against Abstraction: On the Social Thought of Whitehead and Deleuze   121
Kris Klotz

8   The Charge of Resistance: The Influence of Whitehead on Deleuze's Concept of Power   137
Elijah Prewitt-Davis

9   Whitehead, Continental Philosophy, and the Bifurcation of Nature   159
Keith Robinson

Index   179

About the Editor   187

About the Contributors   189

Introduction

Jeremy D. Fackenthal

Readers of this book no doubt are quite aware that the problems facing the twenty-first century are numerous and complex. The effects of climate change, emboldened racism, growing nationalism, and economic and class division all reach and affect us in multiple ways. We might say that these are problems with an old face now manifesting in new dress. To be sure, racism, class divide, and nationalism in a variety of forms have been present in preceding periods, oftentimes in obviously memorable and horrifically remarkable forms. Yet despite this sad tradition of struggles, we experience each problem as new inasmuch as each new occurrence arises uniquely out of the welter of the past and must be addressed uniquely in its own setting. Moreover, these issues cannot be neatly divided but fold in on each other in increasingly novel and more overtly pernicious ways. Hunger and poverty, sadly, are not original to our time period but are problems that have been around as long as some humans have taken for themselves more than is necessary. Yet in the twenty-first century, hunger and poverty are compounded and increased by growing desertification in parts of Africa, by sea level rise in the South Pacific, and by increasing population size with decreasing means of sustainable food production in countless areas around the globe. Each problem traces a lineage back to previous generations and cultural epochs but now emerges with new force as a result of the multiple layers folded in on one another. It is to these multifaceted issues that we now attempt a response.

This book will both draw out some of the specific issues to be addressed as we move toward more sustainable modes of life and will also query what philosophy has to offer, or indeed if any meaningful or helpful response can arise from philosophy at all. Contributors to this book hope that in some small way hosting conversations between twenty-first-century philosopher

Alfred North Whitehead and various European philosophers will provide new insights that dislodge our thinking and move us in new, and perhaps unexpected, directions.

Alfred North Whitehead, the progenitor of process thought, spent the later years of his life in the 1920s and 1930s developing a speculative philosophy that refutes the substantialist claims of metaphysicians before him. Whitehead's speculative work takes interrelation as primary and describes the "growing together" of individual moments or actual occasions, which are the most basic components of reality. His mathematical and scientific background paired oddly with his respect for Kant and for the British empiricists, whom he brought together in unique and fascinating ways. In some regard, Whitehead was already building overlapping planes on which multiple modes of thought might move around and find occasion to converse. And indeed our task today is to locate the planes on which Whitehead thinks not only with those who came before him, but also with those who succeeded him—twentieth and twenty-first-century European philosophers, many of whom may be labeled as postmodern or poststructuralist. While to some, this pairing of conversation partners may seem oddly out of alignment, to the authors of this volume it is a most natural and indeed most helpful coupling; moreover, we remain convinced that conversations pushing us out of alignment are increasingly necessary in the twenty-first century.

When faced with the task of responding to such complex problems, we might look to the past in order to understand how previous generations tackled similar issues. Learning from our mistakes as well as from our successes may enable us to think through similar patterns or seek to replicate responses in new, but not altogether different, situations. Whitehead, with some glimmer of hope, remarks in *Adventures of Ideas*, "The history of ideas is a history of mistakes. But through all mistakes it is also the history of the gradual purification of conduct" (Whitehead 1933, 25). Much can be said for this backward-looking method. Inasmuch as the past contains a wealth of information, even wisdom, that can be offered or conferred on each new occasion, to proceed by drawing from the past means connecting with streams of tradition and all the insight held therein as we address our situation in the present.

Moreover, the backward-looking vision enables us to retain a kind of continuity with the past even as we address new or different situations in the present. We know, of course, that we can never step into the same river twice. Yet a certain continuity with the past helps us recall the sensation of stepping into a river. While both we and the river are no doubt very different from our previous encounter, we have some familiarity with each other, and so the occasion may not be so foreign. We will react differently because we *are* different, the situation *is* different; as Whitehead puts it, "No thinker thinks twice; and, to put the matter more generally, no subject experiences twice" (Whitehead 1978, 29). But we may also recollect some grouping of past occasions that allow us to continue what has occurred in the past.

An alternate response to complex problems might be to start over, scrap the worn-out or broken-down systems and create anew. At certain times, something must dislodge us from "the tameness of outworn perfection," (Whitehead 1933, 257) moving us into novel becomings that seek the new and different. This forward-looking vision may eschew the past and critique what has come before in order to focus on what is to come and what has not yet become.

As process thinkers indebted to Whitehead's speculative philosophy, and as philosophers immersed in various strands of European philosophy, the contributors to this book embrace what might be called a *double vision*—backward and forward looking—from the past and into the future. The world's future "though influenced by the immanence of its past, awaits for its complete determination the spontaneity of the novel individual occasions as in their season they come into being" (Whitehead 1933, 255). As thought is concretized via the immanence of the past, novelty provides the discord necessary to dislodge our current thinking from patterns of repetition and toward creative responses to problems that both recur and arise in new and more destructive ways. Double vision recalls what has already become, celebrates that which has led to peace and beauty, unfolds and examines what has led to destructive evil, and actualizes the possibility of the future in order to move toward more sustainable and equitable becomings.

The chapters in this book address the question of what hope European philosophy together with Whitehead can offer the world when faced with these interwoven economic, ecological, and political crises of the twenty-first century. The authors question which trajectories from European philosophy and Whitehead could lead to a more sustainable future. The unique combination of Whitehead's thought with that of philosophers from Europe provides precisely the dislocations necessary to propel our ideas toward new alternatives, new ways of formulating problems, and new attempts at providing responses.

Whereas previous scholarship has focused on comparisons between Whitehead and various continental philosophers, this volume is about how Whitehead's thought in tandem with continental thought might construct alternatives and propose creative responses to economic, ecological, and political crises. Rather than asking, "how do Whitehead and continental philosophers think similarly?" we ask, "how can Whitehead and others think together on the most pressing topics of the twenty-first century?" What ideas from European philosophy and Whitehead might enact change in the world? How can we rethink sustainability within a Whiteheadian and Continental framework?

These chapters also take up the question of whether it is possible to arrive at concrete change from out of a system of ideas. If we heed Marx's thesis that the goal of philosophy is not merely to describe the world but to change it, then how do we move from speculative philosophy, theories of aesthetics, and descriptions of technology, society, and economics to meaningful action that fosters a sustainable future? Is it possible for a traditionally reflective mode of philosophy to enact change in the world? And perhaps more to the point, can we step beyond critique toward constructive proposals for alternative ways of becoming? Whitehead reminds us that "the primary function for theories is as a lure for feeling" (Whitehead 1978, 184; see also Shaviro, 2009, 14). How might the theories described in this text lure us beyond themselves and toward the conceptual insight that unfolds the basis for novel becoming?

The chapters in this book converge around the task of thinking toward sustainable civilization, to imagine differently and afresh how civilization could become sustainable. This undertaking, of course, raises two questions: what do we mean by sustainable, and what do we mean by civilization? I will not offer clear and distinct definitions of either term in this introduction, since positing a univocal and settled meaning of either "sustainable" or "civilization" seems anathema to the conversational task at hand. Rather, we will allow each contributor to unpack what might be meant by the terms in the context of how, through Whitehead and European thought, we arrive at them. While not each chapter explicitly includes or explicates these terms, each chapter does in some way raise questions about sustainable civilization or the conditions under which sustainability can occur. The authors think broadly with regard to each term, attempting to destabilize the too narrow definitions that we all carry with us from our inherited pasts. These chapters will question what "sustainable" means for human and nonhuman subjects, for subjects in relation to technology, and for the modes of thought that we hope will extend into the future. Likewise, and taking a lead from Whitehead, the authors take aim at traditional notions of "civilization," particularly in historical situations in which naming civilization means drawing an arbitrary and exclusionary boundary.

The book is divided into three parts, each raising various sites where dislocations might occur. Such dislocations, as in Whitehead's thought, provide the occasion for new and renewed thought; they are the events that trigger the sort of double-vision required to address the multiplicity of multifaceted problems in the twenty-first century. For Whitehead, adventure—namely an *Adventure of Ideas*—is the way in which imagination "produces the dislocations and confusions marking the advent of new ideals for civilized effort" (Whitehead 1933, 279). The dislocations are not the novel, creative ideas themselves, but are the occasions, the temporal and spatial moments, in which something new may be realized. Each part in this book examines some spectrum of such occasions, noting possibilities for thinking toward a sustainable future.

In part I, "Technological and Systematic Dislocations," the authors take up questions related to political and capitalistic hegemony, noting that both technology and robust philosophical systems can, and indeed do, introduce new layers of late capitalistic fervor and political anesthesia. In his chapter, "Creativity and Adversity," William S. Hamrick thinks with Whitehead and Maurice Merleau-Ponty to derive a "new ontology" capable of grounding a deep ecology. This new ontology denies any bifurcation of nature, reexamines the relationship between technology and nature, and derives what Hamrick calls an "aesthetic naturalism." While ontology does not impose an ethics or politics, it can, according to Hamrick, suggest certain ways of responding to social, economic, and political situations. Bo Eberle employs Whitehead, Natasha Dow Schüll, and contemporary media theorists to suggest a different perception of how wearable technology and personal tracking devices aggregate and "feed forward" certain personal data. His chapter, "Interrogating the Quantified Self," examines how Whitehead's concept of causal efficacy enables us to consciously critique the ways in which such technology "games" use or are used in the service of advanced capitalism. In their chapter, "Can Whitehead Save the World?," J. R. Hustwit and Carl Dyke take up systematic and systemic dislocations through discussion of the hegemonies that invariably arise within robust and complex systems. Using Ricoeur to think with Whitehead, they propose a means of preserving an imperfect sort of agency capable of working against the hegemony inherent in any system.

In part II, "Human/Nonhuman Dislocations," the authors use Whitehead and European philosophers to problematize the traditional distinction between subjects and objects and to further dislocate human subjectivity from a grounded, univocal self. In the chapter "Process Philosophy and Neo-Materialism," I put Whitehead and Rosi Braidotti in conversation to consider interrelational becoming through a process ontology. Doing so lends weight toward Braidotti's (and Deleuze's) notion of becoming-imperceptible as a means of enabling a sustainable future. Deena Lin likewise pairs Whitehead with Braidotti, alongside Judith Butler, as she examines the Syrian refugee crisis via the lens of a global interrelation and cosmological immanence. Her chapter, like others, leads to an ethical/political evocation of ontological ideas, situated particularly in our global response to refugees. Tano Posteraro's chapter, "Conceptual Prehensions, Worlds of Experience," applies Whiteheadian metaphysics, and the notion of feeling within actual entities, to Jakob von Uexküll's biological account of nonhuman organisms. Together, the two thinkers lend us a new means of exploring experience in nonhuman subjects that might broaden our conception of the world beyond a narrowly anthropocentric view.

Part III, "Time, the World, and Abstraction," the final part of this text, takes aim at three themes—abstraction, power, and time—all of which are thought and rethought by Whitehead and Continental philosophers. Reconceiving each via process ontology enables the authors to posit new modes of sustainability that push back against exclusion and coercion. Kris Klotz's chapter, "Philosophy against Abstraction," considers the critiques of abstraction offered by Whitehead and by Deleuze and Guattari, in both of which abstraction covers over the possibility that philosophy might examine conditions for novelty. Through these critiques, Klotz seeks to recover what or who is normally excluded by such abstractions, thereby creating room for novelty on the part of those who would otherwise find themselves inhibited or delimited by the way in which abstractions operate. In "The Charge of Resistance," Elijah Prewitt-Davis examines power in both Foucault and Whitehead with the help of Deleuze's reading of Foucault. In doing so, he argues that power is not an exertion within the process of becoming but a means of retaining agency. As a result, Prewitt-Davis begins to rethink resistance from a process ontological perspective. Finally, Keith Robinson's chapter, "Whitehead, Continental Philosophy, and the Bifurcation of Nature," discusses understanding of time as inherent in the problem of the "bifurcation of nature." Since a bifurcation of nature into nature "as it really is" and nature as we experience it undermines our efforts at sustainable civilization, Robinson employs Whitehead's and Deleuze's re-conceiving of time in order to overcome this false dichotomy. In doing so, he examines how both thinkers understand the present and the becoming of the present in order to undo this bifurcation of the world.

Each chapter invariably deals with the underlying question: can philosophy and theory provide us with concrete ideas to be enacted in the name of sustainable civilization? And the authors of this volume conjecture a tentative "yes." We are able to say yes because, following Whitehead, we begin with the concrete. Whitehead's speculative scheme, while constituting a philosophical theory that lies beyond complete verifiability or finality, takes seriously what he names the fallacy of misplaced concreteness: "neglecting the degree of abstraction involved when an actual entity [the most basic component of existence] is considered merely so far as it exemplifies certain categories of thought" (Whitehead 1978, 7–8). In other words, accepting the theory as concrete and attempting to shoe-horn actual situations into that theory is the wrong way to proceed. Instead, we begin with the concrete by examining experience, every drop of experience, and especially those bits of experience that have typically been abstracted out of the way (Klotz). Like Whitehead's flight of the airplane, which begins in one specific field of inquiry or realm of experience, we take off in order to fly through the air of abstraction and land again in another region of experience in order to test the generalities produced by the flight (Whitehead 1978, 5). Perhaps we will find that our theories fail, in which case we revise and retest them. But on the other hand, perhaps we will discover that beginning within specific occurrences and then building generalities with fidelity to the occurrences lends us a means to rethink sustainable civilization.

REFERENCES

Shaviro, Steven. 2009. *Without Criteria: Kant, Whitehead, Deleuze, and Aesthetics.* Cambridge, MA: The MIT Press.
Whitehead, Alfred North. 1933. *Adventures of Ideas.* New York: The Free Press.
———. 1978. *Process and Reality: Corrected Edition.* Ed. David Ray Griffin and Donald W. Sherburne. New York: The Free Press.

Part I

Technological and Systematic Dislocations

Chapter One

Creativity and Adversity

Building an Ecological Civilization

William S. Hamrick

Building an ecological civilization is a daunting task in which nature and culture are inseparably intertwined. It is, therefore, a much broader and more complex project than dealing with climate change. Yet, climate change and its associated destructive effects, which turn largely on global warming, comprise the most threatening part of the challenge. For reducing carbon emissions, among other things, is essential to the very existence of future generations. The recent NASA forecasts of sustained drought over many decades testify to this fact.

Scientists are now both sounding the alarm about human-caused climate change as well as working on various strategies to combat it. Yet what, if anything, can philosophers do? Philosophy could well seem to be a useless fifth wheel, an impression easily reinforced by the fact that it begins when science has said all it can say, as Maurice Merleau-Ponty states somewhere.

However, we have different practical tasks as well as a more fundamental and pressing theoretical one. On the practical side, as a duty of citizenship, we need to find ways to communicate more forcefully and effectively basic and irrefutable facts about nature and science to the general populace, corporations—and now especially, those in government. On the one hand, we should acknowledge the existence of irresolvable, legitimate conflicts of interests that are economic, political, and moral in our relationships with nature. Yet on the other hand, we must not give in to the fraudulent (and disgraceful) notion of "alternative facts." We must also stress the distinction between particular interests and the common good, and that balancing competing interests is not a simple matter of "us" against "them." We must continue to emphasize that climate health is a key necessary condition of human flourishing, for when our environment goes, we go.

This is not to say that nature and environment are identical or that thinking about them follows the same logic. As Jason Wirth points out, "Nature cannot be measured by the anthropocentric reference point implicit in the notion of the environment" (Wirth in Wirth and Burke 2013, 11). Nevertheless, as a practical matter, when philosophers take up such issues in order to influence public opinion, beginning with environmental impact concerns is likely to form an important source of motivation for the public at large. The reason is that, I would argue, Hume was correct that reason by itself cannot motivate, and that it therefore needs some stimulus of feelings, or "sentiment," to be operative.[1] Environmental threats have mobilized appropriate feelings of ecological concern.

However, the more fundamental theoretical task is to advance an ontology to find a way to think adequately our most basic, fundamental relationships to nature and therefore to ground a "deep ecology," to use Arne Naess' phrase. Accordingly, the purpose of this chapter is to provide a sketch of such an ontology that derives from Whitehead's philosophy of nature as well as from Maurice Merleau-Ponty's last writings. In them, he began to frame a "new ontology" (1970, 91)[2] during what turned out to be the last five years of a life ended much before its time.

I

Merleau-Ponty's ontology is centered in the notion of "flesh" (*la chair*). He first used the term in his 1951 address, "Man and Adversity" ("*L'homme et l'adversité*"), at the *Rencontres Internationales de Genève*, to indicate the fundamental interrelatedness of body and soul as against Descartes' dualism and its progenies. "Man and Adversity" and the second "private conversation" with various scholars that followed it two days later are highly pertinent to the challenge of building an ecological civilization in ways that do not directly concern the flesh, and it will be worth our while to spend a few minutes with those texts before delving into ontology.[3]

Building an ecological civilization involves a struggle with considerable adverse interests. In the "second private conversation," Merleau-Ponty defines adversity as "the dead weight that one feels behind oneself when one reflects" (Prunair 2000, 334). In the lecture itself, he speaks of "a sort of inertia, a passive resistance, a failure of meaning—an anonymous *adversity*" (Merleau-Ponty 1964a, 239/304; translation revised),[4] of which there are several sources. First, adversity can manifest itself as the dead weight of tradition, against which he appeals for expression "to begin again the initial creative work" (Prunair 2000, 345). Merleau-Ponty's philosophy was consistently one of free creative expression in all possible forms, a subject to which we shall return in terms of ontology. With regard to climate change, it is scarcely necessary to point out that there is also a significant struggle against inertia and passive resistance due to skepticism about science—including at the highest level of the federal government—and the unwillingness of affluent societies to consider the case for restraining their consumption of fossil-fuel-produced goods.

Second, there was the intellectual polarization between materialists and idealists that characterized much of early twentieth-century philosophy (Merleau-Ponty 1964a, 226/287) and made up a significant part of "the dead weight" and "failure of meaning" of Merleau-Ponty's past. On his view, values are neither the product of mechanistic natural functionings nor imposed on us from a transcendent source. They appear as "resistant kernels" (*noyaux résistants*) (Merleau-Ponty 1964a, 226/287) in and through our relationships with nature, other people, and the world around us. In Whiteheadian terms, values are eternal objects only *as ingressed*—the invisible in the visible, the latter context of which contributes to their intelligibility and validity. "The solidarity of values and facts, of power and ideology, is a truth. . . . Lucidity does not consist of thinking politics solely in light of values or ideas. It consists in thinking truly the total state of the world at the hour we are concretely" (Prunair 2000, 354, 355).[5] In Whitehead's words, "Value refers to Fact, and Fact refers to Value. [This statement is a direct contradiction to Plato, and to the theological tradition derived from him.]" (Whitehead 1951, 684).[6]

For example, the value of reducing the use of fossil fuels does not wear its meaning on its sleeve; it is not invariable regardless of context. Rather, its meaning takes on the cast and hue of the society in which it is advocated. It thus signifies desirable restraint in wealthy first-world countries such as the United States, but something else again in desperately poor countries trying to achieve even a faint resemblance of American prosperity. One unavoidable result of this contextualization of values is the "overlapping" (*empiétement*) of I and the Other—the enmeshment of being for self and being for others (Merleau-Ponty 1964a, 231/293), both individually and on a societal level.

A third source of adversity for Merleau-Ponty consisted of a generalized fear of contingency and lack of certitude that became the predominant feature of the times (1964a, 239/303; 242/307). With regard to climate change and the seemingly increasing number of extreme weather events, the same ubiquity of contingency and fear of it also characterize our lives today. Merleau-Ponty notes that there is a contingency of evil, but more pressingly, also of goodness: "Progress is not necessary with a metaphysical necessity; we can only say that experience will very likely end up by eliminating false solutions and working its way out of impasses"[7] (1964a, 239/304). In fact, he goes on to say in the same place, "We cannot even exclude in principle the possibility that humanity, like a sentence which does not succeed in drawing to a close, will suffer shipwreck on its way."[8]

Both this model of progress and the possibility of species failure haunt ecological thinking today. We have no absolute certainty that humanly caused climate change is in progress, though there is copious evidence that it probably is. Too, a multitude of adverse interests aided by various levels of governments try to mobilize that uncertainty to block environmental regulations. Thus we may be the first species ever to engineer its own destruction. Contingency is such that "the human moment par excellence [is one] in which a life woven out of chance events turns back upon, regrasps, and expresses itself" without "giving way to the retrospective illusion of realizing the valuable in advance" (Merleau-Ponty 1964a, 240/305, 304).[9] Fear of contingency also causes convulsive debates, Merleau-Ponty concludes, that (then as now) eliminate the possibility of harmonious, peaceful discussions (Merleau-Ponty 1964a, 242–43/308).

II

There are at least two other sources of adversity that stand in the way of building an ecological civilization. They are intertwined in a deficient ontology of nature and a concomitant concept of science and technology. The first source is the conception of nature as an object apart from us, with which we exist in external rather than internal relationships. The second source is, as Martin Heidegger phrased it, a technological interpretation of nature as *Bestand*, as a "standing reserve"[10] (1977, 17) of resources to be used. We shall consider these in turn.

Merleau-Ponty formulated his "new ontology" of flesh to overthrow the long shadow of Cartesianism that still hung over French philosophy in the mid-1950s. In addition to Descartes' dualism, he also rejected any kind of Platonic heaven of ideas and eternal truths, and held that, contrary to Leibniz, "there is not a single truth of reason that does not contain a coefficient of facticity" (Merleau-Ponty 2012, 414/451).[11] This is another way of endorsing Whitehead's view that "Value refers to Fact, and Fact refers to Value" as opposed to the fallacy of "vacuous actuality."

Merleau-Ponty agrees with Whitehead, therefore, in rejecting the view that the intelligibility of nature is imposed on it from a transcendent source—be it consciousness or God—and is instead inherent in it. Merleau-Ponty also joined Whitehead in identifying the source of that view—what *Science and the Modern World* terms "scientific materialism" that "ruined" modern philosophy (55), the progenitor of which is the Galilean-Cartesian physics. This doctrine interprets nature as "senseless, valueless, purposeless. It just does what it does, following a fixed routine imposed by external relations which do not spring from the nature of its being" (Whitehead 1925, 17). This is "the theory of a materialistic, mechanistic nature, surveyed by cogitating minds" (Whitehead 1925, 145). As Jason Wirth expresses Schelling's rejection of this disconnection, "We are no longer *of* Nature, but rather *in* Nature, as if we were separate from it" (Wirth and Burke 2013, 6).[12] Or, as Heidegger put it helpfully, "nature is represented as something standing-over-against, as an object. Neither the ancients nor the medievals represented being as an ob-ject [*Gegen-stand*]" (2001, 133–34).[13]

Merleau-Ponty calls the two halves of scientific materialism the "ontology of the object" and "surveying thought"—*pensée de survol* (1968, 222).[14] On his view, as with Whitehead and indeed for Heidegger as well, reality does not consist of an objective plenum of Being of which consciousness is an external spectator. "Even the action of thinking is caught up in the push and shove of being" (Merleau-Ponty 1964a, 14/21), as Schelling and Whitehead also knew.[15]

The Cartesian dualism is only one example of such a scheme that evacuates human beings from being active participants within nature and reduces them to onlookers disconnected from it. For Schelling, Descartes' dualism is the "fundamental error" that infected all subsequent philosophy that descended from it (Schelling 2000, 50).[16] But in whatever form, Merleau-Ponty and Whitehead by contrast hold that nature and we are intimately intertwined. In the former's words, "nature is not simply the object, the accessory of consciousness in its tête-à-tête with knowledge. It is an object from which we have arisen" (1970, 64/94). As he stated in his inaugural address to the Collège de France and reiterated many times, "I am of it [nature]" (*J'en suis*) (1973, 16).[17] Merleau-Ponty's sense of "object" here is, therefore, different in kind from a Heideggerean "Gegen-stand" and Cartesian material substance. Nature is an object with which we exist in internal rather than external relations, the world and my body "are made of the same stuff" (Merleau-Ponty 1993, 125)[18] and objective Nature consists of creative process (Merleau-Ponty 2003, 214–15).[19]

To find a way to think adequately about relationships between minds and bodies, and between our bodies and the rest of nature, Merleau-Ponty sought to replace the ontology of the object with an "ontology of the existent" in which our primary relationships to Being would be expressed in the Husserlian concepts of *Offenheit* and *Ineinander*, "the *Ineinander* of human being, human body, and Nature" (Merleau-Ponty 2003, 214–15). "*Ineinander*," he continues, means "the inherence of the self-in-the-world or of the world-in-the-self" (1970, 108/152; translation altered).[20] That to which we are open, that in which we are already involved in a network of relationships, Merleau-Ponty terms "the flesh" (*la chair*). This sense of flesh expresses the fundamental connectedness of all that is: what Charles Hartshorne terms "the 'solidarity' or interrelatedness of things making up 'the world' or 'Being'" (1983, 340). The flesh is what Robert J. Valenza, writing about Whitehead, describes as "an ontological fabric that accommodates the internal and the external as parts of reality, as different aspects of the same thing" (2014, 8).

"Flesh" has more than one meaning. On the one hand, it means carnality: my own flesh, the flesh of others, and the flesh of the world. It also stresses the "inextricable implication"[21] between them while not denying differences between individuals. This inextricability aligns Merleau-Ponty's thought with Whitehead's three-fold view that "Connectedness is of the essence of all things of all types. . . . No fact is merely itself" (Whitehead 1938, 13); that it is impossible to establish an exact boundary between my body and the external world (1938, 30; Merleau-Ponty 1968, 138/182); and finally that the human body is "that region of the world which is the primary field of human expression" (1938, 30). For both thinkers, the body and other natural entities, perceivers and perceived, are particularizations or differentiations of the same ontological tissue.

There is a second meaning of flesh, for which "there is no name in traditional philosophy" (Merleau-Ponty 1968, 139/183). Flesh is not a "what" because it is not an object. It is therefore easier to say what it is not than what it is. It is not "matter," not "some 'psychic' material," not a physical or mental fact or set of them, a mental representation, a substance, or mind (Merleau-Ponty 1968, 139/184). Rather, its proper descriptor is, "the old term 'element,' in the sense that it was used to speak of water, air, earth, and fire, that is, in the sense of a *general thing*, midway between the spatio-temporal individual and the idea, a sort of incarnate principle that brings a style of being wherever there is a fragment of being" (Merleau-Ponty 1968, 139/184).[22]

"The flesh is in this sense an 'element' of Being," he continues in the same passage.[23] Flesh is neither bodies nor minds, subjects nor objects, but an ontological matrix or source anterior to both. It is the "formative milieu of the object and subject" (Merleau-Ponty 1968, 147/193). It does not occupy a unique time and place—the "fallacy of simple location"—but rather consists of a "concrete emblem of a manner of general being" (Merleau-Ponty 1968, 147/194). Mind and body, lived and objective bodies, consciousness and object, spirit and nature, self and others, life and matter—all of the previous dualities—are reintegrated as aspects of the more fundamental unity of flesh in order to think their relationships adequately.

In the Nature lectures, Merleau-Ponty states that, while nature is not identical to the flesh, it does form our primary and indispensable access to ontology. It is primordial because it is "the non-constructed, the non-instituted." As against the notion of "vacuous actuality," nature exists "anywhere there is a life that has a meaning"; it is, in fact, "the autoproduction of meaning" (2003, 3/19) and its creative expressions. Its linguistic derivation points to this fact, for it comes from *natus*, the past participle of *nā/scor -sci*, "to be born." In this view also, Merleau-Ponty was substantially influenced by Schelling's indictment of scientific materialism for evacuating life from nature. As with Whitehead, what gets born is not merely a dead effect. Nature is inseparably active productivity and passive product—as is the concrescence of each actual occasion of experience—whereas in modernity, nature "lacks a living ground" (Schelling 2006, 26). This is, for Schelling, modernity's "fateful curse [*Verhängnis*]."[24]

By contrast, for Merleau-Ponty and Whitehead, as well as Schelling, creativity permeates Nature and is actualized in individuals. Given nature's "autoproduction of meaning," that *naturans*, as Schelling wished to revise Spinoza's view of the relationship, stands to *Natura naturata* such that not only can mental and physical attributes not exist apart, but also cannot be correctly thought of as apart. Any given phenomenon of Nature contains both "reality" and "ideality," and "Nature as *natura naturans* takes part in the history of its creation. This is what makes it *natura naturata*, that is, creativity manifesting itself in itself" (Hilt 2013, 192).

This is because, as just noted, the flesh is inherently meaningful as opposed to having its intelligibility imposed on it from a transcendent source. Meaning is invisible in a very specific sense. It is not the contradictory of the visible, but rather "in [the] visible," the "invisible inner framework" of the flesh (Merleau-Ponty 1968, 215/269). Ideas, as Proust showed, comprise the "lining and depth of the visible" (Merleau-Ponty 1968, 149/195). This implies that, for example, every speech act becomes an incarnation, words made flesh,[25] and by the same token, in the expression of ideas, flesh is made words. In slightly different terms, "life becomes ideas and the ideas return to life" (Merleau-Ponty 1968, 119/159).

Whereas in the philosopher's early writings nature achieved its intelligibility as subjectivized,[26] as a correlate of a body consciousness, his last writings refer to a much more profound sense of meaningfulness. Beginning with his first Nature lectures at the Collège de France, he expresses this intelligibility in terms of the Stoics' twin concepts of the *logos endiathetos* and the *logos proforikos* (1970, 74/105–6). The former conveys the intrinsic sense of the world anterior to consciousness, and the latter provides its cultural articulation through all forms of expression—language, diverse artistic media, history, politics, science, philosophy, and on and on. In whatever form, the *logos proforikos* means that understanding consists of translating "into available significations meaning first held captive in the thing and in the world itself" (Merleau-Ponty 1968, 36/58) and creatively modulating it.

The *logos endiathetos* reveals what is disclosed to our "perceptual openness to the world" (Merleau-Ponty 1968, 212/266), "meaning before logic" (Merleau-Ponty 1968, 169/222), and it precedes the distinction between fact and essence (Merleau-Ponty 1968, 174/228). It is the "*logos* that pronounces itself silently in each sensible thing" (Merleau-Ponty 1968, 208/261). It is silent because it is the "Logos of the natural, aesthetic world, on which the Logos of language rests" (Merleau-Ponty 1968, 114/153). The *logos endiathetos*, as with the Stoics, is the "brute unity [of nature] by means of which the universe 'holds' and of which human understanding is the expression rather than the interior condition" (Merleau-Ponty 1970, 74/105–6). The *logos proforikos* clarifies the inherent intelligibility of Nature (the *logos endiathetos*) that in turn "calls for it" (Merleau-Ponty 1968, 170/224). This is another way of stating his earlier view of the indissolubility of truths of reason and truths of fact and his rejection of pure ideality as the product of the *pensée de survol* (Merleau-Ponty 1968, 97/132).

Since the *logos endiathetos* "calls for" the *logos proforikos*, the latter must be creatively active expression instead of a passively conditioned response. Their relationship, which must be internal rather than external, means that there is something in the *Natura naturans* that pushes toward cultural expression, and that there is an overlapping between Nature and culture in which each transforms the other (Merleau-Ponty 1964b, 123/154).

I take Merleau-Ponty's ontology, based on a descriptive generalization of flesh, coupled with Whitehead's more developed descriptive generalization of nature as meaningful, creative acts of interrelated, individualized processes, to provide an adequate ontological foundation for building an ecological civilization. It is true that one cannot *deduce* a normative ethics or a political system from an ontology. However, an ontological foundation does provide sufficient resources for rejecting certain social, economic, and political initiatives as destructive of our unity with nature and with life itself, and therefore with human flourishing. To use again Merleau-Ponty's reference to the contingency of goodness: "Progress is not necessary with a metaphysical necessity; we can only say that experience will very likely end up by eliminating false solutions and working its way out of impasses" (1964a, 239/304).

One of those impasses is the last source of adversity mentioned above for building an ecological civilization—a technological concept of nature and, therefore, of human life itself. No one has done more than Heidegger to underscore the problems such a definition poses. He observes that, "In modern technology, nature is challenged by 'setting-in-order,' which *sets upon* nature. It sets upon it in the sense of challenging it" (Heidegger 2001, 320). So for instance, "Agriculture is now the mechanized food industry. Air is now set upon to yield nitrogen, the earth to yield ore, ore to yield uranium, for example; uranium is set upon to yield atomic energy, which can be unleashed either for destructive or for peaceful purposes" (Heidegger 2001, 320).

It is not that technology itself runs counter to ecological concerns, for in pre-modern times, technology "challenged" or "set upon" the earth as soon as spades and plows turned up fields to grow crops. Rather, Heidegger's concern is that today technology *defines* nature. Nature understood as *Bestand*, or "standing-reserve," is "on call for a further ordering" (Heidegger 2001, 17).

Even human beings do not escape being ordered as a "standing-reserve" of resources. As Wirth notes, "Our bodies, our health, are just more commodities, more *Bestand*.... The desire to 'entrap nature as calculable forces' [Heidegger 1977, 21; Wirth's translation] conceals the questionability of the subject who would have an uncontested domain over all of nature by stockpiling it as *Bestand*. In so doing, humanity itself becomes *Bestand*" (Wirth 2003, 175).

This is why the phrase, "human resources," has both malign and benign resonances, as does "supply" in the case of patients for care homes or students for classes—students as instruments of student credit hour production. Heidegger's own example is more poignant: he describes the forester following in his grandfather's footsteps who is "ordered by the industry that produces commercial woods, whether he knows it or not. He is made subordinate to the orderability of cellulose, which for its part is challenged forth by the need for paper, which is then delivered to newspapers and illustrated magazines" (Heidegger 1977, 18).

(Other) animals as well are also turned into *Bestand*, and Michael Pollan's *The Omnivore's Dilemma* shows in details both depressing and infuriating how large factory farms "set upon" animals such as chickens, pigs, and cows a definition of "standing reserve" of food in calculable and predictable units. Worse, in a federally funded animal experimentation center, "scientists are using surgery and breeding techniques to re-engineer the farm animal to fit the needs of the twenty-first-century meat industry. The potential benefits are huge: animals that produce more offspring, yield more meat and cost less to raise."[27] Pigs produce up to fourteen offspring, many of which are crushed when their mother rolls over on them. Cows that usually give birth to one calf at a time "have been retooled to have twins and triplets, which often emerge weakened or deformed, dying in such numbers that even meat producers have been repulsed."

However, the lambs may have it worst of all. Scientists are trying to produce "easy care" sheep "that can survive without costly shelters or shepherds." Ewes give birth by themselves in fields where "newborns are killed by predators, harsh weather and starvation." One weekend's results in May 2014 included "25 rag-doll bodies. Five, abandoned by over taxed mothers, had empty stomachs. Six had signs of pneumonia. Five had been savaged by coyotes. 'It's horrible,' one veterinarian said, tossing the remains into a barrel to be dumped in a vast excavation called the dead pit." And all of this is without mentioning the terrible cruelty of painful experiments.

If the technological *definiendum* of Nature is *Bestand*, the *definiens*, so to say, is *Gestell*, "Enframing," which illuminates and reveals. It means "the way of revealing that holds sway in the essence of modern technology" (Heidegger 1977, 20) because it installs "in all things a demand to supply (*herausforderndes bestellen auf... Bestand*)" (Heidegger 2001, 165).

Conceiving nature as *Bestand* also brings to light the mutually reinforcing relationships between *Bestand*, the mechanism at the core of scientific materialism, and modern scientific method. The link between interpreting nature as "standing reserve" and mechanical scientific explanations is predictability and calculability central to modern scientific method. In this regard, Heidegger points to the claim in the sixth and last part of Descartes' *Discourse on Method* that scientific method seeks such calculability. As a result, scientific method "does not simply and vaguely mean 'procedure.' Method is the way and manner of how being, in this case 'nature,' has been thematized.... The modern concept of nature, that is its objectification, is motivated by the idea of representing the processes of nature in such a way that they can be predicted and, therefore controlled" (Heidegger 2001, 133, 134).

In sum, then, the technological *Gestell* of nature viewed mechanically amounts to unending use (*Bestand*) and control guided by scientific method. Such a *Gestell* is plainly inconsistent with establishing an ecological civilization. For, as Wirth points out, "modern industrial humans have lived *in* Nature in order to take *from* Nature." The results have been, apart from the appalling treatment of animals, the "climate emergency, pollution and the general degradation of the earth's various habitats, biodepletion, overpopulation, and the intensive spread of invasive species" (Wirth 2013, 13). As Alexander Solzhenitsyn once said, "Even the simplest village graybeard knows that you can't go on coring the same apple forever."

The root cause of this destructiveness, and what has to be remedied in a new *Gestell* of nature, is the rift between mechanism and life, between bodies and minds, between nature arrayed before the scientist's perceptive study and nature that has a "living ground." We must return to pre-modern insights about nature and our indivisibility from it. It was Schelling's great merit to see that modernity's "fateful curse" created a sickness, and that a healthy life and a healthy earth required healing the fissure by restoring the "living ground," of understanding that "all value, including our value, is *inseparable* and *indivisible* from the value of the Earth" (Wirth 2013, 15).[28]

Merleau-Ponty's incomplete ontology of flesh and Whitehead's process metaphysics offer a way forward to understand that "living ground." For both philosophies put a premium on the creative expression of nature, a respectful interaction with it, and the inability to understand ourselves apart from it. For Merleau-Ponty, the *logos endiathetos* was not something to be set upon and challenged for its use value, but rather to be celebrated in all the diverse forms of cultural creativity (the *logos proforikos*). For Whitehead, deeply influenced as he was by Wordsworth, there was a similar reverence for nature and celebration of its beauty and creativity. In short, both thinkers prized listening to nature and learning its lessons.

Whitehead and Merleau-Ponty might well have found in recent Gaia science support for understanding the "living ground" of nature, as Schelling would have as well. Stephan Harding, for example, makes a plea for regaining "the ancient view of Gaia as a fully integrated, living being consisting of all her life-forms, air, rocks, soil, oceans, lakes, and rivers" (Harding 2010, 122; cited in Wirth 2013, 14).[29]

Edward O. Wilson points out that the Gaia hypothesis, first advanced in 1972 by a British scientist, James Lovelock, claimed that any discrete ecosystem, such as a marsh or pond, was part of the whole biosphere—"a kind of superorganism that surrounds the planet" (Wilson 2002, 11). Wilson believes that there is "considerable merit in looking at life in this grand holistic manner," but he also points out that there are both strong and weak versions of the Gaia hypothesis. The strong version, which most biologists, including Lovelock himself, reject, construes the biosphere as a "true superorganism." The weak version, "which holds that some species exercise widespread and even global influence, is well substantiated" (Wilson 2002, 11–12).[30]

The Gaia hypothesis, at least the strong version, is closely linked to ancient and modern animistic thinking—from the notion of the world soul in the *Timaeus*, passing through Schelling's notion of the world soul to, among others, Rupert Sheldrake. The latter observes, "Both animistic and mechanistic thinking are metaphorical. But whereas mythic and animistic thinking (earth as mother, mother nature, etc.) depends on organic metaphors drawn from the processes of life, mechanistic thinking depends on metaphors drawn from man-made machines" (1990, 6).

Despite the fact that mechanistic thinking in the seventeenth and eighteenth centuries was hardly metaphorical, Sheldrake's observations do helpfully point to the ways that, and how, our views of nature and technology must change to create and maintain an ecological civilization. The Schellingian inheritance present in the works of Whitehead and Merleau-Ponty amounts to two central claims. Mechanism cannot provide a complete account of nature, although nature does work mechanically, as Schelling knew from his immersion in chemistry and medicine. However, second, since all of nature is alive, material and spiritual, mechanism as a doctrine is an abstraction from the whole. As a result, the modernist view is reversed: our "living ground" in nature is not a supplemental, animating principle added on to the mechanical motions of matter. Rather, it's the other way around. The mechanical workings of nature are also manifestations of life. This is why Henri Bergson protested against privileging "inert" matter to which "life" would be added (2005, 101).[31]

Such a reversal also has decisive consequences for our view of technology. Technology devoted solely to conceiving nature as *Bestand* has lost contact with its living ground, the integrity of our biosphere, and therefore from the good. Technology must be reconceived, if possible, as a respectful, appreciative, use of nature. If this can happen—and it's a big if—it will be because people will become capable of self-restraint because they realize that they themselves are inextricably intertwined with the nature they exploit, and harming nature harms them as well. Otherwise, we will fulfill Gabriel Marcel's fear that we have lost control of our own control and lose the opportunity for sanctity that he says the naturalist incarnates. For the naturalist, no species is

> Insignificant. . . . In the passionate study of a particular species he has triumphed for all time over such reactions. The living organism he considers subsists in a dimension of being to which we, the profane, have access only with difficulty. Even leaving aside any belief in a divine creator, the naturalist experiences a kind of wonder before the fineness and the complexity he observes. . . . The saint is someone who has arrived at a way of being that overcomes the current separation between man and nature. (1973, 117–8)[32]

This revised conception of nature could be called "aesthetic naturalism," and we should do whatever we can to implement it in the face of powerful adversities. Both the welfare of the planet and our own health and well being depend on recovering this "living ground."

NOTES

1. See, for example, David Hume, *An Inquiry Concerning the Principles of Morals*, edited, with an introduction, by Charles W. Hendel (Indianapolis, IN: The Liberal Arts Press, 1957), Section I, "Of the General Principles of Morals"; and *A Treatise of Human Nature*, Book III, Section I, reprinted from the Original Edition in Three Volumes and edited, with an analytical index, by L. A. Selby Bigge (Oxford: At the Clarendon Press, 1967 [1888]).

2. Originally published in 1968 as *Résumés de cours, Collège de France 1952–1960* (Paris: Gallimard), 128. Citations to Merleau-Ponty's texts will provide the English and then the French pagination separated by a "/".

3. "Man and Adversity" (Merleau-Ponty 1964a, 224–43) was originally published as "L'homme et l'adversité" in *Signes* (Paris: Gallimard, 1960), 284–308. The "Second Private Conversation" appears in Prunair 2000, 325–71.

4. I have translated "défaillance" as "failure" instead of "dying fall." The French word can also signify blacking out and losing consciousness, hence (possibly) the translator's choice.

5. "La solidarité des valeurs et des faits, de la puissance et de l'idéologie, est une vérité . . . la lucidité ne consiste pas à penser la politique sous la seule lumière des valeurs ou des idées. Elle consiste à penser vraiment l'état total du monde à l'heure où nous sommes concrètement."

6. The brackets are in the cited text. Compare Merleau-Ponty's statement that "The war and the occupation have only taught us that values remain nominal, and do not even count, without an economic and political infrastructure that makes them begin to exist" (1964b, 152). *Sense and Non-Sense* was originally published in 1948 as *Sens et non-sens* (Paris: Nagel), 168. "La guerre et l'occupation nous ont seulement appris que les valeurs restent nominales, et ne valent pas même, sans une infrastructure économique et politique qui les fasse entrer dans l'existence."

7. "Le progrès n'est pas nécessaire d'une nécessité métaphysique: on peut seulement dire que très probablement l'expérience finira par éliminer les fausses solutions et par se dégager des impasses." This view of progress is quite similar to Sir Karl Popper's concept of the process of scientific discovery as one of falsification rather than of verification. See *The Logic of Scientific Discovery* (London: Hutchinson, 1959).

8. "Il n'est même pas exclu en principe que l'humanité, comme une phrase qui n'arrive pas à s'achever, échoue en cours de route."

9. "... le moment humain par excellence, où une vie tissée de hasards se retourne sur elle-même, se ressaisit et s'exprime . . . céder à l'illusion rétrospective, c'est toujours réaliser d'avance le valable."

10. *The Question Concerning Technology and Other* Essays was published originally in *Vorträge und Aufsätze* (Pfullingen: Günther Neske Verlag, 1954), 13–44.

11. *Phenomenology of Perception* was originally published as *Phénoménologie de la perception* (Paris: Gallimard, 1945), 451. "L'éternité n'est pas un autre ordre au-delà du temps, c'est l'atmosphère du temps. . . . Réciproquement, il n'est pas une vérité de raison qui ne garde un coefficient de facticité."

12. Wirth in Wirth and Burke 2013, 6. He also states in the same introduction, "For Schelling, *Naturphilosophie* was not an account of something called Nature, but it was rather philosophy endeavoring to think with, of and from Nature" (10).

13. The *Zollikon Seminars, Protocols—Conversations—Letters* was originally published as *Zollikoner Seminare, Protokolle—Gespräche—Briefe Herausgegeben von Medard Boss* (Frankfurt am Main: Vittorio Klostermann GmbH, 1987). "[*Gegen-stand*]" is Heidegger's insertion.

14. *The Visible and the Invisible* was originally published as *Le Visible et l'invisible, suivi de notes de* travail, ed. Claude Lefort (Paris: Gallimard, 1964), 276.

15. Cf. Marcia Sá Cavalcante Schuback: "Consciousness is born within Nature. It is in this sense a work of Nature." "The Eye and the Spirit of Nature: Some Reflections on Merleau-Ponty's Reading of Schelling Concerning the Relationship between Art and Nature" (Wirth and Burke 2013, 311).

16. At p. 105 Schelling continues, "Descartes, the founder of modern philosophy, lacerated the world into body and spirit and hence, the unity was lost in favor of duality. Spinoza had unified them into a single, albeit dead, substance and had lost duality in favor of unity."

17. *In Praise of Philosophy* was originally published in 1953 as *Éloge de la philosophie* (Paris: Gallimard), 25–26.

18. *Eye and Mind* was originally published as *L'Œil et l'esprit* (Paris: Gallimard, 1964), 19.

19. *Nature: Course Notes from the Collège de France* was originally published in 1994 as *La Nature, Notes, Cours du Collège de France*, ed. Dominique Séglard (Paris: Édition de Seuil), 278. See part II, chapter 2, "The Idea of Nature for Whitehead."

20. The original text contains no hyphens: "l'inhérence du soi au monde ou du monde au soi, du soi à l'autre et de l'autre au soi."

21. A nice phrase from Emmanuel de Saint Aubert (2006, 213).

22. "... le vieux terme d' 'élément,' au sens où on l'employait pour parler de l'eau, de l'air, de la terre et du feu, c'est-à-dire au sens d'une *chose générale*, à mi-chemin de l'individu spatio-temporel et de l'idée, sorte de principe incarné qui importe un style d'être partout où il s'en trouve une parcelle."

23. Although the philosopher writes, "un 'élément,'" it is regrettable that he did not live long enough to complete what came to be titled *Le Visible et l'invisible*. In what we do have, and in all of the unpublished texts of which I am aware, he does not refer to any other "elements."

24. Wirth 2013, 7. In the *Freedom* essay, Schelling also held, "God is not a god of the dead but of the living. It is not comprehensible how the most perfect being could find pleasure even in the most perfect machine possible" (2006, 26).

25. Compare Whitehead's remark, "Expression is the one fundamental sacrament. It is the outward and visible sign of an inward and spiritual grace" (RM, 127). I am grateful to Jan Van der Veken for this reference.

26. See Rudolf Bernet (1994), especially "Perception et vie naturelle (Husserl et Merleau-Ponty)," 163–85.
27. Moss 2015, 1. All quotations in this and the following paragraph come from this article.
28. Wirth 2013, 15. Earlier Schelling had written, "So long as I myself am *identical* with Nature, I understand what a living nature is as well as I understand my own life" (1988, 36).
29. Stephan Harding, "Gaia and Biodiversity," in *Gaia in Turmoil: Climate Change, Biodepletion, and Earth Ethics in an Age of Crisis*, ed. Eileen Crist and H. Bruce Rinker (Cambridge, MA: The MIT Press, 2010), p. 122. Cited in Wirth, *op. cit.*, BP 14.
30. For example, he notes, "the oceanic phytoplankton, composed of microscopic, photosynthesizing bacteria, archaeans, and algae, is a major player in the control of the world climate. Dimethysulfide generated by the algae alone is believed to be an important factor in the regulation of cloud formation" (2002, 11).
31. See, for example, "De quel droit met-on l'inert d'abord? [Par contre] Les anciens avaient imaginé une Ame du Monde qui assurerait la continuité d'existence de l'univers matériel." "By what right does one place the inert first? [By contrast] The ancients had imagined a World Soul that would assure the continuity of the existence of the material universe." Bergson apparently did not read Schelling, but he was substantially influenced by Ravaisson who did.
32. Marcel was also substantially influenced by Schelling.

REFERENCES

Bergson, Henri. 2005 [1938]. *La pensée et le mouvant*. Paris: Presses Universitaires de France.
Bernet, Rudolf. 1994. *La vie du sujet: Recherches sur l'interprétation de Husserl dans la phénoménologie*. Paris: Presses Universitaires de France.
Crist, Eileen, and H. Bruce Rinker, eds. 2010. *Gaia in Turmoil: Climate Change, Biodepletion, and Earth Ethics in an Age of Crisis*. Cambridge, MA: The MIT Press.
Harding, Stephan. 2010. "Gaia and Biodiversity." In *Gaia in Turmoil: Climate Change, Biodepletion, and Earth Ethics in an Age of Crisis*. In Crist and Rinker, 107–24.
Hartshorne, Charles. 1983. *Insights and Oversights of Great Thinkers: An Evaluation of Western Philosophy*. Albany: State University of New York Press.
Heidegger, Martin. 1977. *The Question Concerning Technology and Other* Essays. Translated and with an introduction by William Lovitt. New York: Harper & Row, Publishers. Originally published in 1954 in *Vorträge und Aufsätze*. Pfullingen: Günther Neske Verlag.
———. 2001. *Zollikon Seminars: Protocols—Conversations—Letters*. Ed. Medard Boss, translated from the German and with notes and afterwords by Franz Mayr and Richard Askay. Evanston, IL: Northwestern University Press. Originally published in 1987 as *Zollikoner Seminare: Protokolle—Gespräche—Briefe Herausgegeben von Medard Boss*. Frankfurt am Main: Vittorio Klostermann GmbH.
Hilt, Annette. 2013. "Freedom as the Experience of Nature." In Wirth and Burke 2013, 189–209.
Marcel, Gabriel. 1973. *Tragic Wisdom and Beyond: including Conversations between Paul Ricoeur and Gabriel Marcel*. Translated by Stephen Jolin and Peter McCormick. Evanston, IL: Northwestern University Press. *Tragic Wisdom and Beyond* was originally published in 1968 as *Pour une sagesse tragique*. Paris: Librairie Plon. *Conversations between Paul Ricoeur and Gabriel Marcel* was originally published in 1968 as *Entretiens: Paul Ricoeur, Gabriel Marcel*. Paris: Éditions Aubier-Montaigne.
Merleau-Ponty, Maurice. 1964a. *Sense and Non-Sense*. Trans. Hubert L. and Patricia Allen Dreyfus. Evanston, IL: Northwestern University Press. Originally published in 1948 as *Sens et non-sens*. Paris: Nagel.
———. 1964b. *Signs*. Translated by Richard C. McCleary. Evanston, IL: Northwestern University Press. Originally published as *Signes*. Paris: Gallimard.
———. 1968. *The Visible and the Invisible*. Translated by Alphonso Lingis. Evanston, IL: Northwestern University Press. Originally published in 1964 as *Le Visible et l'invisible, suivi de notes de travail*. Ed. Claude Lefort. Paris: Gallimard.

———. 1970. *Themes from the Lectures at the Collège de France, 1952–1960.* Translated by John O'Neill. Evanston, IL: Northwestern University Press, 1970. Originally published in 1968 as *Résumés de cours, Collège de France 1952–1960.* Paris: Gallimard.

———. 1973. *In Praise of Philosophy.* Translated by John Wild and James M. Edie. Evanston, IL: Northwestern University Press. Originally published in 1953 as *Éloge de la philosophie.* Paris: Gallimard.

———. 1993. *Eye and Mind.* Translated by Michael B. Smith. In Galen A. Johnson, ed. *The Merleau-Ponty Aesthetics Reader.* Evanston, IL: Northwestern University Press. Originally published (in book form) in 1964 as *L'Œil et l'esprit.* Paris: Gallimard.

———. 2003. *Nature: Course Notes from the Collège de France.* Translated by Robert Vallier. Evanston, IL: Northwestern University Press. Originally published in 1994 as *La Nature, Notes, Cours du Collège de France,* ed. Dominique Séglard. Paris: Édition de Seuil.

———. 2012. *Phenomenology of Perception.* Translated by Donald A. Landes. New York: Routledge. Originally published in 1945 as *Phénoménologie de a perception.* Paris: Gallimard.

Moss, Michael. 2015. "In Quest for More Meat Profits, U.S. Lab Lets Animals Suffer." *The New York Times,* Tuesday, January 20.

Pollan, Michael. 2006. *The Omnivore's Dilemma: A Natural History of Four Meals.* New York: The Penguin Press.

Prunair, Jacques, ed. 2000. *Maurice Merleau-Ponty, Parcours deux, 1951–1961.* Paris: Éditions Verdier.

Saint Aubert, Emmanuel de. 2006. *Vers une ontologie indirecte, sources et enjeux critiques de l'appel à l'ontologie chez Merleau-Ponty.* Paris: J. Vrin.

Scheldrake, Rupert. 1990. *The Rebirth of Nature: The Greening of Science and God.* London: Random Century Group, Ltd.

Schelling, F. W. J. 1988 [revised edition 1803]. *Ideas for a Philosophy of Nature.* Trans. Errol E. Harris and Peter Heath, with an introduction by Robert Stern. Cambridge: Cambridge University Press.

———. 2000 [1815]. *The Ages of the World,* Third Version. Translated with an introduction by Jason M. Wirth. Albany: State University of New York Press.

———. 2006 [1809]. *Philosophical Investigations into the Essence of Human Freedom.* Translated with an introduction by Jeff Love and Johannes Schmidt. Albany: State University of New York Press.

Schillp, Paul A., ed. 1951. *The Philosophy of Alfred North Whitehead.* New York: Tudor Publishing Company, second edition.

Schuback, Marcia Sá Cavalcante. 2013. "The Eye and the Spirit of Nature: Some Reflections on Merleau-Ponty's Reading of Schelling Concerning the Relationship between Art and Nature." In Jason M. Wirth and Patrick Burke, 307–19.

Valenza, Robert J. 2014. "Harmony and Science: Toward a More Inclusive Scientific Worldview." *Process Perspectives,* Spring, 5–8.

Whitehead, Alfred North. 1951 [1941]. "Immortality." In Paul Arthur Schillp, ed., *The Philosophy of Alfred North Whitehead,* Evanston, IL: Northwestern University Press, 1941: 682–700.

———. 1925. *Science and the Modern World.* New York: The Free Press.

———. 1938. *Modes of Thought.* New York: The Free Press.

———. 1996. *Religion in the Making.* New York: Fordham University Press.

Wilson, Edward O. 2002. *The Future of Life.* New York: Vintage Books.

Wirth, Jason M. 2003. *The Conspiracy of Life: Meditations on Schelling and His Time.* Albany: State University of New York Press.

———. 2013. "The Reawakening of the Barbarian Principle." In Jason M. Wirth and Patrick Burke, 3–22.

Wirth, Jason M., and Patrick Burke, eds. 2013. *The Barbarian Principle: Merleau-Ponty, Schelling, and the Question of Nature.* Albany: State University of New York Press.

Chapter Two

Interrogating the Quantified Self

The Technological Reinterpretation of Causal Efficacy

Bo Eberle

In her insightful and thorough ethnography *Addiction by Design: Machine Gambling in Las Vegas,* Natasha Dow Schül investigates the way Las Vegas and particularly its video slot machines have been carefully concocted to draw players in and subtly guide their actions and gambling habits. Particularly striking is the way Schül reveals techniques for manipulating player behavior via the process of obfuscating cause and effect in the experience of play (Schül 2014, 86). The player is intentionally misled in complex ways as to how random values and odds are converted into reel stops on the screen of play while gambling. It is in that intermediate step—between the algorithm producing random values and creating the experience of a reel stop on the screen—that allows programmers to do all sorts of "wonderful things," as gaming expert John Robinson observes (Schül 2014, 86). Perhaps the most obvious of these wonderful things is the lengthening of odds with the departure from physical reels; after all, players more easily identify long odds if playing with a wheel with 72 stops than a video screen concealing thousands while only displaying 22. In sum, program design and micro-processing capabilities allowed game designers to produce a large disparity between actual and virtual reels, which in turn exponentially drove profits by concealing odds from the players. More than concealing odds, however, the newly designed video machines also enticed players and misled them in other ways. This gambling technology was designed at great expense to mislead players into having a false sense of control over being able to physically stop the reels, incorporating other non-gambling mechanisms such as simple video games into the gambling experience to prolong the time a player is at the machine, and ensuring that the overall aesthetic and ergonomic experience was optimal for prolonged play. While this is only the briefest exploration of some of the work Schül has accomplished in regard to video gambling, it will hopefully become clear how it relates to her next and current area of ethnographic and theoretical analysis: personal tracking devices. I wish to take Schül's work as a "lure" to think about how these personal tracking devices, following technology and strategies developed in the gambling industry, manipulate our experience of our own bodies. Adding a Whiteheadian metaphysical account to the technology in question will help us understand the multiple levels of layers of subject formation and experience such technologies produce at the level of and beneath conscious experience. Hence, to think through some of the consequences of the phenomenon now known as the "quantified self," we will think with Whitehead, particularly his concept of causal efficacy, as to how these devices subtly "game" our behavior.

WHITEHEAD ON MEDIA

In his book *Feed Forward: On the Future of 21st Century Media,* Mark Hansen makes important claims regarding forms of media that are no longer meant for or targeting our conscious experience. A Whiteheadian account, for Hansen, is "capacious enough to account for the ways in which . . . supposedly foundational and categorical divisions in fact involve complex overlappings of different levels of experience, none of which is intrinsically more worthy than others" (Hansen 2015, 9). Whitehead's reform succeeds in this by reforming agent-centered perceptual modality towards what Hansen calls "environmental sensibility," which acts as a neutral theory of experience that applies to humans and nonhumans alike. For Hansen, there is a need to think networks of various kinds of entities impressing upon each other horizontally. Importantly, Whitehead provides a framework to analyze media non-prosthetically and non-anthropocentrically. Media theory of the twentieth century, especially in the work of Marshall McLuhan, falls prey to this tendency to think of media as a prosthetic or extension of the human. Other important media theorists such as Jacques Ellul remained suspicious of technological development, or *technique* as Ellul writes, while others such as Paul Virilio and his theory of dromology lament the speed at which the world now operates. Whether or not these are valid concerns is not at issue here, for it seems far too late to take a critical stance toward new media and microprocessing technologies. Instead, with Hansen it is prudent to take this historical moment to resuscitate *metaphysical* concepts that help us understand the way in which consciousness has always already been imbricated with the environment. Whether or not developers are aware of certain metaphysical principles, what seems to be happening with the proliferation of wearable technology and data collection is the leveraging of something like Whiteheadian concepts of the philosophy of the organism *in order to change the way we perceive ourselves and the world.*

One of the most crucial claims Hansen makes in his study of new media is the displacing perception with sensation, which he calls "worldly sensibility" (Hansen 2015, 46). Again, this is necessary in his view because media technologies such as micro sensors and processors in ubiquitous machines like cell phones do not grant us awareness or ordinary perception as they carry out many of their functions. Rather, these devices gather a monumental amount of sensory information from the environment, and are capable of "feed forward" operations (rather than feedback mechanisms) that operate at a level above (and below) our conscious perception, even to the extent of *standing in for consciousness itself.* Sense perception itself is now open to a far greater swath of its environment than it has been before. Media is now in the position of mediating *sensibility itself* outside of the realm of conscious perception. In other words, media forms the "sensory basis for experience as such" (Hansen 2015, 47). To again draw the connection back to Whitehead's metaphysical preemption of any of these observations, the payoff is broadening of the scope of *perception* (Hansen 2015, 48).

More explicitly, Hansen continues, "Consciousness is no longer the relevant level of experience" (Hansen 2015, 59). Micro-processing technology has stepped in as the primary form of world-sensing and interpreting, replacing the human mind. One example employed by Hansen is that of the devices designed to regulate insulin. These new devices, Hansen describes, measure not only insulin levels, but also indicate when seizures are most likely to occur. These devices, then, bypass consciousness entirely, tapping into elements of our body that operate on the level of what Whitehead calls causal efficacy rather than presentational immediacy, creating "digital insight" that bring into our conscious awareness (artificially) and participate in our awareness of our own bodies (Hansen 2015, 60). These devices bring to light some of the nearly infinite bodily processes that occur beneath our perception, but instead of certain physical feelings remaining the grounds for conceptual feelings on a conscious level, they are collected and interpreted *on our behalf*, and the devices are able to act on their own interpretations well before we can become aware or feel the forces they are measuring. Whitehead, then, begins to help us see the complex causal ground, as Hansen articulates it, for new kinds of media experiences that work on the feed-forward model.

While feed-forward technology might be new, the principles by which it functions are clearly articulated in Whitehead's philosophical system. Whitehead's thought helps address Bruno Latour's challenge to avoid the bifurcation of nature. Latour warns against splitting the universe into different kinds of things, or primary and secondary qualities. Media theory of the twentieth century does precisely this whenever technology or media is thought of as a prosthetic, or something secondary grafted onto the body and thought of "primary" sorts of things like minds and experience. When Whitehead proclaims of every actual occasion "The many become one, and are increased by one. In their natures, entities are disjunctively 'many' in process of passage into conjunctive unity," we can see that actual occasions, whether in the human mind or a particle of dust, are never comprised of only some kind of thing and not another (Whitehead 1978, 21). Put simply, nothing that exists in any kind of concrete unity can be thought of as un-networked, or lacking connection to everything else. Any attempted work of purification, for Whitehead, would simply be a fallacy of misplaced concreteness: "It lies in the nature of things that the many enter into complex unity" (Whitehead 1978, 21). The world, in other words, is complex and fluid, and any event that occurs is impacted and shaped by what comes before it, significantly caused by what effects it. This kind of framework then allows Hansen to think about humans and forms of media as complex nodes in a broader environmental context, reframing human experience (or conscious experience) as only one, sometimes very limited component of our relationship to media and technology. This is partly why Whitehead defines philosophy as "the self-correction by consciousness of its own initial excess of subjectivity" (Whitehead 1978, 15). We must overcome our own limited perspective, not to achieve a "view from no-where," but to adapt to the idea that what appears to us in consciousness is indeed part of multifaceted feed forward apparatuses built into the fabric of reality, no less our technology. Twenty-first-century media give us ever increasing insight into some of the causal forces that go into producing consciousness, which is precisely why Whitehead is more important than ever as a philosopher who emphasizes the causal ground of experience and consciousness. Whitehead calls to us to overcome seeing ourselves as discreet entities not already intensely networked into the world. Failing to then think critically about the kind of data, and even why particular data, is being fed forward into conscious perception is the key critical question.

But now that we have briefly explored how Whitehead might reframe our approach to contemporary media from an environmental perspective, we must also begin to ask more critical questions about the employment of these kinds of media technology. Building on the work of Schül and Hansen, a useful way to go about such questions might be to think about how wearable tracking devices such as the Fitbit, Lumo Lift, Muse headband, and various sensors in our phones and now Apple Watches redistribute sense perception in Whitehead's concept of "symbolic reference." Symbolic reference is Whitehead's way of talking about the interplay of affect, causality, and conscious perception. In symbolic reference, ordinary sense perception is formed by symbolically referencing feelings given in the form of causal efficacy. Actual physical feeling passed from the physical world to our physical organs and flesh relate us to our environment and the events happening around us in the mode of causal efficacy, while shortly afterward we integrate a propositional feeling, like that of color, onto the physical prehension (Whitehead's word for experience not dependent on consciousness) linking us to the world. Put simply, seeing the blue sky above me is not simply a matter of experiencing something like the qualia or sensation of blue, but the integration, through symbolic reference, of causal events and propositional concepts, or eternal objects, that conceptually allow me to perceive the sky as blue. In other words, Whitehead is describing a process, seemingly overlooked by many philosophers in the wake of Hume and Kant, by which physical events or stimuli are abstracted into conscious perceptual awareness via our body *and* our imagination. In the past many philosophers only spoke of perception in the register of presentational immediacy, clear and distinct sensuous perceptions, but Whitehead calls our attention to how we come to these sense perceptions through our bodies and organs, arguing that we are not directly perceiving something like the color "blue" but only perceiving *through* the mediation not only our bodies but our environment. As Whitehead puts in in his book *Symbolism*, this is "the perception of the pressure from a world of things with characters in their own right, characters mysteriously moulding our own natures" (Whitehead 1927, 44). While Whitehead may not have had the kind of technology in question here in mind, nevertheless these "characters" are in some cases becoming more aware of their role in forming our conscious perception.

With Whitehead's theory of perception broadly outlined, and keeping in mind Hansen's important work on twenty-first-century media, we can now turn toward the movement known as the "quantified self," which has helped popularize the fitness tracking phenomenon as well as developing technologies like the insulin regulator mentioned above. Through the intervention of technology, the hope of the movement is improved self-knowledge via self-tracking. While the "movement" itself is multifaceted, and also includes things like body modification and body hacking (in the realm of "transhumanism"), the focus of this inquiry will be more modest pieces of technology like the wildly popular Fitbit personal fitness tracker. Personal tracking devices have steadily increased in popularity and now constitute an industry with an estimated worth approaching one billion dollars. Building on initial fitness technology designed to track an individual's daily step count, devices have proliferated to provide their user (and in some cases, other entities) with detailed information purporting to represent important internal information about the individual's body and/or bodily activity. Such as heart rate, sleep quality, and stress levels. I should point out that by "device" I mean not only physical pieces of technology like a Fitbit around one's wrist, but also sophisticated software applications that work in conjunction with detailed sensors built into devices such as mobile phones that many carry with them most of the time. Hence personal tracking devices range from sports heart monitors to phone "apps" that help one track their hydration level and sleep patterns, to headbands that claim to be able to detect brainwaves.

It does not seem outlandish to postulate these devices, as they grow in popularity, changing the way humans have generally been aware of their own perceptions. Harkening back to my introduction regarding Schül's video slot machines using advanced micro-processing technology to obscure cause and effect for the player at the machine and predicting players' movements even before they become aware of them, it is quite possible to imagine tracking devices acting similarly insofar as they also bring into presentational immediacy representations about ourselves *on our behalf* rather than the process working within our own consciousness as Whitehead described. Following the aforementioned Whitehead quote, causal efficacy entails characters "moulding our natures" in a mysterious manner, but perhaps now the mysterious process has been coopted by for-profit bodily tracking. Many of these so-called quantified-self devices therefore seek to quantify and then represent, usually numerically, complex bodily processes that usually remain beneath conscious perception and bring them straight into perception in the mode presentational immediacy. In doing so, there is either an explicit or implicit assertion that *particular* metrics, such as step count or heart rate, are the *cause* of various states of well-being. Rather than allowing a myriad of complex sub-perceptive forces to aggregate and come to form a perception in the form of presentational immediacy, micro-processing devices essentially extract acute metrics from complex webs in order to make the user consciously aware of either movements, such as steps, or bodily measures such as heart rate that would usually contribute to how our perceptions of the world are formed—for example a quickened heart rate may cause heightened perceptual sensitivity due to anxiety or fear, or a sedentary period may dull one's senses due to lack of energy or motivation, whereas with devices measuring our bodies *before* perceptions such as these are formed may affect how we think before we are allowed to perceive via the process Whitehead describes as symbolic reference. Put another way, micro-processing devices have the capacity to wedge themselves in between causal efficacy and presentational immediacy, potentially obscuring or simplifying causes in order to produce specific effects. Not unlike the video slot machines that are programmed to keep their odds and determined outcomes a secret in order to produce prolonged play of the user, devices that measure and quantify bodily processes might be interpreted to cover up the complexity of one's own body, one's relationship to their environment, and even the mode of perception itself in order to encourage or prod a certain kind of action. It is not difficult to think, after all, about the kind of subject a Fitbit aims to form—an "active subject" who has enough free time to "get their steps in," elevate their heart rate at least once per day, and generally maintain a kind of inertia that is considered "normal" by the programming. Other devices can be even more extreme. The Muse headband, for instance, claims to be able to monitor the wearer's brainwaves in order to play different sounds, which it pumps into your ear canal based on whether it detects you are calm or anxious. These devices hence "get to" your consciousness before environmental stimuli get to it themselves—they are much quicker than you, able to, in some cases, interpret causally efficacious stimuli and represent them to your conscious mode of perception in a planned, goal-oriented fashion. "Quantrepeneurs," as developers of these kinds of devices sometimes call themselves, have faith that through greater knowledge of the self we will ultimately become more controlled, even more ethical people.

A Whiteheadian theoretical intervention is so helpfully applied to this phenomenon because of the nuanced approach to perception that allows us to see how these devices intervene *between* the two major poles of perception, whereas so much theory of perception is limited to what Whitehead calls presentational immediacy. If we are limited to a presentational immediacy approach—thinking about perception as merely the qualities we experience—it is more difficult to see the kind of perception made possible by advanced micro processing media of the twenty-first century. Moreover, as Whitehead argues in *Process and Reality,* it is perception in the mode of causal efficacy, not presentational immediacy, that is "the uncontrolled basis on which our character weaves itself" (Whitehead 1978, 174/271). Here Whitehead is of course highlighting the extent to which past experiences, and by extension the social environment in which we are socially formed, determines our capacity for creativity and action. Applied to the Quantified Self movement we can also see how, through altering our perception in a calculated way by bringing straight into perceptual awareness that which usually lies beneath the surface of conscious awareness, there can also be modifications to our subjectivity and character. This is the stark characteristic of passive sensing technologies collecting massive amounts of data—we are no longer the most complex sensing agents in the world we live in. Following Hansen's argument, we can no longer have object- or body-centered theories of perception because sense data is constantly collected and massively distributed, calling for a radically environmental approach. Media do not simply impact our experiences or intensify them, as prosthetic theories such as McLuhan's suggest: media impact experience diffusely at the level of causal efficacy.

Massively distributed data, or what Hansen calls "reality mining," gives us ever increasing and astounding access to environmental processes never before available for our conscious appreciation. On the other hand, the more reality, and particularly our own physical and emotional behavior is mined, the more it becomes *predictable.* As Theodore Porter has argued, quantifying biometrical data in order for predicating outcomes has been a part of our society for a long time (Porter 1996). Porter's study concerns one particularly ubiquitous measurement, that of blood pressure, which he argues was not an innovation made in the name of medicine but by insurance companies. It was, according to Porter, actuary tables that demanded the most reliable way to predict the likelihood of someone's death—not doctors. Porter also shows that while blood pressure is certainly a useful metric in many circumstances, its function is financial and for insurance purposes more than it is for individual patient care. The aggregation of millions upon millions of statistics about blood pressure allowed for the creation of more accurate tables and hence more profitable insurance policies. In relation to our discussion here, twenty-first-century media as analyzed by Hansen and Schül extrapolate out what it might mean for this kind of operation to be carried out by always collecting microprocessors and algorithms in our computers and our pockets. If it is indeed true that microtemporal behaviors inform higher order perceptions at the level of causal efficacy, once these microtemporal behaviors can be registered and interpreted on their own time scale, which is much faster than our consciousness, consciousness can simply be bypassed entirely. When this occurs and predictions are carried out, operations can then be implemented based on predictive models of events and behaviors derived from the mined data. Twenty-first-century media then can be characterized by their capacity to capture information that directly concerns our behavior and tendencies but to which we ourselves lack direct access (Hansen 2015, 181). This is what Hansen calls the *precognitive* vocation of twenty-first-century media, that "targets infrastructural or causally efficacious elements informing future behavior with the aim of reliably predicting such behavior before it happens" (Hansen 2015, 187). Of course, this is of great interest to global capital as many have pointed out with terms like "networked capitalism," the collection of data itself becomes the production of a new kind of surplus value produced almost automatically. Hansen's question is thus what becomes of perception in the wake of the capitalist conquest of forethought? Rather than granting us intensification of experience by vastly increasing our perceptive capacities, new media technology is appropriated for neoliberal economic and biopolitical purposes.

STAVING OFF THE PATHOLOGICAL

Georges Canguilhem, early twentieth-century philosopher of science and physician, is well known for his interrogation of the concept of health. In his seminal work, *The Normal and the Pathological*, Canguilhem defends the thesis that any concept of the "normal" scientists or physicians may employ is only sensible in relation to the study of what is deemed "pathological." For example, constructions of the normal structure of organs and tissues were historically derived from observations of samples deemed pathological due to the appearance of lesions. Lesions, rightly seen as irregular, were then in time correlated with pathology or sickness, and Canguilhem sets his sights on correcting the assumption that irregularity = pathology, and by extension that regular (or normal) = healthy. It may be the case that irregularity is representative of a deeper issue of health and wellness; however, the leap from treating an irregularity as a possible sign to a marker of the pathological is greater than it appears, and results in a kind of medical practice and wisdom that occludes the individual. In the process of constructing categories of normal and pathological based on trends, statistics, and aggregates for what usually appears and appears to be the case, norms for particular subjects are made invisible, and that which is singular can only appear as a dangerous aberration.

Therefore for Canguilhem, "adaptation to a personal milieu is one of the fundamental presuppositions of health" (Canguilhem 1989, 129). One is healthy, in other words, when she is "capable of several norms . . . more than normal" (Canguilhem 1989, 132). Disease decreases our ability to adapt. Something is pathological, by extension, when it does not fit a specific milieu it is measured against (Canguilhem 1989, 128). Whereas physicians might well be justified in taking biological measurements and comparing them against certain norms in the present, changing social milieus may constitute bodily or biological responses that can only appear pathological if a single, context independent norm or function is assigned to a body. As Canguilhem notes, this understanding would compel physicians toward the *subjective* element of the patient, inquiring about the experiences of various events in the patient's life, rather than objectivized data that represents particular processes. It should go without saying that Canguilhem is certainly not suggesting an abandonment of any measure of objectification, but sternly warning his readers of the danger residing in being unreflective about the way we use statistics and norms to put the individual under erasure.

Personal tracking devices may have both a friend and a foe in Canguilhem. There is little doubt that these devices rely on monitoring the individual in relation to statistical norms. To take the most prevalent form of the technology, the Fitbit, as an example, we can see that the step-counting device simultaneously measures one's own activity against personal averages, but at the same time great pressure is applied on the user to meet fitness goals and achieve "badges" for completing certain challenges set by the manufacturer. Additionally, the social component of many of the quantified self technologies encourage users to post their activity to social media and compete with "friends" to achieve the "best" statistics for a given period (e.g., the most steps or the most glasses of water consumed—Fitbit strongly encourages keeping other metrics alongside steps, including sleep patterns as well as caloric and water intake).

It appears that in theory, the advent of technologies like the seemingly ubiquitous Fitbit either seen adorning wrists or hidden in pockets all around you, would be a boon for Canguilhemian approaches to personal health. One must take the technological ability to potentially aggregate an enormous amount of data about the individual with a grain of salt, however, due to the inevitable ways in which the data is put to use. First of all, as I will return to below, data, in this case in the form of steps, is a potentially misleading and extraordinarily simplified measurement of well-being. Though I do not want to act as if consumers are as naïve as to think that any one life style improvement will cure them of any impediment, it must be held in mind that there is great interest in portraying a single metric, such as steps, as more efficacious in improving one's health than perhaps is warranted due to the nature of the marketing. Additionally, and as alluded to above, even as date about the individual proliferates, it is then almost *immediately* then set against data from other individuals. Not only are devices pre-programmed with recommended goals and "averages," a significant part of the quantified self "experience" is social in that one is encouraged, if not forced via automation, to see one's data set against the data of others, from which norms and averages are then derived. This is then a good time to move toward a greater exploration of the process of quantification itself. From a Canguilhemian perspective, then, it is not clear that technologies such as the Fitbit offer a substantial lifestyle improvement.

Two news stories point in diverging directions in relation to the use of personal tracking technology and healthcare. It was recently reported that emergency room physicians were able to use the Fitbit app in a patient's phone to "identify the time his heart arrhythmia started, which allowed them to treat his new-onset atrial fibrillation with electrical cardioversion and discharge him home" ("Can Your Fitness Tracker" 2015). Allegedly, this is the first time that personal tracking technology has been used in medical decision making. Using the software linked to the device worn by the patient on a daily basis, the physicians identified exactly when the patient's heart rate erratically jumped from 70 BPM to over 190 and also showed that the fibrillation only persisted for a few hours within a 48 hour window, allowing for a more specialized, individualized medical diagnosis than if doctors only had access to symptoms present when the patient was admitted. A case like this might hint at a kind of personalized medical practice enabled by wearable technology. Doctors and nurses might be able to take readings from a patient who wears a Fitbit or something similar to see long term averages *for that patient* rather than constantly comparing readings to what is considered "normal" for a large population. Unfortunately, it seems that while there may be a lone case of diagnosis via Fitbit, data taken up by these kinds of tracking devices is becoming much more valuable to insurance agencies (the original masters of statistics, e.g., blood pressure measurements) and even private religious universities wishing to aggregate data about their student populations.

In the time since 2016, many insurance companies have taken to relating premium prices to fitness and activity level for customers who wear devices like Fitbits. Ultimately, one insurance industry expert noted, a device that can track glucose levels would be ideal since it would let adjusters know almost exactly what their customer's diet is like (Olson 2014). Prudential Insurance has a program called "Vitality" through which its customers can receive up to a 15 percent discount for tracking their activity and regularly achieving certain goals (Pagliery 2015). What remains unclear, however, is the "black box" through which rates might ultimately be determined. Is a user's biometric data compared to what has been concerned "normal" by the adjusters, as has been seen in the extreme weight given to blood pressure measurements by life insurance adjusters for decades? With the advent of personal tracking, insurance providers have the opportunity to take an individualized approach to adjusting rates, but there is no evidence that suggests they are in the process of doing so.

Another significant deployment of wearable technology is at the fundamentalist Christian Oral Roberts University in Tulsa, Oklahoma. Incoming freshman in 2016 were required to wear a Fitbit and record 10,000 steps per day with the data being made available to professors (Chasmer 2016). Oral Roberts couches the program in terms of a mode of education oriented toward the "whole person," though it is noted that university administrators can also access GPS data from the tracking devices to see where students eat, work out, and even sleep. Commentators have pointed out potential links between this technology and the fundamentalist Christian rules employed at Oral Roberts. While it is conceivable that this program is indeed for the purpose of increasing the overall health of its students, it can also be seen as a kind of biopolitical measure allowing the university to make sure that students are not sleeping together, spending time off campus in places like bars, and generally adding another requirement that students must fulfill with their bodies in their free time. As Fitbit has also stated publicly in a class action lawsuit statement, "It's also important to note that Fitbit trackers are designed to provide meaningful data to our users to help them reach their health and fitness goals, and are not intended to be scientific or medical devices" (Chasmer 2016). As another commentator points out, fitness tracking also fits right in with the long tradition of Christian universities monitoring students' behavior. Oral Roberts has been requiring certain fitness tests and tracking via journal since the 1970s (Root 2016). Hence one might look at the contrasting goals of Fitbit and how Fitbit is implemented in both contexts of Oral Roberts University and Prudential Insurance. Fitbit claims that it was established to help *individuals* achieve their fitness and wellness goals. In both cases of Oral Roberts and Prudential, larger entities essentially aim to use Fitbit to reorient the activities of a mass of bodies for purposes of statistical and social control and regulation, respectively. While I will not take this antimony further here, or morally denounce either of these uses, it is sufficient to note the normative drift that is taking place in respect to personal tracking technology: it is becoming less personal.

Against Fitbit's own stated intentions, we might also examine that while Fitbits and other such devices offer individuals abilities to measure their own statistics against themselves rather than averages, this is discouraged through the programming of the devices and the move to immediately compare oneself to others. Moreover, and as we will see in greater detail, the devices are still only offering quantification of biology and experience, rather than offering any kind of outlet for the subjective element of healthcare Canguilhem laments is disappearing from modern medical practice.

CONCLUSION

As the world descends into ecological ruin, it is hardly surprising that neoliberal capitalism, the most virulent form of capitalism we currently inhabit, which may be defined by its absolute commodification of everything, if not especially human life itself, might be very happy to direct our attention inside of ourselves, turning us into little detectives of the self, rather than focusing on the maladies of the earth itself. As conditions worsen and perhaps pollution puts the less wealthy at higher risks, devices that "know us better than we can know ourselves" may be marketed even more aggressively appealing to the survival instincts of the upper class (no doubt the only ones who can afford the advanced devices). As the Microsoft ad quoted above also intimates, there is even a quasi-religious appeal to "become a better person" via the kind of Hegelian self-mastery these devices offer.

Following Schül and others, we must begin to think about not only how design of tangible environments might influence our perception and behavior, but the design of algorithms that are far too nimble for us to detect if we aren't on our guard. But of course, simply recognizing that our worlds are being manipulated by various kinds of technology may not change anything. One important conclusion from Schül's work on video slot machines was that even when people *did* understand the con and the odds, their desire to play remained or even intensified. Likewise, pointing out the arbitrary, unverified, and in some cases manipulative function of wearable technology probably will do little to curb our desire for Fitbits and Apple Watches. I certainly do not wish to conclude with a technophobic injunction against wearing various kinds of technology that may well help many to become more active and shed light on aspects of our life we might improve with the help of new data. Rather, those interested in Whitehead's account of perception might be in prime position to ask the right questions as wearable tech becomes more adept and ubiquitous. As devices transform from simply other objects in the world physically bearing on our sense organs to interpreting the world (including our own bodies) before and for us, at issue will be what we do with this manner of sensing. Rather than taking the Luddite approach of condemnation, instead I will just point out that it is not surprising that a billion-dollar industry has arisen to prod individuals to track and obsess over their own individuality.

As the world descends into ecological ruin and capitalism makes life more precarious, we will be increasingly bombarded with pressure to improve ourselves as individuals, and this will be possible only for those with the resources to invest in their own bodies. On the other hand, data is certainly full of potential. Whitehead is very clear about different kinds of potential:

> We always have to consider two meanings of potentiality: (a) the "general" potentiality, which is the bundle of possibilities, mutually consistent or alternative, provided by the multiplicity of eternal objects, and (b) the "real" potentiality, which is conditioned by the data provided by the actual world. General potentiality is absolute, and real potentiality is relative to some actual entity, taken as a standpoint where the actual world is defined. It must be remembered that the phrase "actual world" is like "yesterday" and "tomorrow," in that it alters its meaning according to standpoint. The actual world must always mean the community of all actual entities. (Whitehead 1978, 65)

New ways of bulk data collection could also lead to increased access to "real potential" insofar as we are selectively expanding our view of the actual world. As Whitehead points out, this "real potentiality" is relative insofar as it represents the potential for a particular actual entity in a specific time and place. The advent of big data collection does not inaugurate an age of the view from nowhere, but certainly Whitehead's observation that "yesterday" and "tomorrow" change their meaning as our recording of yesterday is exponentially expanded via data collection, and hence the predictive models that come with the collection may radically alter what tomorrow might become. There is no extricating ourselves from the new world of big data and micro-sensing, so continually thinking about what kinds of nodes we want to become in a hyper-networked world will be imperative. The stakes are no less than who gets access to the "real potential" of reality and the construction of the "actual world."

REFERENCES

Canguilhem, Georges. 1989. *The Normal and the Pathological.* New York: Zone.
Chasmar, Jessica. 2016. "Oklahoma University Requires Freshmen to Wear Fitbit, Track 10k Steps Per Day." http://www.washingtontimes.com/news/2016/jan/11/oklahoma-university-requires-freshmen-to-wear-fitb/. January 11.

EurekAlert! The Global Source for Science News. 2015. "Can Your Fitness Tracker Save Your Life in the ER?" http://www.eurekalert.org/pub_releases/2016–04/acoe-cyf040516.php April 5.
Hansen, Mark. 2015. *Feed Forward: On the Future of Twenty-First-Century Media.* Chicago: University of Chicago Press.
Olson, Parmy. 2014. "Wearable Tech Is Plugging into Health Insurance." http://www.forbes.com/sites/parmyolson/2014/06/19/wearable-tech-health-insurance/#3a23b4fe5ba1. June 19.
Pagliery, Jose. 2015. "Would You Wear a Tracker to Get an Insurance Discount?" http://money.cnn.com/2015/04/08/technology/security/insurance-data-tracking/ April 8.
Porter, Theodore. 1996. *Trust in Numbers.* Princeton: Princeton University Press.
Root, Jonathan. 2016. "How Fitbit Helps a Conservative Evangelical College Monitor Students' Bodies for Christ." http://religiondispatches.org/where-oral-meets-orwell/. March 16.
Schül, Natasha Dow. 2014. *Addiction by Design: Machine Gambling in Las Vegas.* Durham: Duke University Press.
Whitehead, Alfred North. 1927. *Symbolism: Its Meaning and Effect.* New York: Fordham University Press.
———. 1978. *Process and Reality.* Corrected Edition. New York: The Free Press.

Chapter Three

Can Whitehead Save the World?

Complex Systems and the Limits of Activism

J. R. Hustwit and Carl Dyke

A core tenet of Whitehead's process metaphysics is that novelty continually ingresses into the world. This creative transformation accounts for variety in physical processes, human experience, and the development of human societies. Philosophers, theologians, and educators have been inspired to combine philosophy and social activism—coherent metaphysics put in the service of social justice. It is not surprising that many scholars of Whitehead have advocated that his metaphysical system itself should ingress into societies as a lure toward creative transformation. But we contend that philosophical activists should dampen their expectations. Civilizations are systems too complex to be managed.

This does not seem to be a popular view. Many philosophers seem to be confident that the world's troubles would be righted if only more people accepted the proper conceptual scheme.[1] For Whiteheadians, the proper scheme usually includes an event-based ontology and a non-coercive model of deity. There are many Whiteheadian scholar-activists who draw a direct line between a benighted substance-based metaphysic and social injustices. We recall one colleague, when his article on Whitehead had been ungently rejected from an academic journal, complained he was the victim of the editor's "classical model of God at work!" If only all of our frustrations could be attributed to the incoherent metaphysical beliefs of others.

Our aim is not to criticize Whitehead's philosophies, or argue against their ameliorative potential for civilization. At least one of this chapter's authors believes that Whitehead's metaphysics are better than the alternatives by a long shot. Nevertheless, both authors wish to vigorously complicate the correlation between accepting a metaphysical system, publicly advocating for that system's acceptance, and causing civilizational transformation.

We postulate that most systems worth saving are *complex adaptive systems* that endlessly generate hegemonies, and so transformative social activism cannot reliably generate ends specified in any dimension. Stated positively, activism does *something*, just as all action does *something*. But where change in complex adaptive systems is concerned (vs. maintenance of existing systems, which is an altogether different sort of project), what action *does* is not predictable. Individuals and groups do have power to contribute to the collapse of a civilization or birth of a new age, and have done so over and over again in history.[2] But it is a power realized only in hindsight, which means it cannot be managed or relied upon. The owl of Minerva flies only at dusk.

WHITEHEAD ON THE TRANSFORMATION OF CIVILIZATION

Whitehead has written much about moral ideals imperfectly realized in civilization, and the meandering progress of value that is infused into individual occasions from the primordial nature of God. But for this chapter, we will suspend his grandest speculation, and focus on the intersubjective situation of individual human persons attempting to change their intersubjective environments. Particular to this focus, Whitehead argues that the manipulation of symbols is key to effecting societal change, and that symbolic manipulation has

> two aspects; one is the subordination of the community to the individuals composing it, and the other is the subordination of the individuals to the community. Free men obey the rules which they themselves have made. . . . The art of free society consists first in the maintenance of the symbolic code; and secondly in fearlessness of revision. . . . Those societies that cannot combine reverence to their symbols with freedom of revision, must ultimately decay either from anarchy or from the slow atrophy of a life stifled by useless shadows. (Whitehead 1927, 88)

Echoing his technical metaphysics, Whitehead here argues that the manifold elements of society must submit to the one shared constellation of meaning, just as that unity must in turn submit to requirements of the many. The ability to transform society is precisely tied to the metaphysics of language: healthy communities must be able to both establish semantic stability, but also revise that constellation of meaning when required. But here, Whitehead may be overly sanguine about the fact that "free men" make the rules in a society.[3] The conditions under which a unity of meaning emerges from a vast multiplicity of individuals are not at all straightforward.

CASE STUDY: HEGEMONY IN MASS MEDIA

The media are among the most effective power assemblies for symbolic manipulation, and media channels wield the power of the past (i.e., Whitehead's doctrine of conformal feeling),[4] more effectively than other comparable occasions. For better or worse, televisions, newspapers, websites, blogs, billboards, radio, and even the little stickers on supermarket apples convey messages that are part of the constitutive field of a person's reason, values, and will. Information is abundant, diverse, and powerful.

In 2015, California was experiencing the most severe drought in at least 1,200 years (Nagourney 2015). Environmental scientists reported that this was not normal cyclical dryness, but the result of a long-term decrease in precipitation and a long-term increase in warming in the state (Nagourney 2015). In short, the climate is changing, and not in a way friendly to the current human infrastructure. A drought, unlike other natural catastrophes, endures over an extended period of time, so it can be ameliorated, both in the short and long term, by public efforts at conservation—activism! Drought (and famine) relief is especially dependent on public awareness and education. Curiously, in the month following the governor's spring announcement of a drought relief package (March 19–April 19, 2015), the top four television networks (ABC, NBC, CBS, FOX) in the two largest markets in the state (Los Angeles and Bay Area) aired 980 segments about the drought, but only 15 of those segments—less than 2 percent—connected the drought to climate change. Of those 15 segments, nine of them "balanced" the coverage by also offering statements of climate science denial, specifically those of Senator Ted Cruz (R-Texas) that "the alarmists on global warming [have] got a problem because the science doesn't back them up" (Halhoefer 2015).

But Ted Cruz, perhaps disappointingly, is not our villain. Nor is/are "the media." Let us be wary of misplacing concreteness. There is no single actor named "the media." Furthermore, media operate within larger fields that can be both damping and amplifying, at various scales.[5] Perhaps (routinely) overwhelmed, the news coverage of the drought skewed away from a scientifically sound and practically necessary bit of information: that the Earth's climate is changing in irreversible ways. A useful orienting concept here is that of hegemony, developed by Italian Marxist Antonio Gramsci. Gramsci, frustrated in the early twentieth century that the supposedly inevitable class revolution had not occurred in Western Europe, explained the entrenchment of the bourgeoisie by means of hegemony—a process by which one group or confederation of groups establishes a cultural superstructure that wins the "commonsense" participation of the populace. The hegemonic group's goals and interests are constituted and embedded in ways of life and thought; others are suppressed, diverted, or incorporated.

Concretely, Gramsci looked to folklore, religion, and education as venues in which the formation of popular thought or "common sense" comes to be aligned with that of the hegemonic class (Gramsci 1971, 57–59, 79, 339, 421). He saw a complex system composed of multiple interrelated and interdependent subsystems.[6] The press is the most dynamic part of this ideological structure, but not the only one. Everything that influences or is able to influence public opinion, directly or indirectly, belongs to it: libraries, schools, associations and clubs of various kinds, even architecture and the layout and names of streets (Gramsci 1985, 389). Even in just the cultural complex including family, education, media, and other primarily ideological functions, effective hegemony and therefore effective opposition to it

> requires an extremely minute, molecular process of extreme, capillary analysis, the documentation for which is made up of an immense quantity of books, pamphlets, review and newspaper articles, conversations and oral debates repeated countless times, and which in their gigantic aggregation represent this long labor which gives birth to a collective will with a certain degree of homogeneity—of the degree necessary and sufficient to achieve coordinated and simultaneous action in the time and space in which the historical event takes place. (Gramsci 1975, 8 and 195)[7]

Revolution is hard. Hence his famous motto, "pessimism of the intellect, optimism of the will."

Today we could certainly add radio, television, the web, and social media as venues of the formation of hegemony. Every half-heard television news story or skimmed Facebook post contributes to the agglomeration of information that is cemented unconsciously into the "common sense" of the population. In fact, the "viral" nature of new social media means that the more popular a piece of content becomes, the more people share it, the higher the quantity of impressions it makes on an individual. Television news stories run twice a day no matter what, but an internet meme could be served up in a single Facebook feed fifteen times in an hour, and each accompanied by the tacit endorsement of our friends and loved ones. Whitehead supposes that "Each little emotion directly arising out of some subordinate detail refuses to accept its status as a detached fact in our consciousness. It insists on its symbolic transfer to the unity of the main effect" (Whitehead 1927, 86). The result is a gestalt participation in a cultural hegemony. One begins to see that Whitehead does indeed appreciate just how profoundly individuals are subordinated by, and contribute to a shared unity of meaning in and through media. Despite his optimistic invocations of reason and progress, one should not read Whitehead as assuming that humans blithely alter their cultural superstructure whenever reason demands it. Revision is ultimately necessary, but there is hegemonic momentum working against those who seek change. Successful transformation has to "go with the flow," to be working with currents already generated from within the hegemony; the action is not to change everything, but to work with and encourage emergence. This means that hegemonic momentum has to somehow be working FOR those who seek change. Trying to force it is what gets you terrors, gulags, and killing fields.

FROM CONSPIRACY TO COMPLEXITY

Gramscian hegemony is frequently read as the accomplishment of human will, whereby the dominant classes intentionally manipulate media outlets from behind the scenes for self-serving, if not nefarious purposes. But this "evil mastermind" trope of vulgar Marxism yielded thin analysis of no use to effective political action in Gramsci's day or ours, and was therefore precisely what Gramsci was attempting to think beyond.[8] There is no one person or cabal named "the media"; it stands for the interrelated network of corporations, individuals, material artifacts, and narratives that disseminate symbols to the public. Each of the actors of this network have different pasts, different projects, and different horizons of imagined possibilities.[9] If we return to the climate change example, we may find that try as we might, there is no identifiable party directly responsible for the global warming cover-up. It is entirely plausible to imagine that the news anchors reporting the story actually objected to the incomplete coverage of the drought, but felt obligated by their contracts to read the scripts given to them. Content is the responsibility of the producers. The producers may find the programming lopsided, but are trained to keep segments short and light so as to not tax viewer attention. Let the trained scientists be responsible for public education. Perhaps the executives would rather their networks report the matter differently, but are obligated to their stockholders to maximize revenue. Each of these sins is minor—there are no tyrants here. Where does the nefarious power reside? Nowhere in particular. The media system itself is an emergent hegemonic agent, but not because of intelligent design. As media scholar Neil Postman observes, "The President does not have the press under his thumb. The *New York Times* and the *Washington Post* are not *Pravda*; the Associated Press is not *Tass*. And there is no Newspeak here.... All that has happened is that the public has adjusted to incoherence [of new media] and been amused into indifference" (Postman 1985, 110–11). This is not to deny that there may be explicit pressure somewhere in the system to stifle discussion of climate change. The more complete explanation, however, describes pressure emerging from the uncountable micro-transactions between viewers, readers, producers, performers, and other interested agents, including many that clamor from positions of hegemonic authority and prestige (Al Gore, Bill Gates, the "scientific establishment") for *more* and *better* discussion of climate change.

In the absence of a centralized puppet master, we must look to the distributed micro-transactions for the emergence of ideological narratives, and though a hegemony emerges, that hegemony cannot be reduced to the decisions and interests of the individuals who make up the system. Hegemony is no more a singular entity than media. This revised, emergent hegemony can be explained by complexity science, which according to James Glieck, offers "new kinds of laws. They are laws of structure and organization and scale, and they simply vanish when you focus on the individual constituents of a complex system—just as the psychology of a lynch mob vanishes when you interview individual participants" (quoted in Weinberg 1992, 60).[10] For the past forty years or so, scientists, mathematicians, and philosophers have observed that in software, species populations, politics, and other collective societies, there seem to be two kinds of systems. One is a multi-agent system, or ordinary system. In an ordinary system, the behavior of the system is nothing more than the sum total of the behavior of its individual components. The molecules in a cloud of gas will bounce every which way, but the cloud as a whole drifts aimlessly with the net aggregation of molecular vectors, most of which cancel each other out. There is no emergent novelty, and the organization quickly dissipates due to entropy. Such a system is complicated, not complex.

But sometimes, a system can behave unexpectedly. Properties emerge that defy reductive teleology, even while maintaining unidirectionality (Funtowicz and Ravetz 1994, 569). The system takes on a life of its own, demonstrating *autopoeisis*, self-organization. We call these complex adaptive systems. A number of traits define a complex adaptive system (CAS). A CAS (1) contains *non-linear interactions* in which the tiniest perturbation can feed back into progressively large and systemic effects. The famous "butterfly effect" by which a butterfly's flapping wings can ultimately cause a typhoon halfway around the world is a prime example. Likewise, consider the fourteenth-century proverb:

> *For want of a nail the shoe was lost.*
> *For want of a shoe the horse was lost.*
> *For want of a horse the rider was lost.*
> *For want of a rider the message was lost.*
> *For want of a message the battle was lost.*
> *For want of a battle the kingdom was lost.*
> *And all for the want of a horseshoe nail.*

An initially inconsequent event has increasingly wide-ranging effects. Because effects feedback on themselves, amplifying some traits while suppressing others, complex systems create hierarchical order and dynamical simplification. Emergent complexity is therefore strongly correlated with hegemony, cultural or otherwise (Deacon 2011, 243). There are many examples of this. One biological population will come to consume more and more of an environment's resources until it collapses, only to be replaced by the dominance of an alternate species. Unregulated economic markets tend toward consolidation and concentration of wealth (cf. Orrell 2010).

A complex system will also (2) *resist entropy*. Structures of the system that maintain stability far from entropic equilibrium develop (independent of individual agents). As particular behaviors feedback on themselves, one element of the system (a species, an ideology, a behavior) gains dominance over the others, and the system self-organizes to actively maintain that structure.[11]

Complex adaptive systems are (3) atomically ateleological. This does not entail a philosophical determinism, but rather indicates that behaviors of the system cannot be reliably attributed to members of the system.[12] In this complex system, where does the power reside? Who is ultimately responsible for the behavior of the system? No one. The system itself emerges and evolves as an agent by constraining and entraining the agency of its components. The moral responsibility is diffused among a great many moral agents, each of whom is unable to see the whole scope of her behavior's consequences, and unable to predict the chaotic effects of her decisions. This is not to absolve those who act in bad faith. But even Rupert Murdoch, identifiable as the chairman of some of the most misleading media organizations today, is himself constrained by the system he would control. We must not only look to the acts of individuals, but to the legal and economic constraints that incentivize such behavior, to the sociological facts of Murdoch's childhood, to the material and spiritual qualities of Western culture in the later twentieth century, Saturday morning cartoons (Burke and Burke 1998), FCC regulations, Superbowl Sundays, Nielsen ratings, televised presidential assassinations, dietary adaptations of gut bacteria. Again, countless micro-events were necessary to produce the milieu in which our particular media hegemony emerged.

This leads to the next trait of complex systems, that (4) individuals in the CAS frequently remain ignorant of the system as a whole. This is where ethical complication occurs. We do not hold a person responsible for consequences that are unintended and unforeseeable. Yet in a complex system, any action could have profound and unpredictable consequences. Many of us could easily be complicit in destructive complex systems without even knowing it. Racism, sexism, heterosexism, genderism, and imperialism are a few salient examples. The 1976 film *Network* provides a pathetic illustration. Television anchor Howard Beale's famous protest of "I'm as mad as hell, and I'm not going to take this anymore," is especially poignant because the viewer knows that Beale's own defiance, which is eventually echoed by thousands of his viewers, is futile given the hegemonies in place (*Network* 1976). In short order, the slogan no longer echoes from the open windows of the viewing public, is gone as quickly as it came, forgotten. Ultimately,

Beale's critique was in fact co-opted by the network, and used to propagate its success.

The Network example also illustrates another important aspect of successful hegemonies. They must (5) tolerate contradictions. This is especially so among the mass media, where at least a superficial diversity of content is required in order to maintain viewer interest. Todd Gitlin notes that television networks in particular accommodate "legitimated forms of opposition" where "major social conflicts are transported into the cultural system, where the hegemonic process frames them, form and content both, into compatibility with the dominant systems of meaning" (Gitlin 1979, 263–64). Without this ability to reframe and co-opt dissent, the hegemony becomes fragile, making itself vulnerable to challenge. But when the terms of the debate can be reframed to include issues that are only superficially challenging to the status quo, the hegemony can adapt with democratic dissent in order to cathartically forestall more serious challenges. In 1984, Neil Postman predicted that one of the only recourses against television's cultural hegemony was to create a television program that would self-referentially parody the medium. The goal would be to "induce a nationwide horselaugh over television's control of public discourse." Of course, Postman concludes, TV would have the last laugh, as the very critique must itself be entertaining and endorsable by advertisers in order to make it to air, and so the entire critique would be co-opted by TV, and incorporated into the ideology of amusement (Postman 1985, 161–62). This describes exactly the role of Comedy Central's *The Daily Show* with Jon Stewart (1999–2015). Incidentally, shortly before his death, Postman did appear on *The Daily Show*, not as a serious media critic, but as the punchline in a spoofed interview in which Postman was portrayed as an eccentric technophobe, and accused of waging war against toasters ("Lies of the Machines" 2003). Touché.

The ambivalence of subversive programming—critiquing the system while bolstering it—is an example of another trait of complex systems. A complex system will always demonstrate (6) adaptive novelty in order to suppress those elements that challenge its ascendancy.[13] We see both of these traits when we consider the ways in which both disease-causing and symbiotic organisms evolve resistances to various drugs and treatments, or when media conglomerates continue to merge and simultaneously lobby against anti-trust regulation. The system itself is ateleologically adapting to maintain hegemony.[14]

Finally, scientists have observed that the hegemonies that emerge from complex systems eventually undergo (7) autolysis. They break themselves apart. Funtowicz and Ravetz call this the *ancien régime* syndrome. The incumbents in a hegemony tend to filter or suppress novel or threatening information, resorting to distraction, irrelevant narratives, and other techniques. In the short run, these techniques shore up the hegemony's stability, but in the long run, erode the efficacy of the hegemony. The timescale involved may be long or short, but one of a number of scenarios generally ends the stability. Sometimes, a system devotes increasing amounts of energy into suppressing challenges that it can no longer produce effective results (in governance, communication, technology), and is toppled by an external catastrophe (Funtowicz and Ravetz 1994, 571–72). So, though hegemonies are by nature constraining, they are also by nature finite, and the temporal analysis of complex systems reveals an oscillation between hegemony and fragmentation. But this liberation is short-lived as the previously marginalized or "slaved" elements of the system will concatenate upwards into a new hegemony. It takes great care and energy to maintain a truly democratic pluralism in such systems.[15]

Complexity theorists portray complex systems as volatile entities, especially treacherous because of their (a) large scale, especially when humans are involved, (b) non-linear tendency toward hegemony, which blunts the efficacy of individual action, and (c) disjunction between individual agency and systemic consequences. If we suppose that hegemony is a generally undesirable thing in human communicative media, we must still wonder what could replace it.

Bringing down a hegemony is impossible to strategize.[16] The distributed nature of complex systems entails that although the environment is target rich, there's no way to pick the ones to take out. You could remove Rupert Murdoch or gendered pronouns from the face of the Earth, and it might not make much difference. Gramsci therefore offered a comprehensive assault of "extremely minute molecularity," which is still the best account of a complexity-aware political practice available. Yet apart from its overwhelming scope, that account still gives us a politics in pieces rather than an actionable sense of complexly adaptive functionality. "But we have to do *something*" is true, but unhelpful.[17] The results of an action are not your own, but shared with thousands or millions of other causal interactions. It may be a mistake to think in terms of problems and solutions with complex systems.

Although linear problem solving is ineffective, there are two ontological features of symbolic communication that allow for the possibility of counter-hegemonic discourse. Of course, countering one hegemony only leads to another hegemony in a CAS. Our thesis is not that Ricoeur and Whitehead provide the tools for smashing hegemony any more than magnets and rocket fuel smashed the laws of physics—in both examples, one finds a new mode of comportment within the system. There are multiple ways to maneuver within a hegemony; one need not be wholly determined by it. These are not features of whole systems, but occur at the level of individual viewers and readers. Ideological resistance can go forward with hope and modest aspiration by means of a symbol's vagueness and its structure.

THE MISCHIEF OF VAGUENESS

Hermeneutics, the study of individuals interpreting symbols, has traditionally struggled with the possibility of ideological critique. Hans-Georg Gadamer, who is arguably the most influential hermeneutic philosopher of the twentieth century, argues that an individual's most basic ontological relation is that of belonging to a tradition. It defines the horizon of possibilities for each person. Traditions do not belong to us, we belong to them. The worry here is that if we are first and foremost creatures of the traditions to which we belong, then an ideology's hold over us is pernicious, complete. There can be no Archimedean point from which to critique hegemonic symbols when our very common sense and standards of rationality are constituted by the symbols in question.

In this debate we see Whitehead's dueling concerns about mutual subordination in a free society, which were mentioned above: the individual must submit to the collective unity "in reverence," and the collective unity must submit to the individual for critique. But theories of hegemony and complex adaptive systems have shifted the likelihood of Whitehead's original requirements for a free society. It now seems obvious that the individual cannot help but submit to the symbolic meanings of the community in almost all cases. This submission is sometimes benign—we must learn the rules of a language to communicate, and participate in shared symbolic meaning to fully communicate our experience. But this submission also implies that ideological content acts on us profoundly, after making us originally. Whitehead's second requirement for a free society now seems further out of reach.

Paul Ricoeur is particularly useful in this discussion of critical resistance, as he seeks to find some common ground between critical theory and hermeneutics. Though a synthesis between the two approaches is not likely, Ricoeur argues that there is a "critical moment" in hermeneutics (Ricouer 1981, 91–93). We can humbly acknowledge the conditionedness of all thinking while also maintaining the ability to resist ideology and prejudice. This critical moment is the result of the interplay between a symbolic text's structure and its vagueness.

Ricoeur notes that symbols are vague because once they are written, they are distanciated from the intention of their authors. This distanciation provides space for the symbols to be interpreted variably.[18] While we may project back our own construals of intentions, cultural context or audience, such things are never positively given to us. As a result, the symbols are plurivocal, or to use Whitehead's term, "vague." They offer a surplus of meaning to readers and viewers, each of whom applies their own concerns and prejudgments to construe an available meaning.

Marxist cultural critic Stuart Hall laments that formal semiology "has too often neglected this practice of interpretative work, though this constitutes, in fact, the real relations of broadcast practices in television" (Hall 1993, 514). Plurivocity of symbols entails that mass media are less of a propaganda tool and more of an ideological battleground. His "Encoding / Decoding" essay points out that because viewers *interpret* what they consume, consent of the public is not a foregone conclusion. You cannot upload ideology directly into the minds of the audience. Instead, a television audience is able to "misunderstand" the connotation of a broadcast, and this "is the door via which a residual pluralism evades the compulsions of a highly structured, asymmetrical, and non-equivalent process" (Hall 1993, 514). Because texts are vague and have a surplus of meaning, subversive construals of media content can and will occur.

Though the viewer's decoding of that content is variable, all interpretations are not equal. There is a dominant cultural order, which demands a "preferred reading," which has "the whole social order embedded in them" (Hall 1993, 513). Most viewers will adopt the (a) hegemonic position, which interprets the message more or less in a way that perpetuates the hegemony. But not all viewers will take the hegemonic position. Some will take the (b) negotiated position, which "acknowledges the legitimacy of hegemonic definitions to make the grand significations (abstract)," while using oppositional exceptions to these rules at the local level (Hall 1993, 516): "This country is suffering an obesity *crisis*! Also, people shouldn't be judged by their bodies." Contradictions abound here. Finally, some viewers will take an (c) oppositional position, which grasps the literal and connotative meaning of the code, but "detotalizes the message in the preferred code in order to retotalize the message within some alternative framework of reference" (Hall 1993, 517). *Adbusters*, for example, is "a global network of artists, activists, writers, pranksters, students, educators and entrepreneurs who want to advance the new social activist movement of the information age" (Hall 1993, 517). Based in Vancouver, their magazine regularly spoofs ads and other content, playing on common media texts to undercut the sanctioned connotation. Adbusters portrays Joe Camel, the slick tobacco mascot, languishing in a hospital bed and undergoing chemotherapy. An Absolut vodka bottle slumps flaccidly in its ad-space, the logo "Absolut Impotence" emblazoned in the company's branded typeface. These acts of "culture jamming" may or may not have a widespread subversive effect—the magazine is not distributed as widely as *The New York Times* or *Cosmopolitan*. But they do offer glimpses of unsanctioned narratives operating in alternate fields.

Whitehead's remarks on symbolism are applicable here. Social revolution is largely possible because of the novel meanings that are available for adoption. Though symbolic language "binds a nation together by the common emotions which it elicits," in an ideological function, language is also "the instrument whereby freedom of thought and of individual criticism finds its expression. . . . The self-organization of society depends on commonly diffused symbols evoking commonly diffused ideas, and at the same time indicating commonly understood actions" (Whitehead 1927, 68 and 76). Societies continue in a particular manner because the overall structure holds. Whitehead imagines that social life in Virginia after the War of Independence was not much different from antebellum colonial life, as the customary symbolic meanings from before the revolution continued unbroken (Whitehead 1927, 77). George Allan counterbalances the diffusion of common ideas by also emphasizing the plurivocity of symbols, specifically the connotatively rich aesthetic symbols, as essential to countering hegemony, and also essential to uniting disparate causes together:

> For one person, the predominant feature of freedom might be the right to pursue his economic interests without government interference, for another the protection of her unorthodox religious beliefs from the wrath of the orthodox, for a third the opportunity to marry someone of the same gender or of a different race or religion. Yet they stand side by side at the barricades, their rifles aimed at the approaching enemies of freedom, believing in their mutual equality and finding comradeship in their common purpose. Their shout of "freedom" is a portmanteau ample enough to hold them all. (Allan, 10–11)

Of course, while vagueness is useful for uniting diverse propositions under a common signifier, it can also be employed to diffuse critical discourse. Revolutionary symbols can be co-opted and their meanings can be shifted. Late in the 2016 U.S. presidential race, the term "fake news" was used to describe incredible stories of dubious origin that spread virally through social media—a disinformation campaign. After the 2017 inauguration, Donald Trump appropriated the slogan "fake news" to refer, early and often, to any news story critical of his administration. The plurivocity of symbols, which makes it so easy to slide from fake-as-disinformation to fake-as-illegitimate-criticism is one of the conditions for the possibility of non-linear complexity. Meanings are free to multiply exponentially and unidirectionally in content and number when they are distanciated from their material conditions. Vagueness greases the wheels of ideology as much as it greases the wheels of subversion. Without a principle of communicative limitation, the cycle of hegemonies oscillates without inhibition.

Ricoeur argues, however, that symbols are not entirely frictionless. His interpretation theory is unique in that it employs a dialectic between understanding and explanation. That is, after an initial guess at a text's meaning (only accessible because of the symbol's vagueness), one may examine the structure of a text—its grammar, ostensive references, *langue* as opposed to *parole*. The code itself is a product of a linguistic community and is not up for grabs, it constrains possible meanings assigned to the text. The television news story about the California drought may say many things to us about meteorology, anthropogenic climate change, civil responsibilities, but the code is not infinitely flexible. One cannot assert the story tells us anything about the existence of extraterrestrials, the apostle Paul, or football statistics. Symbols are plurivocal, but only within certain constraints.

So, for Ricoeur, a text's structure—its grammar and depth semantics—participate in a dialectic with Gadamer's "tradition" or Whitehead's "conformal feeling." Human understanding is capable of genuine novelty, and therefore genuine subversion. This novelty comes from the otherness fixed in the text's structure, which is always transformed, but also resists assimilation to prejudice. Ricoeur calls this process "appropriation," which is commonly construed to mean assimilation, but for Ricoeur means a dialectic between that and otherness (i.e., transformation without assimilation). Here we find our principle of communicative limitation. A symbol's meaning is constrained, and those constraints also present the viewer with the structure of something other—an otherness that sometimes cannot be managed by hegemony.[19]

Structure without vagueness leaves no room for creative transformation of media messages. Vagueness without structure offers no constraints to limit the dominant media narratives. But when symbols are flexible, but not too flexible, they can seep into the cracks. Both traits together provide a stance from which individuals have the right combination of freedom and limitation to subvert ideological media.

This structural otherness is further bolstered by the referential dimension of a text. For Whitehead, reference is a foregone conclusion, built into the structure of his metaphysics. Perception in the mode of symbolic reference attributes causal realism to presentational immediacy. But Ricoeur was engaged in other debates with "linguistic imperialists." Ricoeur resists this imperialism by asserting that a symbol cannot fail to be about something, to point beyond itself to a non-linguistic dimension. When interpreting any text, the reader projects "a world, the pro-position of a mode of being in the world that the text opens up in front of itself by means of its non-ostensive references" (Ricoeur 1976, 94). This reference is not an idle tale, but changes the reader. Ricoeur argues that texts transform the ego (pre-reflective collection of prejudices) to a self "enlarged by the appropriation of the proposed world which interpretation unfolds" (Ricoeur 1976, 94–95). In short, symbolic communication, whether through Facebook or newsprint, contains, by means of its structure, the seeds of subversion. A text refers beyond the present situation, and by appropriating its alterity, I have "unrealized myself" and confront "imaginative variations of the ego" (Ricoeur 1981, 94).

Interestingly, Ricoeur identifies poetry as the most subversive of genres. Poetic discourse in particular contains "the power-to-be . . . the subversive force of the imaginary" (Ricoeur 1981, 93–94). Nevertheless, any text, regardless of genre of medium, possesses the power "to open a dimension of reality [and] implies in principle a recourse against any given reality and thereby the possibility of a critique of the real" (Ricoeur 1981, 94). We are more than automata of our milieu.

THE LIMITS OF ACTIVISM

Ricoeur's answer to Whitehead, by way of Gramsci and complexity science, is an affirmative one. Some hegemonically generated agency can be reflexively critical, though that agency is profoundly nerfed.[20] First, we are able, with effort, to achieve true critical distance from the hegemonic paradigm (via textual autonomy, structural explanation, and oppositional decoding).

Second, the media system cannot be effectively managed. It would be better to realize that individual agency is both constrained and enabled by the non-linear dynamics of the hegemony. The narrative of a will or wills that directly control the hegemony is counter-productive. Effecting change cannot be done decisively and expansively. Only local and micro-subversions are effective, and not predictably so.[21] Conventional social activism will almost always be frustrated, fragmented, and dispersed, and so the chief problem with a morally / ecologically / financially unhealthy society is not the hegemony itself, but the way that individuals think about social dynamics. As a result, we should look for some relief from the generalized anxiety of the injustice presented to us on an hourly basis. It is not any individual's obligation to remedy social ills, because that is not how social ills are remedied. At the same time we may know that it is not entirely futile to act. For the vagueness of symbols allows for mischief, and the structure of symbols welds that mischief to the accepted language of the hegemony. Who knows which of our acts will feed back into a significant shift in the cultural order? The more important point is that social change does not result from our modern notions of causation and individual agency. It may not be the case that changing our beliefs about agency and causation will make social activism more effective, but it will perhaps be therapeutic to those who are fatigued, frustrated, and discouraged by the failure of their efforts to produce expected results.

NOTES

1. "A very common error is that of thinking that every social stratum elaborates its consciousness and its culture in the same way, with the same methods, namely the methods of the professional intellectuals. . . . It is childish to think that a 'clear concept,' suitably circulated, is inserted in various consciousnesses with the same 'organizing' effects of diffused clarity: this is an 'enlightenment' error. . . . When a ray of light passes through different prisms it is refracted differently: if you want the same refraction, you need to make a whole series of rectifications of each prism" (Gramsci 1985, 417).

2. "It is not unknown to me how many men have had, and still have, the opinion that the affairs of the world are in such wise governed by fortune and by God that men with their

wisdom cannot direct them and that no one can even help them; and because of this they would have us believe that it is not necessary to labour much in affairs, but to let chance govern them. This opinion has been more credited in our times because of the great changes in affairs which have been seen, and may still be seen, every day, beyond all human conjecture. Sometimes pondering over this, I am in some degree inclined to their opinion. Nevertheless, not to extinguish our free will, I hold it to be true that Fortune is the arbiter of one-half of our actions, but that she still leaves us to direct the other half, or perhaps a little less" (Machiavelli 1908, ch. XXV).

3. On the inability of the concept "society" to specify any stable entity and therefore to ground a priori any theory of semantic stability or transformation, see Latour 2007. This is arguably consistent with Whitehead's society of occasions and affords the same limited opportunities for creative reconfiguration discussed re: Ricoeur, below. Lots of bets are off if "society" as such does not exist.

4. The doctrine of conformal feeling is Whitehead's metaphysical term for affective inertia. In a series of actual occasions, the present occasion tends to feel the vast majority of feelings of the past occasion with the same subjective form as the subjective forms within the previous occasions (cf. Whitehead 1978, 108 and 113).

5. "[W]e see any given field as embedded in a broader environment consisting of countless proximate or distal fields as well as states, which are themselves organized as intricate systems of strategic action fields" (Fligstein and McAdam 2002, 3). One among a lifeworld of pertinent illustrations is almond milk, which both emerged as an everyday option in the supermarket from concern over the environmental and ethical impact of dairy farming, and demands vast water resources in a drought-prone state turned to commercial agriculture only through massive investments of public and private infrastructure. Options, supermarkets, concerns; environments, impacts, commerce; investments, publics, privates, infrastructure. How does almond milk work, among and across these linked networks of actors and actions? What would we have media, politicians, consumers, citizens, and the activists of various causes and persuasions make of this simple beverage, resource, byproduct, alternative, asset, commodity, in the context of climate change? (cf. Saner 2015 and Ho et al. 2016).

6. "In fact, for Gramsci ideology represents a 'complex form of the social world,' not only in the sense of 'complicated,' but more precisely—and etymologically speaking—in the sense of a non-linear object, composed of different parts and several elements, that depends on various determinations" (Filippini 2016).

7. Trans. Carl Dyke.

8. The other pole of critique for Gramsci and many other "Western Marxists" of the early twentieth century was "automatic Marxism," the idea that capitalism would through the unfolding of its own inexorable, impersonal logic bring about its own collapse and transcendence (cf. Jacoby 1971, 119–46).

9. "It is unusual for CAS agents to converge, even momentarily, to a single 'optimal' strategy, or to an equilibrium. As the agents adapt to each other, new agents with new strategies usually emerge. Then each new agent offers opportunities for still further interactions, increasing the overall complexity" (Holland 2014, 9).

10. Cf. Ian Barbour, "Five Models of God and Evolution," *Philosophy, Science, and Divine Action*, ed. F. LeRon Shults, Nancy C. Murphy, and Robert John Russell (Boston: Brill, 2009). We acknowledge and regret that this is an insensitive analogy, but also one that's grimly illuminating of the perplexing disconnect between racism as an individual attitude and as a structured and structuring dynamic.

11. "Dominance" may be a misleading term here. "J. R." and "Carl" are hegemonies too. We exist as diversified systems by virtue of resisting entropy through the energetic dominance of resources such as atoms, molecules, the light of the sun, foodstuff plants and animals, cultural codes of gender, sexuality, and race, employment opportunities, and so on. We might also refer to these various constitutive relationships as cooperative associations, and for many purposes it might be both healthy and accurate to do so. However, the discourses of transformative activism tend to amplify the dominance trait of systems while suppressing their cooperative dimensions as a way of maintaining organizational structure. In these cases we refer to the

formation of organized, coherently simplified ideological systems as "interpretation," or "politics."

12. "The characteristic of 'wetness' cannot reasonably be assigned to individual H2O molecules, so we see that the wetness of water is not obtained by summing up the wetness of the constituent molecules—wetness emerges from the interactions between the molecules. Similarly, common properties of markets, such as 'bubbles' and 'crashes,' are not well-described by summing (say averaging) the acts of individual traders—these larger, emergent effects depend upon the interactions of the traders" (Holland 2014, 49).

13. "Resilience arises from a rich structure of many feedback loops that can work in different ways to restore a system even after a large perturbation. A single balancing loop brings a system stock back to its desired state. Resilience is provided by several such loops, operating through different mechanisms, at different time scales, and with redundancy—one kicking in if another one fails" (Meadows 2008, ch. 3).

14. "To maintain hegemony" would normally be a teleological statement. We discuss systems as ateleological in order not to become entangled in the homunculus traps of legacy agency and intentionality discourse. In *Incomplete Nature*, Deacon introduces the term "ententionality" to enable analysis of end-orientation in complex adaptive systems without falling into those traps. We didn't think getting into that would be helpful yet here. The point again is that there is no intelligent design. (Cf. Juarrero 2002).

15. Democratic pluralism may not be an ideal state at all. Nick Lane suggests that all life needs to be understood in terms of energy sources, flows, and constraints. Complex life emerges from, creates, and depends upon gradients. If hegemony is just another word for the ordering processes of life itself, generating a critical standpoint out of ecological commitment requires some careful attention to both the democratic and undemocratic dynamics of pluralistic interdependence (Lane 2015).

16. "Self-organizing, nonlinear, feedback systems are inherently unpredictable. They are not controllable. They are understandable only in the most general way. The goal of foreseeing the future exactly and preparing for it perfectly is unrealizable. The idea of making a complex system do just what you want it to do can be achieved only temporarily, at best. . . . We can't control systems or figure them out. But we can dance with them!" (Meadows 2008, ch. 7).

17. "It is easy to be overly simplistic about these implications and to see the alternatives as either control or chaos, either certainty or uncertainty, either management or laissez-faire. It is tempting to see complexity science as a source of new and possibly more complicated tools for the toolkit—but still to want them to fit within our existing, familiar approach to defining and solving the problem as we see it. But maybe the issue is less to do with tools and more to do with perspective" (Boulton et al. 2015, 5).

18. To be specific, Ricoeur notes three dimensions of textual autonomy. Texts, once fixed in writing (or meme), are liberated from their author's intentions, the cultural situation of the text's creation, and their original intended audience (Ricoeur 1981, 91).

19. Constraint enables agency, and agency produces constraint. "The ability to produce highly diverse and yet precise constraints . . . thus makes possible a nearly unlimited capacity for selves to intervene in the goings-on of the natural world" (Deacon 2011, 479).

20. NERF, of course, is a company that makes foam darts, foam bullets, and other toys that mimic violence but cause no real damage. In online gaming communities "nerfed" is slang—an appropriated symbol—for a power or capacity possessed by a player character that has been substantially weakened, either by an in-game element or a change in the rules of the game.

21. "When your experiments go awry, as some inevitably will, learn from them and try not to be discouraged" (Katz 2003).

REFERENCES

"About Adbusters." Adbusters Media Foundation. Adbusters.org. Web.
Allan, George. "The Art of Free Society." unpubl.

Barbour, Ian. 2009. "Five Models of God and Evolution." *Philosophy, Science, and Divine Action*. Edited by F. LeRon Shults, Nancy C. Murphy, and Robert John Russell. Boston: Brill.
Boulton, Jean G., Peter M. Allen, and Cliff Bowman. 2015. *Embracing Complexity: Strategic Perspectives for an Age of Turbulence*. Oxford: Oxford University Press.
Burke, Timothy, and Kevin Burke. 1998. *Saturday Morning Fever: Growing Up with Cartoon Culture*. New York: St. Martin's Griffin.
Deacon, Terrence. 2011. *Incomplete Nature: How Mind Emerged from Matter*. New York: W. W. Norton.
Filippini, Michele. 2016. *Using Gramsci: A New Approach*. London: Pluto Press.
Fligstein, Neil, and Doug McAdam. 2002. *A Theory of Fields*. Oxford: Oxford University Press.
Funtowicz, S., and J. R. Ravetz. 1994. "Emergent Complex Systems." *Futures* 26, no. 6: 568–82.
Gitlin, Todd. 1979. "Prime Time Ideology: The Hegemonic Process in Television Entertainment." *Social Problems* 26, no. 3: 263–64.
Gramsci, Antonio. 1971. *Selections from the Prison Notebooks*. Edited and translated by Quinton Hoare and Geoffrey Nowell-Smith. New York: International Publishers.
———. 1975. *Quaderni del carcere*. Edited by Valentino Gerratana. Turin: Einaudi.
———. 1985. *Selections from Cultural Writings*. Edited by David Fogacs and Geoffrey Nowell-Smith. Translated by William Boelhower. Cambridge, MA: Harvard University Press.
Halhoefer, Kevin. 2015. "STUDY: California TV Stations' Drought Coverage Gave Short Shrift to Climate Change." Media Matters for America. May 21. https://www.mediamatters.org/research/2015/05/21/study-california-tv-stations-drought-coverage-g/203650.
Hall, Stuart. 1993. "Encoding/Decoding." *The Cultural Studies Reader*. Edited by Simon During, 507–17. New York: Routledge.
Ho, Jacqueline, Ingrid Maradiaga, Jamika Martin, Huyen Nguyen, and Linh Trinh. 2016. "Almond Milk vs. Cow Milk Life Cycle Assessment." *UCLA Environment* 159. June 2.
Holland, John H. 2014. *Complexity: A Very Short Introduction*. Oxford: Oxford University Press.
Jacoby, Russell. 1971. "Towards a Critique of Automatic Marxism: The Politics of Philosophy from Lukács to the Frankfurt School." *Telos*, no. 10 (Winter).
Juarrero, Alicia. 2002. *Dynamics in Action: Intentional Behavior as a Complex System*. Cambridge, MA: MIT/Bradford.
Katz, Sandor Ellix. 2003. *Wild Fermentation: The Flavor, Nutrition, and Craft of Live-Culture Foods*. White River Junction, VT: Chelsea Green.
Lane, Nick. 2015. *The Vital Question: Energy, Evolution, and the Origins of Complex Life*. New York: W. W. Norton.
Latour, Bruno. 2007. *Reassembling the Social: An Introduction to Actor-Network Theory*. Oxford: Oxford University Press.
"Lies of the Machines." 2003. *The Daily Show with Jon Stewart*. Comedy Central. July 14. Television.
Machiavelli, Niccolò. 1908. *The Prince*. Translated by W. K. Marriott. J. M. Dent & Sons: London: E. P. Dutton & Co.
Meadows, Donella H. 2008. *Thinking in Systems: A Primer*. White River Junction, VT: Chelsea Green.
Nagourney, Adam. 2015. "As California Drought Enters 4th Year, Conservation Efforts and Worries Increase." *The New York Times*. March 17.
Network. Sidney Lumet, director. United Artists, 1976. DVD.
Orrell, David. 2010. *Economyths: How the Science of Complex Systems Is Transforming Economic Thought*. London: Icon Books.
Postman, Neil. 1985. *Amusing Ourselves to Death: Public Discourse in the Age of Show Business*. New York: Penguin Books.
Ricoeur, Paul. 1976. *Interpretation Theory: Discourse and the Surplus of Meaning*. Fort Worth: Texas Christian University Press.

———. 1981. *Hermeneutics and the Human Sciences*. Edited and translated by John B. Thompson. Cambridge: Cambridge University Press.
Saner, Emine. 2015. "Almond Milk: Quite Good for You—Very Bad for the Planet." *The Guardian*. Oct 21.
Weinberg, Steven. 1992. *Dreams of a Final Theory*. New York: Pantheon.
Whitehead, Alfred North. 1978. *Process and Reality*. Corrected edition. Edited by Donald Sherburne and David Ray Griffin. New York: The Free Press.
———. 1927. *Symbolism: Its Meaning and Effect*. New York: Fordham University Press.

Part II

Human/Nonhuman Dislocations

Chapter Four

Process Philosophy and Neo-Materialism

Nomadic Subjectivity and Evanescing toward Sustainability

Jeremy D. Fackenthal

Over the last two decades, Rosi Braidotti has produced a body of work citing both a process ontology and a neo-materialism aimed at creating sustainable alternatives to the current regime of global capitalism. This chapter will introduce Braidotti's work and analyze her concept of nomadic subjectivity as a sustainable means of becoming before examining such subjectivity alongside Whitehead's metaphysics. In doing so, I will reframe Braidotti's concept of inter-relational becoming in explicitly Whiteheadian terms to see if lending her a more robust process ontology fits with her project and increases the strength of her claims. At the end I'll cite her more recent work that calls for Deleuze's notion of becoming-imperceptible arrived at via a sort of secular spiritualism and propose some ways in which the superjective nature of becoming-imperceptible contributes to sustainable civilization and a more verdant, life-giving future.

As the twenty-first century proceeds, we can understand the ecological crisis as tied to capitalism, or the effects of capitalism: the voracious desire to consume, with little regard to the effects of our consumption, has grossly depleted our resources and led to global climate change, ultimately bringing our civilization to the brink of radical alteration or even destruction. In agreement with countless present-day philosophers and critical theorists, including Braidotti, this chapter starts with the assumption that resisting the effects of capitalism, and therefore also the system itself, might help us move toward a more sustainable civilization. Producing and consuming fewer "disposable" goods, focusing less on the financial bottom line as the metric of success and progress, and moving away from the anthropocentric marketplace as the primary means of global interaction would all go a long way toward an eco-centric worldview and sustainable future on this planet.

SCHIZOPHRENIC CAPITALISM IN THE TWENTY-FIRST CENTURY

Rosi Braidotti is a feminist critical theorist who includes in her field of influences Gilles Deleuze, Marxist philosophy, process ontology, and post-humanist thinkers like Donna Haraway. Between the mid-1990s and the early 2000s she wrote a trilogy of books that unfold an explanation of subjects in a post-structuralist and neo-materialist milieu, titled *Nomadic Subjects, Metamorphoses: Towards a Materialist Theory of Becoming,* and *Transpositions: On Nomadic Ethics,* respectively. Early on, her work on materialism and subjectivity signaled a turn away from traditional Marxist materialism—the type of materialism that provides a strong critique of capitalism while also heralding its demise and the in-breaking of a new, socialist economic reality. What Braidotti advocates instead she terms neo-materialism, which has also come to be called new materialism. In an interview published in Rick Dolphijn and Iris van der Tuin's book *New Materialism: Interviews and Cartographies,* Braidotti describes the gradual emergence of neo-materialism as critical theorists and philosophers from the late 1960s onward realized that historical or dialectical materialism needed to be re-thought in light of "recent scientific insights," including the then burgeoning field of psychoanalysis, and vis-à-vis the awareness of significant changes in so-called "advanced capitalism" (Dolphijn and van der Tuin 2012, 20). As the decades ticked by the various strands of post-structuralism became more divided, and neo-materialism formed the banner under which those dissatisfied with the linguistic branch could gather to find "a method, a conceptual frame and a political stand . . . stressing instead the concrete yet complex materiality of bodies immersed in social relations of power" (2012, 21). Not only marking the difference between post-structuralist strands that allowed and avowed a type of ontology, on the one hand, and the more deconstructive strands, on the other, neo-materialism also birthed a form of "oppositional consciousness" that "combines critique with creativity" (2012, 22). Braidotti and others working in the mode of neo-materialism are not interested in merely haunting the system of capitalism, but want to move creatively beyond disruption toward actively producing alternatives to the dominant economic and philosophical systems that become increasingly unsustainable and unstable. One may find a certain hauntology, in the mode of Derrida's *Spectres of Marx,* a necessary and useful task (Derrida 1994); yet the neo-materialist project of constructing sustainable alternatives strikes me as a more fruitful long-term endeavor, and one that aligns well with a process ontology of becoming in which subjectivity can be conceived differently in hopes of forming fissures in the already unstable model of late or advanced capitalism.

Braidotti, who completed her philosophical training at the Sorbonne, encountered Gilles Deleuze and Felix Guattari's work early in her career. Their notion of capitalism as schizophrenia takes a central role in her writing on nomadic subjectivity. In the two volumes of *Capitalism and Schizophrenia—Anti-Oedipus* and *A Thousand Plateaus*—Deleuze and Guattari describe the increasingly apparent double pull toward individualism (individual expression) and autonomy, on the one hand, and the re-territorialization of desire in support of commercial profit, on the other. We want the personalized, custom-made material objects that make us unique individuals, just the same as everyone else. Think of the "artist" targeted by Apple or the modern-day hipster targeted by myriad fashion lines, tech start-ups, and accessory manufacturers. Goods that allow a person to create or to stand out can now be mass-marketed and mass-produced such that everyone becomes a creator, and everyone stands out in much the same way. In Braidotti's analysis of this schizoid position, "it reasserts individualism as the unquestionably desirable standard, while it reduces it to name brands and logos" (Braidotti 2006c, 3). Braidotti clearly intends the word "logos" to be a double-entendre (both brand symbol and *logos*), read and employed in this way: a branding that also endows a sense of order or meaning for those who dawn it. "I shop therefore I am," she writes (Braidotti 2006c, 3). In this mode of capitalism as schizophrenia the subject is supposed to remain a unitary, autonomous individual, but in reality is left fragmented without realizing it, vulnerable to the whim and fancy of the designers of technology and fashion. The becoming of the subject occurs along lines dictated by capitalist forces, not only in terms of material objects, but also in terms of life-long desires and claims toward success. Advertisers and for-profit companies dictate what the subject wants, both now and in the future, and so the subject acts in ways suggested by the flow of capital that serve to feed and sustain the flow. Yet all the while the subject believes individualism to be the end game providing her or him with monetary gains, luxury goods, and happiness.

According to Braidotti, there are subtle ways to get oneself out of this morass, and in fact her nomadic subjectivity is a response to schizophrenic capitalism. In *Nomadic Subjects* and *Metamorphoses,* she outlines her conception of the non-unitary subject, which she also terms the nomadic subject. In *Transpositions,* her more recent work on subjectivity and sustainability, she summarizes her previous descriptions of non-unitary subjectivity by stating that it means "a nomadic, dispersed, fragmented vision, which is nonetheless functional, coherent, and accountable, mostly because it is embedded and embodied" (2006c, 4). This non-unitary or nomadic form of subjectivity is a materialist understanding of subjectivity because of this embodied and embedded-ness. We are located and situated subjects with agency in the world, and this "materialist, nomadic philosophy of becoming" serves as an "alternative conceptual framework, in the service of sustainable future" (2006c, 4).

Before I offer a more complete explanation of Braidotti's nomadic subjectivity alongside Whiteheadian modes of subjectivity, I wish to trace what she means by sustainable and articulate again why unitary notions of subjectivity, for her, are *not* sustainable and do *not* promote a sustainable civilization. Sustainability becomes a central node around which she discusses the environment, to be sure, but also feminism and anti-racism. In a sense, Braidotti is concerned with sustainable civilization, insofar as "sustainability" extends beyond merely a discussion of ecology. In order to be sustainable, something must give evidence of endurance, must include processes of becoming that provide resistance against the rigidity of dominant systems. Her own words betray the subversive agency required for sustainability: "sustainability is a very concrete social and ethical practice—not the abstract economic ideal that development and social-planning specialists often reduce it to" (Braidotti 2006c, 160). In following process ontology, her understanding of sustainability is one that includes novelty and promotes difference rather than homogeneity. Her major project in *Transpositions* becomes rethinking nomadic subjectivity as sustainable, and she does this by reconceiving what gives a subject endurance, both temporally and spatially.

Braidotti's view of civilization may well differ (at least somewhat) from Whitehead's understanding of civilization, which emerges in the later chapters of *Adventures of Ideas*, and it certainly differs from other dominant notions of civilization in Western culture. Whitehead defines a civilized society as "exhibiting the five qualities of Truth, Beauty, Adventure, Art, Peace" (Whitehead 1933, 274). If we examine what each of these qualities means, we see that Whitehead's version of civilization also bucks any connection to normative understandings of civilized versus primitive culture. "Truth," he writes, "is the conformation of appearance to reality" (Whitehead 1933, 241). Beauty involves both the lack of mutual inhibition among prehensions during concrescence and the production of new contrasts among objective content. Adventure provides the ripples of change that preserve freshness within a civilization, while Art aims at producing a singularity within a multiplicity, and Peace becomes the "removal of inhibition" and thereby "enlarges the field of attention" (Whitehead 1933, 285). Thus, civilization for Whitehead must be about promoting novelty, fostering creativity, and avoiding homogeneity in the world's unfolding. Braidotti, who speaks of cosmopolitanism, but not civilization explicitly, might evince some resonance in what we can construct of her perception of civilization. If Whitehead is trying to move away from purely historical, Age-based constructions of civilization (i.e.,

Greek civilization, Mayan civilization, etc.) and toward a construction more temporally coordinated, then Braidotti seems to be moving toward the same construction but by means of a different approach. Cosmopolitanism is concerned with location, with embodied and embedded persons existing within a buzzing, chaotic space. The term "cosmopolitan" itself gives the sense that these persons are crossing borders and are "at home" in many places, and so the location does not need to be narrow. She also realizes that constituents of this type of civilization are temporally situated as well. The buzzing, chaotic nexus of embodied life—spatially and temporally coordinated—could be a sort of cosmopolitan civilization for Braidotti, and the emphasis in this notion must be placed on the transposable capability of the subjects constituting the civilization. If such a civilization exists or could exist, then it is (or would be) already sustainable by virtue of its nomadic possibilities, its skill in traversing/transversing boundaries and living outside the rigid confines of advanced capitalism. What this idea shares with Whitehead's understanding of civilization is the requirement for novelty, difference, and contrasts; but what it articulates differently is the embodied and spatially located nature of this nexus of subjects comprising civilization.

NOMADIC SUBJECTIVITY

As I have said, Braidotti's work has been about articulating a non-unitary account of subjectivity such that one might break free from the schizophrenic double pull of advanced capitalism in order to create alternative modes of becoming. The term "non-unitary" likely resonates with most process thinkers, and indeed Braidotti writes frequently that she is working out of a process ontology. However, she avoids writing explicitly about Whitehead's metaphyics, and it seems that most of her draw toward process thought comes through people like Haraway. Nevertheless, I think we can walk alongside both thinkers to make the connections more explicit. In the rest of this chapter my goal will be, first, to outline more thoroughly what she means by non-unitary and nomadic subjectivity and, then, to think with Braidotti and Whitehead about the implications such subjectivity has for sustainability, broadly construed.

Following Deleuze and Guattari's entreaty in *A Thousand Plateaus*— "Don't be one or multiple, be multiplicities!" (Deleuze and Guattari 1987, 24)—Braidotti conceives of nomadic subjects not as quantitative pluralities, "but rather qualitative multiplicities" (Braidotti 2006c, 94). Pluralities can be sameness reproduced over and over, whereas multiplicities trace many patterns of becoming with different and changing intensities, forces, and possibilities for expression. As an example, she writes that one might be woman/adult/white/human/lesbian/healthy/urbanized/English-speaking. No one of these adjectives can adequately describe the embodied person and therefore none of them serves as a center or essence of one's being, but rather they constitute the qualitative multiplicities that coalesce toward a person's becoming. All of these variables can be located in both time and space. Spatially, they are all embodied, in an organic, living person; and temporally, as she notes rather playfully, "one is not a Muslim on Tuesday and a European on Wednesday, or a woman on Monday, black on Sunday and Lesbian on Thursday afternoons" (Braidotti 2006c, 94). Rather these variables overlap and intersect in a temporal co-existence, which means that oftentimes they not only overlap, but may in fact clash or crash into each other in those difficult moments that make up the reality of our lives. At the same time, Braidotti realizes that the qualitative multiplicities aren't held at a conscious level: "one's consciousness of oneself does not always coincide with all of these variables *all* the time. One may, for a period of time, coincide with some categories, but seldom with them all" (Braidotti 2006c, 94).

What it means to be a nomad, for Braidotti, is to transverse each of these categories or constituent parts at various points in the process of becoming. She also borrows the nomad terminology from Deleuze and Guattari, who write of nomadology and nomadism in *Anti-Oedipus* and *A Thousand Plateaus,* where they suggest that a nomad, while being located temporally and spatially, is never sedentary or bound to a particular state (meaning nation-state). The nomad crosses borders and boundaries and wanders across a thousand plateaus, which serves to form or extend the rhizome (Deleuze and Guattari 1987, 22). The nomad travels across these multiple planes, feeling equally "at home" in each, but not bound by or to any one particular plane, plateau, or state. In *A Thousand Plateaus* Deleuze and Guattari differentiate among the nomad, the migrant, and the sedentary, remarking that the "life of the nomad is intermezzo," always in the middle and without beginning or end (Deleuze and Guattari 1987, 25). In Whiteheadian terms we can say that the nomad is always in the process of becoming. Moreover, the nomad deterritorializes without reterritorializing—as opposed to the migrant and or the sedentary, who reterritorialize either after moving or through some other apparatus. By virtue of this deterritorialization without reterritorialization, the nomad may be in a position to disrupt capitalism. Deleuze and Guattari's diagnosis of capitalism is that, "There is no universal capitalism, there is no capitalism in itself; capitalism is at the crossroads of all kinds of formations, it is neocapitalism by nature. It invents its eastern face and western face, and reshapes them both—all for the worst" (Deleuze and Guattari 1987, 20). Capitalism deterritiorializes, always with the aim of profit in mind, and this is how it remains at the crossroads and how it infiltrates multiple fissures simultaneously. For Deleuze and Guattari, the economic system no longer requires a state, but could operate equally as well outside of a state. Thus, the boundaries are removed in and for capitalism, just as they are for the nomad.

Because of this deterritorialization, because it is boundless, there can be no stepping outside of capitalism—the lines are always already redrawn to include the occasion that seeks to lie beyond. The nomad, as deterritorializing without reterritorialization, already holds the tools to function well within a deterritorialized world, as opposed to the sedentary, who always seeks to reterritorialize via a state or other apparatus and may not ever realize the deterritorializing effects of capitalism.

Braidotti's own use of the nomad moves in a similar direction. The nomad finds herself transitioning between potential contradictions and realizes herself as multiple, stepping from plateau to plateau among contradictions that may well be constitutive of her own becoming. The multiplicity inherent in nomadic subjectivity can't and shouldn't be homogenized into a whole, but rather Braidotti embraces the nomad as well-equipped to transverse boundaries and move among deterritorialized locations. Nomadic subjectivity should also certainly be seen as ecological in the sense that it is made up of its environment, shaped by the multiple points it inhabits and the paths leading between those points. Here she takes spatiality most seriously, reminding us of the subject's embedded and embodied materiality.

Her work in *Transpositions* makes the connection between nomadism, capitalism, and sustainability explicit. Braidotti seems well aware that poststructuralist philosophers typically argue for resistance from within whatever system is in place. Since it isn't possible to step outside of systems (like capitalism) that constantly re-inscribe every attempt at escape, she joins this argument in favor of enacting subtle resistance from within through qualitative change.[1] She writes that "processes of becoming are such forms of resistance," when enacted for non-profit. Thus the "production of empowering and affirmative differences is a qualitative change of gears within the system of advanced capitalism" (Braidotti 2006c, 134). Her nomad embodies and affirms such difference within him/herself and, as a self-avowed process ontologist, she describes the nomad as in a perpetual mode of becoming. "Becomings are the sustainable shifts or changes undergone by nomadic subjects in their active resistance against being subsumed in the commodification of their own diversity. Becomings are unprogrammed as mutations, disruptions, and points of resistance" (Braidotti 2006c, 137). Returning to the notion of schizophrenic capitalism, Braidotti realizes the fragmentation at work in advanced capitalism and recognizes that attempting to resist being split or to piece back together a unitary subject would be fruitless and almost non-sensical. Instead, she accepts her fate and embraces the schizophrenia, aiming to work from within its already deterritorialized modes.

The best one can do then is to tell nomadic stories about our normadic selves, which means weaving narratives that conform appearance to reality—or, in Whitehead's view, narratives that are true. Since narratives describing the subject as univocal or entirely territorialized always push some aspect of the subject, some constitutive part, away or down under the fold, then conforming appearance to reality means expressing the subject as the type of nomadic subject Braidotti describes. True here does not mean an expression of some essentialism or universal characteristic, but rather it means that we do not tell stories to deceive ourselves, as capitalism would have us do. Such true narratives are the ones necessary for building a sustainable civilization insofar as, for Whitehead, truth is one of those basic components of civilization and, for Braidotti, the nomadic self is the only one that can truly be "at home" in the cosmopolitan world she would call sustainable. And these true stories originating from the nomadic subject can become one of the subtle ways of pointing out the reality of nomadic life against a world constantly deterritorialized and yet also reinscribed by schizophrenic capitalism.

PROCESS-RELATIONAL NOMADISM

In an article entitled "Posthuman, All Too Human: Towards a New Process Ontology," Braidotti articulates her process position as affirming the primacy of relations over substances (Braidotti 2006b). She herself does not delve into Whiteheadian metaphysics, though she also doesn't seem allergic to such projects. And despite her reliance on Haraway rather than Whitehead for her process ontological underpinnings, there are at least two places of resonance that I wish to point out with the hope of strengthening Braidotti's nomadic subjectivity as a sustainable means of becoming in resistance to advanced capitalism.

Braidotti is clear that a subject does not necessarily correspond to an individual or to a body. Despite subjectivity being embodied, one cannot reduce the subject to a body. The subject is embedded, but is also more than a body. Whitehead is less clear about the connection between the notion of subjects and human subjectivity broadly construed. He doesn't spend much time dealing with human subjectivity, though he does surprisingly discuss the soul a good bit. Whitehead's basic meaning when he uses the term subject is an entity constituted by the process of feeling. A subject emerges from the world, from the wealth of objective data available for prehension in the becoming of an actual entity. The entity feels this objective data as it grows together. And of course, once the becoming of a single actual entity is complete, it then joins the objective data that consequent entities will feel in their own processes of becoming. Thus, the many become one and are increased by one (Whitehead 1978, 21). Beyond the most basic level of the actual entity lies the society—a group of occasions drawn together by some social order, meaning that they share a common element of form and all positively prehend this form from antecedent occasions that are a part of the society. One of the characteristics of a society is that it demonstrates endurance, temporally and continuously, and such an enduring percipient Whitehead names a human (1933, 205). This human as an enduring percipient constituted by a society or societies of actual entities cannot be much set apart from other higher levels of societies. Nevertheless, Whitehead does write about the living person to say that: "The defining characteristic of a living person is some definite type of hybrid prehensions transmitted from occasion to occasion of its existence . . . a 'hybrid' prehension is the prehension by one subject of a conceptual prehension, or of an 'impure' prehension, belonging to the mentality of another subject" (Whitehead 1978, 107). Through such hybrid prehensions the living occasions receive a "character and depth" and are "canalized" into individual originality (Whitehead 1978, 107).

The canalization process of the society as living person brings about the depth of originality required for what Braidotti calls subjectivity, but it also reminds us that the subject can never be conceived as static or as already having come to be. Rather, the living person as society holds relation as primary and recognizes the multiplicity inherent within the occasions that constitute the living person. Without trying to harmonize Braidotti and Whitehead on this primacy of relation, it is safe to say that both see multiple relations and multiple ways of relating at the core of either the living person or the nomadic subject. The nomadic subject is already fragmented and variously constituted by a wealth of relations that are in some way coordinated spatially and temporally into a body. Whitehead's living person, while "canalizing," cannot be reduced to a unity or sameness, but continues to gain originality by way of its multiplicity of relations. And in this way one could say that Whitehead's conception of the human as made up of societies, each containing a multiplicity of relations, lives up to Deleuze and Guattari's imperative—be multiplicities! (Deleuze and Guattari 1987, 24).

When thinking about subjects as embodied and embedded, the Whiteheadian scheme only increases the multiplicities of relations involved in the continual becoming of societies constitutive of a person. A human body is composed of societies of societies—multiplicities of groups of actual occasions held together spatially and temporally by some social order. Bodies endure, more or less, over time and thus require a serial ordering of occasions, constituting multiple enduring objects that then make up a "corpuscular society" (Whitehead 1978, 34–35). Within this togetherness of the occasions constitutive of a body lie multiplicities of relations and interrelations both as prehensions of occasions composing the corpuscular society and prehensions of occasions beyond it. In fact, Whitehead writes in *Modes of Thought* that one can never be precisely sure where the body ends or begins. Whereas we tend to think of humans as complex unities of body and mind, the reality is that "the body is part of the external world, continuous with it. . . . Also, if we are fussily exact, we cannot define where a body begins and where external nature ends" (Whitehead 1938, 29–30). To be embodied or embedded for Whitehead must mean experiencing multiplicities of relations from within a specific sphere. Indeed, he writes: "The Human Body is that region of the world which is the primary field of human expression" (1938, 30). By expression here he means the "activity of finitude impressing itself on its environment"; it is the "diffusion, in the environment, of something initially entertained in the experience of the expressor" (1938, 28–29). Yet this body cannot be a unified or bounded whole, but rather being embodied only means that one is always open to and composed of relations with occasions or enduring objects beyond "oneself." The nomadic subject then is fragmented in the sense that many aspects hang together tenuously through routes of relation; yet in its togetherness the subject might also impress itself upon the larger environment in which it is embedded and with which it is inevitably related.

Additionally, lest one think that becoming nomad occurs easily or without sharp contrast or conflict, Braidotti reminds us that the nomad often experiences a clash among the variables that constitute one's subjectivity. Insofar as the subject constantly shifts and refigures itself as nomadic, one can say that these contrasts do not utterly decompose a person, though they do certainly cause pain and discomfort from time to time. For Whitehead such contrasts are inherent in the production of novelty but must be weighed so as to promote contrast without reaching a complete disjunction. The term he reconceives so as to provide this gentle limitation, while also encouraging certain disruptions, is Beauty. As mentioned before, Beauty is one of the categories that constitute civilization for Whitehead. Beauty, Whitehead writes, is the "mutual adaptation of the several factors in an occasion of experience," such that the various prehensions involved in a given concrescence do not inhibit each other but lead to the increase of novelty by producing new contrasts among objective data of the past (Whitehead 1933, 252). While insisting upon the mutual adaptation of factors in an experience, in order to highlight these contrasts Beauty also necessarily includes an amount of discord: "the contribution to Beauty which can be supplied by Discord . . . is the positive feeling of a quick shift of aim from the tameness of outworn perfection to some other ideal with its freshness still upon it" (Whitehead 1933, 257). Thus, discord aids in the production of Beauty by providing the contrasts necessary for novelty, halting the sequence of rote repetition, or ensuring that the "tameness of outworn perfection" does not continue indefinitely. While harmony among various factors might be preferable in the constitution of an actual entity, disharmony also aids the increase of novel becomings, and according to Whitehead a certain amount of discord actually assists in the process. Whitehead writes: "The objective life of the past and the future in the present is an inevitable element of disturbance. Discord may take the form of freshness or hope, or it may be horror or pain" (Whitehead 1933, 266). What matters, whether an experience evokes harmony or disharmony, is the strength of the experience. Intense experiences may include either, despite the fact that "Harmony is bound up with the preservation of the individual significance in detail, and Discord consists in its destruction" (Whitehead 1933, 263). Yet insofar as discord resists the stasis of anaesthetized perfection, discord continues its role in the production of novelty and in this sense can be said to be productively positive.

If we now return to Braidotti we can conceive that when the multiple variables constitutive of nomadic subjectivity bump into each other, or intersect and overlap, they result in productive discord. Yes, synchronization (in Braidotti's words) of the variables occurs at times, but never in such a way that all of the pieces can be said to be put together (2006c, 176). In Whitehead's terms, the fragmentation remains as the discord necessary to produce certain dislocations productive of novelty, but an adaptation of mutual factors of experience can also be cited. If we can consider the nomad as productive of dislocations that lead to novelty, then perhaps this sort of discord is what is required for creative subversion of dominant systems. These systems, as Braidotti, Deleuze, and Guattari assert, are quite good at both fragmenting entities and then reinscribing the fragmentation into the system. But if the nomad is already at home in the fragmentation, then s/he is able to work in the fissures to produce novel disruptions within the system. In this sense she describes becoming (and becoming nomad) as an intransitive process—humans aren't becoming anything in particular, but rather becoming "is an ethical and political sensibility that begins with the recognition of one's limitations as the necessary counterpart of one's forces or intensive encounters with multiple others" (Braidotti 2006c, 163). She is neither naïve about the limitations inherent in the creative resistance from within, nor is she hopeless about the potential results of such action.[2]

EVANESCING TOWARD SUSTAINABILITY

Yet Braidotti also takes her creative subversion further (and perhaps further than Whitehead might wish to go) when she draws on Deleuze's concept of becoming-imperceptible. She explains this process as Deleuze's affirmative restatement or rethinking of Foucault's death of the subject. "You have to die to the self in order to enter qualitatively finer processes of becoming. To do that, to be able to sustain it, you can draw the strength from the future, and thus engender an event here and now" (Braidotti 2006c, 261). While Deleuze's concept of becoming-imperceptible remains somewhat opaque, Braidotti unpacks it her article "The Ethics of Becoming-Imperceptible." Here she notes the dominant understanding of the notion as pointing toward death. But this death, the evanescence of the subject into the web of relations constitutive of that subject, does not mean the end. Rather it is an opening up of new possibilities, new creative potentials, as a result of becoming-imperceptible. Moreover, if becoming is always in process, then becoming-imperceptible is also a process and not a definite or finite step. The remainder of this chapter will explore possibilities for becoming-imperceptible as an ethical movement toward sustainability, positing that the notion need not *only* mean the termination of an individual life. But rather might it be possible that becoming nomad results in becoming-imperceptible as the most thorough means of fitting into the cracks and fissures of the systems that continually deterritorialize and reinscribe us? Here I will begin with Whitehead's notion of satisfaction as the end of becoming for a particular actual occasion, then return to Braidotti's discussion of becoming-imperceptible, before finally bringing the two into dialogue and moving toward constructive and concrete possibilities for evanescence as sustainability.

While Whitehead's metaphysics provides the temporal theory to affirm a sense in which the future might be felt in the present through anticipation in later phases of concrescence, for Whitehead the loss of subjectivity ends the individual becoming of a particular occasion. Perhaps the tragic evil inherent in loss might be productive of future contrasts in occasions yet to become, but for the occasion itself a becoming-imperceptible heralds a loss: having reached satisfaction or the end of the process of growing together, the superjective nature of the occasion increases the many by one and thereby adds itself to the welter of occasions available to subsequent occasions. It has reached objective immortality (Whitehead's status for past occasions that enter into the multiplicity of data to be felt by other occasions as they concresce) but can't be said to sustain itself in any other means. The movement from conscrescing subject to objective datum does not result in a change in value for Whitehead, though it is a change in status. Each present moment as it comes together carries with it the objective data of the past, and that data has import for the becoming of the present and future. While the present moments are the ones registering feeling, making qualitative judgments, and expressing quantitative duration or extension, the objectively immortal past fades into the past only to be recalled again by the present and future in various ways. Yes, there is a loss, but objective immortality does not constitute a final loss.

Braidotti too seems to acknowledge this loss as she notes that becoming-imperceptible "marks the death of the self to any notion of identity." When this phase of becoming begins, "all a subject can do is mark his or her assent to the loss of identity" (2006c, 261). The subject diminishes oneself to the point of imperceptibility—no longer carving out a personal identity but becoming an "affirmative subjectivity" or an affirmation of interconnections. The self evanesces to the point of becoming one with his/her habitat, leaving only an empowerment of the collective community behind. In *Transpositions,* just before she describes this evanescence she writes about a type of post-secular spirituality of immanence that disavows any relation to a particular religion or to transcendence at all. Nevertheless, this spirituality for her seems to inculcate the types of practices and secular-pietism that might lead one to becoming-imperceptible. To be sure, her notion calls out for a strong anti-anthropocentrism and an affirmation of other forms of life (which she refers to as both *bios* and *zoe*, to include technological or hybrid forms of life). But moreover, it appears as a type of empowerment of the community or of what we might call a sustainable civilization.

Despite this phase of becoming to which she calls her readers, and which calls for the loss of identity, Braidotti still finds hope in the subversive action of her neo-materialism. This sustainable, nomadic subject "practices a humble kind of hope, rooted in the ordinary micro-practices of everyday life: simple strategies to hold, sustain and map out thresholds of sustainable transformations . . . for the hell of it and for love of the world" (Braidotti 2006c, 278). Ultimately, she takes quite seriously the idea that one is not becoming anything in particular, in fact in the end one is not becoming any *thing* or any *one*, but becoming imperceptible:

> I think the becoming-imperceptible is the point of fusion between the self and his/her habitat, the cosmos as a whole. It marks the point of evanescence of the self and its replacement by a living nexus of multiple interconnections that empower not the self, but the collective; not identity, but affirmative subjectivity; not consciousness, but affirmative interconnections. (Braidotti 2006a, 154)

Affirming the community empowerment of becoming-imperceptible, she writes at the end of *Transpositions* about synchronizations of nomadic selves in community and as community: "Co-synchronizations constitute communities. Fitting in with the world in order to help it along the horizon of hope and sustainability indicates *amor fati* as an evolutionary talent" (Braidotti 2006c, 278). Co-synchronization as constitutive of community marks the beginnings of a sustainable civilization. If one always becomes in and through community and then co-synchronizes one's becoming, one's nomadic activity with community, then one can evanesce into the community, no longer calling out for recognition as an individual subject but only as a constituent of a wider community of life. What remains is the (not solely human) community in and through which one is formed. And if this is the case, then is becoming co-synchronous with the wider community to which we are always already intertwined the fullest meaning of nomadic subjectivity? I suggest that if one is nomadic through and through, then the boundaries of the nomadic self are disrupted and disavowed in ways that make becoming-imperceptible not only possible but the logical conclusion of nomadic activity.

It is possible that Whitehead's perishing and Deleuze's becoming imperceptible are not so far apart. Braidotti seems to read the imperceptibility as both an inevitability and a process by and through which future occasions may come together. The subversive act of becoming-imperceptible makes space (temporally and spatially) for other becomings and produces a superjective element into the world as a sort of beacon (from the past) of how we might become and become imperceptible. If "[s]ustainability does assume faith in a future, and also a sense of responsibility for 'passing on' to future generations a world that is livable and worth living in," then the superjective element of becoming-imperceptible has the potential to yield creative dislocations of the systems, such as advanced capitalism, that deterritorialize for the sake of profit and to the detriment of eco-systems (Braidotti 2006a, 153).

Whitehead's objective immortality appears as a sort of evanescing into the extensive continuum, into the khoric non/space of becoming itself. As Braidotti describes it: "It is like a floodgate of creative forces that make it possible to be actually fully inserted into the *hic et nunc* defined as the present unfolding of potentials, but also the enfolding of qualitative shifts within the subject" (Braidotti 2006a, 155). Both Whitehead and Deleuze/Braidotti affirm the immanence of the evanesced or perished subject. Each past becoming is recollected in/onto a sort of plane of immanence, an extensive continuum that itself shifts, folds and unfolds as the becoming (imperceptible) of future occasions variously increase and alter the interrelations among past occasions along the plane. Likewise, Braidotti notes that becoming-imperceptible is "the ultimate delegation of selfhood to something that we may be tempted to call transcendence, except that it takes us into embodied and embedded perspectives, into radical immanence, not into further abstractions" (Braidotti 2006a, 155).

Becoming-imperceptible has practical implications for human and non-human subjects in the here and now. Opening up creative responses to the systems that dominate us is perhaps the foremost advantage of this type of becoming. It is a

> qualitative leap to a sustainable future, like writing the pre-history of a future, thus fixing us at last in a present that is neither nostalgic, or backward-looking, nor euphorically confident but is actualised here and now. (Braidotti 2006a, 155)

Being able to write this pre-history of a future, being able to influence or persuade the ways in which the future grows together, means being able to write against the narrative being written by schizophrenic capitalism. Like a simultaneous and creative undoing of the deleterious conditions constantly unfolding from the deterritorialization and reinscription on behalf of sameness and profit, becoming imperceptible allows for the novel, communal acts of resistance. If "sustainability is a very concrete social and ethical practice" as Braidotti reminds us, then practically this means giving up the relentless pursuit of individual greatness (in either stature or wealth) in favor of communal growth and flourishing. It means leaving behind notions of progress based on economic growth and viewing progress instead by metrics tied to levels of happiness, contentment, and sustainability within the community. It means the unabashed striving toward a world in which Truth, Beauty, Adventure, Art, and Peace coalesce to provide the conditions for sustainability as the endurance of all forms of life.

To conclude, Braidotti's neo-materialism of nomadic subjectivity, I believe, becomes more robust via the reading of Whitehead provided here. Rather than merely citing a process ontology of interrelation, Whitehead seems a good candidate for lending her an actual ontology that promotes relation as primary and as constitutive of our modes of becoming. Whitehead's concept of Beauty endows Braidotti's multiple variables of nomadic subjectivity with the discord necessary to provide novelty or, in her own words, sustainable transformations that might enjoy some hope of subverting schizophrenic capitalism. And by thinking with Braidotti and Whitehead together, a metaphysical rearticulation of becoming-imperceptible enables creative response to dominant and harmful systems by emphasizing (not-solely-human) communal life and making space for a sustainable civilization resistant to the deterritorializing effects of advanced capitalism.

NOTES

1. One may think here of Judith Butler's subversive repetition. Additionally, Badiou's argument that even leftist or left-leaning political action simply cannot resist commodification denotes the difficulty and subtlety of such resistance.

2. As an aside, she includes a beautiful passage in *Transpositions* where she describes Deleuze's own ability to keep a healthy distance from those aspects of the academy that propel one both to success and self-aggrandizing gestures. She claims that he was able to step out of the "negativity circuit" as he did this.

REFERENCES

Braidotti, Rosi. 1994. *Nomadic Subjects.* New York: Columbia University Press.
———. 2002. *Metamorphoses: Towards a Materialist Theory of Becoming.* Malden, MA: Polity Press.
———. 2006a. "The Ethics of Becoming-Imperceptible." In *Deleuze and Philosophy,* ed. Constantin V. Boundas. Edinburgh: Edinburgh University Press.
———. 2006b. "Posthuman, All Too Human: Towards a New Process Ontology." *Theory, Culture & Society* 23, no. 7–8: 197–208.
———. 2006c. *Transpositions: On Nomadic Ethics.* Malden, MA: Polity Press.
Butler, Judith. 1993. *Gender Trouble.* New York: Routledge.
Deleuze, Gilles, and Felix Guattari. 1987. *A Thousand Plateaus: Capitalism and Schizophrenia.* Trans. Brian Massumi. Minneapolis: University of Minnesota Press.

Derrida, Jacques. 1994. *Spectres of Marx: The State of the Debt, the Work of Mourning and the New International.* New York: Routledge.

Dolphijn, Rick, and Iris van der Tuin. 2012. *New Materialism: Interviews and Cartographies.* Ann Arbor, MI: Open Humanities Press.

Whitehead, Alfred North. 1933. *Adventure of Ideas.* New York: The Free Press.

———. 1938. *Modes of Thought.* New York: The Free Press.

———. 1978. *Process and Reality.* Corrected Edition. Ed. David Ray Griffin and Donald W. Sherburne. New York: The Free Press.

Chapter Five

Welcoming Syrian Life

Recognitions of Immanent Vulnerability

Deena M. Lin

According to a survey by the World Economic Forum, one of the greatest risks the world will face in the next ten years is the large-scale involuntary migration of refugees on a global scale (World Economic Forum 2017). We are now witnessing the largest refugee crisis since the Second World War. The UN Refugee Agency reports that there are approximately 5.6 million Syrians in a current state of crisis, and an estimated 11 million refugees have fled their homes since the Civil War began in 2011 (UN Refugee Agency 2018). Most Syrian refugees are living in extreme poverty and are barely surviving.[1] Some of them face death, women are exposed to gender-based violence, children aren't allowed access to schools, and they lack basic necessities such as water, decent nutrition, and health care. Whether they are surviving in camps, or are fortunate enough to move beyond these border-crossings to achieve sanctuary in new lands, refugees incur tremendous hardships at home and abroad. Syria is now into its eighth year of war without an end in sight. A shift in perspective must take place that will incite us towards exercising a stance of hospitality rather than alienation, such that they may be provided basic conditions that will ensure their survival.

Syrians are at the periphery of our gaze in this country. The aim of this chapter is to critically examine the justifications made for this marginalization, such that we may promote more compassionate policies of engagement with them. The problem to be addressed here is the lack of responsibility the U.S. government has taken towards securing Syrian life. As time passes this discrepancy is becoming more and more troublesome, for the presidency of Donald Trump has only sought to impose stricter regulations on their emigration, to the point where our borders are now closed off to them entirely

(White House 2017). Those who support this are primarily conservatives who identify Syrian refugees as a threat to our national security and characterize them as a people embroiled in radical Islamic extremism.[2]

Since the inception of the War on Terror in 2001, providing sanctuary to large populations of Muslims has not been on the hearts and minds of U.S. citizens.[3] In this chapter I will argue that this way of thinking must change, and the alternative I present requires that America be held responsible for preserving and protecting the basic conditions of Syrian life. The current policies instantiated by the U.S. stem from a narrow vision of the world where value is both derived and imparted to a select population. If one lives outside this frame, they become systemically de-legitimized, and deemed unworthy of grief. To marginalize the most vulnerable in this way is unethical. It is a prejudice that accounts for the survivability of some, and the systemic disposing of others. My hope is that by revealing the inconsistencies of this view and constructing a more responsible alternative, we may recognize the mutual vulnerability and ensure the protection and emigration toward these precarious citizens without a country.

To penetrate a mentality that values autonomy and self-aggrandizement above responsibility and social justice requires a critical probing that values immanence. All lives are deemed valuable when we think globally and in more immanent terms. Humans thrive and are emboldened when we see ourselves as vulnerable with and interrelated to other humans, animals, and the rest of the natural world, for our survival and sustenance depends on them. To make reparations for our current failings towards Syrian refugees, we can appeal to the constructive insights of Judith Butler, Alfred North Whitehead, and Rosi Braidotti. These thinkers recognize life as interconnected and co-dependent, and such a difference in outlook is needed in order to probe policies which fail to acknowledge the innate value of all life.

From an ethical standpoint, America needs to recognize all life as precarious. Syrian refugees must be understood through a lens that values them as more than our global-other. These lives are just as vulnerable as our own, they actively prehend others like we do, and live with us in a deep planetary immanence that risks perishing at any moment. There is a mutual precarity to life, because we all require basic conditions to sustain us. This is the equalizing point, and by examining intellectual pursuits that sustain an impartial valuing of all life, this chapter will be instructive for envisioning a means beyond the exclusionary framework that seeks to protect the sovereignty of our nation above all others.

America is one nation within a global community. We mustn't think that our moral responsibility is restricted to those who live within our borders alone. To build my case, it is necessary to first understand what our current policy towards Syrian refugees entails, as well as underscore the justifications given by the current Administration and its supporters. I will argue that these explanations exude a certain mindset that is out to secure the sovereignty of the nation-state above all else, and this thinking sees no fault in harming the most vulnerable among us. Next, I will clarify Butler's notions of precarity and vulnerability when it comes to agency, identity, and global policy. This will be followed by discussing beneficial aspects of Alfred North Whitehead's cosmology, such that a deeper sense of interrelatedness with our global others may be granted. Lastly, Braidotti provides a further elaboration of immanence by way of her *zoe*-centered egalitarian account of trans-species subjectivity. One may consider these three accounts as integral slices of a broader alternative vision that is critically juxtaposed to the nationalist agenda being put forth by the policies of the current Administration.

The alternative vision that emerges here provides a constructive means to address the unethical power-over structuring of relations that is being upheld by the conservative political elite in this country. Each are integral to understanding how considerations of the subject may employ an ethical probing of policies that protect some lives and not others. Thinking of our lives as interdependent and constantly at-risk is needed such that we may be compelled to finally take accountability for our actions, or in this case inactions toward securing the lives of Syrian refugees. First, we must examine the current Administration's position on Syrian refugees, and better understand the rationale employed that legitimizes its decisions.

PROBING RATIONALES FOR EXCLUDING SYRIAN LIFE

To formulate an alternative approach to address the Syrian refugee crisis requires that we investigate the position of the current Administration more closely to reveal its intentions. We must also address the level of accountability it deems itself responsible for when it comes to Syrian life. These points will elucidate how our policies in regard to the emigration of Syrian refugees is extreme and is built upon a problematic framing of Syrians as proponents of Islamic terrorism. Our media further legitimizes this policy by failing to mention our current military tactics to the general public, and such societal blindness gives way to our passivity on the issue. Failing to recognize Syrian life correlates to a sentiment of disposability, where we do not see them as needing our attention or any hospitality within our borders that may protect them from violence at home. We need to be aware of the conscious efforts made to preserve the sovereignty of our nation by instilling a sentiment of anxiety towards Syrian refugees as opposed to compassion. Breaking open the matrix of intelligibility that rationalizes our current policies and the rhetoric used to justify them shall show the need for this Administration to be made accountable for Syrian life. One may shed light on our level of responsibility in this once a more ethical perspective emerges, where the loss of life and sense of dignity is seen as a mutual vulnerability that we all share.

First we must look more closely at the emigration policy that has been engineered by the current Administration to cope with Syrian refugees. President Trump has been interested in addressing the threat of terrorism in the U.S. since he took office on January 20, 2017. He ran with a campaign promise to "ban Muslims from entering the United States," and followed through with this sentiment by signing an executive order banning the entry of citizens from Syria, Iran, Libya, Somalia, Yemen, Iraq and Sudan seven days after he was inaugurated (Hussain 2017a).[4] This order imposed the strictest exclusion for Syrians, denying their admittance indefinitely. Such restrictions were supported by stating that it is necessary to be forbidding when it comes to refugees and immigrants in order "to combat the threat of terrorism in the United States" (Hussain 2017a). This rationale was met with much criticism, and for good reason.

When this policy was ordered no specifics were given in regard to how our nation was more at risk than it had been previously, and its critics were quick to point out that it omits countries that are not associated with the radicalized Muslims who have done acts of terrorism in the U.S. since 9/11.[5] The deadliest attack committed by a Muslim extremist on our soil since 9/11 has been the Pulse nightclub shooting in Orlando, and this was done by a U.S. citizen born in New York. The shooter's parents emigrated from Afghanistan, but this country was also omitted from the list (Bier 2017). Some criticizers of the ban have argued that the list conveniently excludes Muslim countries where President Trump has business interests, such as Saudi Arabia, the United Arab Emirates and Egypt, which are countries of the extremists who were responsible for killing nearly 3,000 Americans from 1975–2015 (Sommerfeldt 2017). Pointing out discrepancies in these lists, especially regarding the nations that have been origin points for Islamic terrorism, raises conflict of interest concerns on Trump's behalf, and also requires a further probing of the reasoning used to justify this executive order.

The travel ban has been referred to by many (including those in the Administration) as a "Muslim ban" because it concerns seven Muslim-majority countries, and concessions were made for non-Muslims within it. Americans have not only been critical of the order, but several Federal courts have refused to adhere to the mandate altogether. These Federal judges have deemed it unconstitutional and a violation of *The Immigration and Nationality Act of 1965* by denying the admittance of immigrants based on their religion or country of origin. The Administration sought to address inconsistencies in the first order by issuing a second executive order on March 6, 2017. After experiencing diplomatic pressure, Iraq was removed from the list, while Syrian refugees remain banned (see de Vogue et al. 2017). To address the issue of providing any special concessions for non-Muslims, the second order halted the admittance of any and all refugees, irrespective of their religion. No rationale was provided for this more extreme action, other than the need to seem less biased against Muslims.

This is our current policy to cope with Syrian refugees seeking asylum in our country, and yet it is clear that their plight is only getting worse. According to World Vision, 470,000 Syrians have died since the Civil War began, and 55,000 of them are children (World Vision 2017). Indeed, half of the 13.5 million total Syrian refugees are children, and they are all in desperate need of humanitarian aid. These people are not fleeing their homes by choice. Life has become unbearable in Syria, where they are experiencing violence from all sides, whether it be from ISIS fighters, current military forces, rebel fighters from Chechnya, militias from Iraq, or airstrikes by the allied coalition of nations with personal interests in the country. Along with Russia, Turkey, and Iran, the U.S. is currently responsible for the greatest number of civilian casualties, with a disproportionate number of them being women and children.[6]

Importantly, according to the independent reporting company Airwars, the numbers of civilian deaths are only increasing since Trump took office, and this is rarely admitted by the Coalition itself (Hussain 2017b). It isn't surprising that the government should want to remain discrete with these numbers, and yet there is also a lack of interest on the part of the international media to report them. By not reporting these incidents, American citizens fail to see this violence. To be sure, this is a curtailed blindness on the part of the government. By making the egregious consequences of our military regime invisible, it can ensure such tactics will go without criticism or the need for proper justification. Syrians are dying on a daily basis, and according to Kinda Haddad, a Syria analyst with Airwars, those who remain are the poorest and most vulnerable of all because they really have no other option but to stay (Hussain 2017b). If they had the means to flee they would have done so much sooner, and this has been stressed by various human rights organizations aiming to protect them. These are the same organizations who are lobbying for the U.S. to amend the travel ban and allow them to be granted asylum here.

Omar Hossino of the Syrian-American Council has stressed that "no Syrian wants to be a refugee," and yet there are numerous politicians (including President Trump), who have given us the impression that those who are seeking asylum want to emigrate to either take advantage of the social welfare amenities of our nation, or to conduct acts of terrorism (Lennard 2015). During his presidential campaign Senator Ted Cruz (R-Texas) described Syrian refugees as "jihadists," and said that if we allowed them in they would undoubtedly "murder innocent Americans" (Jilani 2015). These comments are in line with the reaction of more than half of the U.S. governors and conservative lawmakers who sought to block entry to Syrian refugees after the terrorist attacks in Paris in November of 2016 (Lennard 2015). A similar sentiment was reflected by Trump at a campaign rally in September of 2015, where he pledged to kick all Syrian refugees out of the country, explaining that "they could be ISIS, I don't know. This could be one of the great tactical ploys of all time. A 200,000-man army, maybe" (Johnson and Hauslohner 2017). Such negative rhetoric justifies a need to act against refugees rather than take responsibility for ensuring their protection. By defining them as security threats, this dehumanizes Syrian life and fails to see them as victims of violence who are as vulnerable to violence as we are.

The rationality used to justify closing our borders to refugees, as well as the military strikes being done by our warplanes on Syrian soil, requires a systemic undermining of Syrian life. The Trump administration exercises its political agency by way of self-preservation. It recognizes and protects lives only in accordance with a narrow lens of value. Syrian lives are ungrievable through this lens, such that any violence done to them is not perceived as murdering innocent civilians, and instead is seen as a necessary consequence to efforts made to ensure the preservation of the nation-state. According to Jay Morse, a senior military advisor at the Center for Civilians in Conflict, civilian harm is always "underrepresented and always underemphasized. . . . But these are the people who are suffering the most" (Hussain 2017b).[7] Our media fails to report on the number of civilian casualties, nor do they shine a light on the horrible conditions Syrian refugees are experiencing in camps in the borderlands or their efforts to emigrate to Europe. When we are alerted to some of the atrocities occurring, often these events are framed by way of xenophobically charged language that defines refugees as threats rather than victims. These accounts incite a sentiment of disinterest in coming to their aid, and the Administration can then continue to exercise its power without being held accountable for its inaction.

Self-preservation of the state rests on a rationale that sees refugees as expendable, disposable, and an economic burden, rather than fellow humans in need. Importantly, by closing our borders to these most vulnerable of people, the Administration is actually producing what counts as life. Such a Muslim ban imparts a system of recognition that defends those who are deemed "safe," and disavows a select group of misfits such that they may be marginalized to the shadows where they needn't be provided basic necessities to live. Judith Butler highlights the importance of the modes of recognition of the nation-state, and reveals their troublesome effects on marginalized populations in her work.[8] Athena Athanasiou co-authors *Dispossession: The Performative in the Political* with Butler, and addresses how the State effectively produces and manages forms of life, stating that "survival is configured and differently allocated by normative and normalizing operations of power, such as racism, poverty, heteronormativity, ethnocentrism, and cultural recognition" (Butler and Athanasiou 2013, 79). By producing what is to be regarded as vulnerable, precarious, and worthy of saving, the State also systemically overlooks the silent populous who fail to have a voice. Relying upon this dichotomization of life to further its interests overseas through the guise of protecting our citizens from potential terrorist attacks is unethical, and the remainder of this chapter will detail a perspective that calls this practice of exclusion into question.

The ethical principle at work here imparts an equal recognition of precarity among all people, regardless of social identifiers such as race, ethnicity, class, gender, sexual preference, religion, or country of origin. Butler states that "lives are by definition precarious: they can be expunged at will or by accident; their persistence is in no sense guaranteed" (Butler 2009, 25). Her work underscores the need to provide and ensure basic conditions that will further one's survival. I share Butler's ethical concerns, and believe our politics should recognize the precarity of life. We are all conditioned with a basic need for food, water, shelter, medical care, work, and legal status to ensure our lives are sustainable, and yet the nation is enacting policies that fail to observe these basic human rights on a global scale. By failing to enact such protections for Syrian life requires that the Administration be held accountable for its overt processes to exclude such people as equally injurable or at-risk.

This mode of recognition and the policies this Administration enacts to systemically exclude Syrian life is what I will take issue with going forward. Without a proper recognition of life, or a framework in place that holds all life as equally recognizable, the lives of Syrian refugees become legally proscribed from appearing as fellow humans who are precarious or grievable. Indeed, according to Butler, we must ratify how the State enforces "certain norms of recognition over others, and so constraining the field of the recognizable" (Butler 2015, 35). The frame of recognition imparted by the State, because of its power to preserve life, effectively produces what counts as livable at the same time. For instance, when the Administration constructs emigration policies that fail to allow the populations who are experiencing the constant threat of violence to seek protection within our borders, this stems from the "norms of recognizability" it corresponds to (Butler and Athanasiou 2013, 88). Importantly, as Athanasiou points out, such modes of recognition have "tangible implications of life and death," where those who are seen are allowed to expand their livability, while the opposite occurs for those who go unrecognized (Butler and Athanasiou 2013, 88).

Some have criticized Butler for being too focused on deconstruction and negativity, as opposed to constructing a positive way to provoke change in her political activism.[9] I find her work to be constructive, because focusing on lack functions as a means to address the prevailing norms. Such provocations are integral for exposing the fact that not all people are allowed basic human rights. Her work produces a much-needed shift in perspective that calls us to protect all lives as mutually vulnerable. That said, the significance of this work is not only to bear witness to the actions done to exclude Syrian refugees, but to show that this failure of recognition affects their ability to live at all.

The thinkers discussed in the remaining pages provide us with insights that support my criticisms of the partial frame of recognition imparted by the policies of this Administration. Butler's ethic of precarity requires that no life should be seen as more in need of securing the basic conditions for livability than another. The next sections will highlight philosophies of interdependency, and their prizing of immanence over transcendence will reveal the detrimental nature of this Administration's policies that alienate and injure Syrian lives. Athanasiou cues us in on what is to come, stating that:

> Perhaps what is at stake here is a shift from the (wounded) narcissism of autonomous and sovereign self-identity, which lies at the heart of the individualistic ontology of modernity, to an ethics and politics of post-identity subjectivities, which are consigned and exposed to the exposure, abandonment, precarity, and vulnerability of others. (Butler and Athanasiou 2013, 136)

There is a common thread sewn among Butler, Whitehead, and Braidotti's philosophy which exposes the need for an analysis of self that will reveal its immanent, interdependent, prehensive, and nomadic character.

By understanding the subject as existing in intimate relations with others, these thinkers show that we are only as protected as others and our environment will allow us to be. Butler states:

> There is no life without the conditions of life that variably sustain life, and those conditions are pervasively social, establishing not the discrete ontology of the person, but rather the interdependency of persons... and relations to the environment and to non-human forms of life, broadly considered. (Butler 2009, 19)

The view advocated here speaks to the immanent value of all life, as opposed to a dichotomy of power-over relations that seeks to disperse livability as the current Administration sees fit. Most importantly, not only does the ontological gaze of its nationalist policies require their own deconstruction to reveal their inherent partiality, but the remainder of this chapter will show that counter to the executive order in place, *our nation must take responsibility for Syrian refugees, and ensure that their basic human rights are recognized and preserved.*

The next section will illuminate the shift in perspective required in order for the State to take responsibility for disenfranchised Syrians. To be clear, Butler, Whitehead and Braidotti have different concerns and aims that emerge out of a variety of contexts, but all are relevant because of their shared emphasis on recognizing the value of all life. To transform policies that exclude Syrians from entry, the State needs to recognize each of us as defined in connection to, as opposed to alienation from others. The concepts and ontologies provided by Butler, Whitehead, and Braidotti assist us with elucidating our mutual precarity, and it is by way of this shared vulnerability that we may better understand lives as interconnected and equally in need of basic conditions that will ensure our shared survival on a global level.

UTILIZING PRECARITY AS AN ETHICAL IMPERATIVE

This chapter is Butlerian in its emphasis, and the ethical principle at work here is her understanding of subjects as precarious and living at-risk of peril. By keeping one attentive to the mutual immanence of life, the consequence of Butler's work is that as interrelational subjects, we must also take responsibility for the preservation of others. In her words, "once life is understood as both equally valuable and interdependent, certain ethical formulations follow. . . . Since other lives, understood as part of life that exceeds me, are a condition of who I am" (Butler 2015, 43). Butler understands human subjects as connected to a biological network of life that exceeds us. Our lives are dependent on a greater sociality, and in this way the lives of others cannot be understood as autonomous to our own. Butler's deep social ontology is porous at its essence, for every boundary is a site of adjacency, boundedness, and exposure to others (Butler 2015, 108). Importantly, we are all precarious in this immanence, for in our shared exposure, others can either ensure our survival or pose as a threat.

Butler's philosophical work has always taken issue with the suffering incurred by populations who are marginalized from dominant (and privileged) categories of gender, race, sexual orientation, class, and/or citizenship. She imparts a hermeneutic of suspicion to expose the rationale given to impart the normative matrix of intelligibility within the field of appearance itself. Constructively, she reveals forms of interdependency with the hope that her criticisms may make a way for the field to be transformed. In *Dispossession* she states that "for me, the insight into interdependency, exposure, [and] precarity, functions as a condition for thinking about ways of countering violent suppression and occupation" (Butler and Athanasiou 2013, 94). In this way, with every moment of deconstruction comes a constructive ethical counter-imperative.

By making precarity an ethical imperative, Butler is not seeking to rehabilitate humanism as such. Her work is egalitarian in its emphasis, for as she describes, "no one escapes the precarious dimension of social life" (Butler 2015, 119). Humans are understood as "relational and social being[s]," where one is dispossessed, interdependent, and in a constant state of vulnerability (Butler 2015, 88). She understands lives as beholden to others, whether they be human, plant, or animal, and this speaks to the ontologies of immanence emphasized in the work of Whitehead and Braidotti as well. Every life is socially-embedded, and we must also understand our lives as vulnerable in their immanence. She describes us as living organisms who "are clearly related to a vast continuum or network of living beings," who can only persist if we recognize that we mutually depend on a greater "matrix of sustaining interdependent relations" (Butler 2015, 86). The subject must not be understood as an ontological outlier to the world, for one can only persist if provided certain conditions that will enable one's survival. As corporeal beings, we all share a certain fragility. Precarity informs Butler's "ethical conception of human relationality," and as the great equalizer, it requires us to be attentive to the social conditions we live with (Butler 2015, 22). Our interdependency makes us vulnerable, and this requires our attention and mutual protection on a global level.

Any mode of recognition that legitimizes one population through a systemic unseeing of another (and thus exposing them to further vulnerability), fails to correspond to the ethical imperative that her notion of precarity emphasizes. Along with mutual vulnerability, we must recognize the unchosen character of our cohabitation with others. Butler describes that:

> Although we can and do choose with whom to share a bed, a house, or sometimes a neighborhood, we cannot choose with whom to share the earth without engaging in genocide. . . . We have obligations to preserve the lives of others whether or not we have contractually agreed to preserve their lives. (Butler and Athanasiou 2013, 122–23)

Living with others is not up for negotiation, such that we may deem certain populations as in more need of our recognition. This fact requires that we be made accountable to others and recognize them indiscriminately. Likewise, our vulnerability to others is not by choice either, nor are the levels of precarity equally dispersed among us. For this reason, recognizing precarity should be an ethical aim, as well as enforcing policies that provide Syrian refugees with basic conditions that will ensure their survival.

By accepting Butler's assessment that all life is at-risk, and the corresponding notion that we have a responsibility to preserve basic conditions to sustain life, closing our borders to Syrian refugees is unethical. We live only if we are granted basic conditions that will enable us to do so. Butler reveals how contingent our lives are, stating that "no human can be human alone. . . . [Where] no human can be human without acting in concert with others and on conditions of equality" (Butler 2015, 88). Precarity operates as "a social and economic condition" that speaks to the conditions of our interdependency for Butler (Butler 2015, 58). In one sense it is essential to the human condition, but as such, it emphasizes that our immanent fragility can be preserved only if the sustaining infrastructures and political institutions recognize life as requiring protection. Political regimes that deem certain lives disposable by failing to enact policies that will secure those lives, are producing what Butler so viscerally describes as "a damaged future in the stomach and in the bones" (Butler 2015, 201). The current conditions of forced emigration and neoliberalism are effectively stealing a secure future away from these people, leaving them without any political belonging.[10]

The economic and political institutions that employ biased exposures to precarity must be made accountable for their allowance of the "differential exposure to death and dying" that occur by way of their policies of exclusion (Butler 2015, 48). Indeed, the current military and emigration policies make it clear that humanitarian goals are not something that this Administration thinks it should be beholden to so that it may execute its will. Butler's work is helpful in coping with this ethical discrepancy, for she is calling for a different frame of recognition to be employed. Rather than re-establishing a normative apparatus of recognition of life (which will inevitably exclude it), the State should allow for the relationship between recognition and normativity to be more malleable.

Butler's constructive move is one that enacts a radical democratic politics in line with the principle of precarity, and such a reckoning can only take place if we become more attentive to an immanent social ontology. Life must be both understood and recognized as equally valuable and interdependent, where all things are connected within a greater biological network. Deep ontological immanence is also taken up by Whitehead and Braidotti, who provide us with an understanding of subjectivity as part and parcel to a greater organic whole. By incorporating aspects of these philosophies along with this consideration of Butler's ethical principle provides a means to inspire a change in perspective towards Syrian life. These thinkers inspire us to enact policies that are sensitive and accountable toward the biopolitical, as opposed to only valuing the means for pursuing State sovereignty.

VALUING PREHENSIVE BECOMINGS AND GREATER DIVERSITY

Thus far I have emphasized the importance of taking up Butler's work as a means to criticize the current policies enacted by the State that systemically exclude Syrian life. As I have mentioned, the lives of these refugees are not valued in the same sense as citizens of this country. The Administration can deny Syrians asylum if we don't see them as grievable. By failing to value their lives, we don't need to recognize their need for basic conditions to ensure their survival. This position is untenable from a moral standpoint. We are responsible for their lives and need to recognize that they are just as precarious and valuable as our own. To encourage us to continue thinking of ourselves as fundamentally bound up with Syrian life requires a further elaboration of an ontological framework where all lives are entangled, interconnected, and mutually becoming. Whitehead assists us in this regard by employing an ontology with a prehensive component where all lives are valued and are understood as integral to one another.

Whitehead's philosophy of organism was constructed as a means to critically probe the cosmologies of scientific materialists and Newtonian physicists of modernity. These prior cosmologies were based on a concept of nature where material beings were understood to be static, self-sufficient, and alienated from one another (see his sentiments towards these early cosmologies in Whitehead 1933, 131–34). As opposed to having any internal connection, entities were perceived as related to each other in an external, or neighborly way. By contrast, Whitehead sees the world as deeply connected, where things are always undergoing change and have value in their actualization of time and space. This valuation of concrete life is based on his view of the subject, which runs counter to substantive notions of presence. According to his "doctrine of mutual immanence," Whitehead understands each life as a factor "in the nature of every other happening" (Whitehead 1938, 164). His view upholds a notion of subjectivity where each is considered integral to the other and allows him to criticize scientific schemes that failed to incorporate any ethical component in them. An ethical repercussion of Whitehead's ontology is a sentiment of mutual accountability for the preservation and sustainability of others.

The interrelationality of Whitehead's system is arrived at by way of his notion of prehension. One integrates other organisms into their own occasion of experience through prehending them. Prehension is intrinsic to the process of concrescence, which is how one experiences the world. When concrescing, one's past experiences become integrated into one's subjective aim within the present occasion of experience or act of prehension. Prehending is how actual entities transfer feelings to one another on a physical as well as a conceptual level. These prehensions then become integrated into prior prehensions that have already been experienced. No one prehension holds greater value than another in this process, and what emerges as an entity concresces is a greater multiplicity of feeling. I've summarized this in another text as a process where "what is experienced is a growing together of prehensions that mutually effect one another and are solidified into one complex unity of feeling" (Lin 2012, 195).

By extrapolating Whitehead's notion of prehension here, we can begin to see how process and becoming are at the forefront of his cosmology. Such notions of action and engagement is how he conveys the perception of entities as integral to one another, rather than enduring soul-substances that remain static over time. Entities are threads of continuity at their essence, and Whitehead further describes them as "drops of experience, [which are] complex, and interdependent" (Whitehead 1978, 18). By prehending the world, subjects are understood as constantly emerging from it, and should never be understood as disengaged from this process (Whitehead 1978, 88). Ivor Leclerc provides a nice synopsis of the interconnectedness of actual entities, stating that:

> The act of an actual entity is an act of prehending other actual entities, relating them to itself. Thus each actual entity is, as it were, a node in a web of interrelatedness. To conceive it as existing in isolation is to falsify its nature. Each actual entity is the unitary synthesis achieved by its prehending activity. Each actual entity is a one prehending the many. There are many ones, each achieving its unity by the synthesis of the many. (Leclerc 1983, 59–60)

Entities are conceptualized as persisting nexuses of experience *with* others. We fail to recognize this when we support policies that deny Syrians to traverse our shores. Whitehead's notion of prehension assists us in our current endeavor to critically probe efforts to blind us to our state of interdependency on all life. By elucidating our present as a state of mutual feeling or prehension, is helpful for recognizing the ethical principle of precarity we should be made accountable to.

Whitehead mentions an ethical impulse that emerges from his notion of conscrescence, for it makes sense that mutually prehending entities would be concerned with the state of others as well (Whitehead 1933, 180). He describes a certain "solidarity of the world" that emanates from the process of concrescence (Whitehead 1978, 7). Prehension does not invoke a filtered view by which it feels others, it simply does so. In the same way, much could be gained by incorporating such impartiality within our emigration policies, such that we may recognize the integral value of Syrians in our midst. Prehensive beings live in immanence, there is no limitation to the unbounded potentiality of all life to be integrated within one another in its ongoing prehension of occasions of experience. Indeed, Whitehead's cosmology does not incorporate any system that may invoke limitations on our valuing of life.

In conjunction with his notion of prehension it is also helpful for us to value his honoring of diversity. For Whitehead, multiplicity needs to be recognized and integrated into one's purview so that novelty, creativity, and beauty can be manifested in the world. It is imperative that we don't overlook this, because in its execution of stricter processes of emigration as well as a continued insistence on border walls, there is also a controlling of heterogeneity being pursued by this Administration. Insofar as they are defined as a risk to our nation, Syrian lives are delegitimized, such that we need not grieve them, nor do we need to enact efforts to ensure their survival. The xenophobic rhetoric utilized by this Administration is done in an effort to value homogeneity and enforce policies of exclusion that only sees the Syrian immigrant as a potential threat to our national security. Such a dichotomization of life effectively curates their enigmatic status as strangers knocking on the door, but never allowed sanctuary.

At this point in our discussion, it is useful to not only think about the importance of implementing a thinking whereby we are all considered mutually precarious and prehensive, but even further, I now want us to consider another motivating factor to be gained by Whitehead's philosophy. There is an often-quoted saying taken from *Process and Reality* that speaks to my present interest, that "the many become one, and are increased by one" (Whitehead 1978, 21). When describing Whitehead's philosophy of nature, Victor Lowe states that it proposes "a system of the world" where self-realization grows out of "previous ones and . . . [adds] a new pulse of individuality and a new value to the world" (Lowe 1990, 223–24). For Whitehead, diversity has innate value because it contributes to greater creativity and beauty in the world. To secure our borders without the proper justifications for doing so not only fails to ensure the survival of fellow human beings, but if examined through a Whiteheadian lens, this also enacts a parsing out of life to maintain an economy of sameness that fails to integrate greater diversity. Enforcing proscriptive modes of recognition foregoes the value of multiplicity and forbids us from experiencing the potential novelty and creativity to be gained through our exposure to increased diversity.

This exploration of Whitehead has provided us with a means to consider our immanence as a deeply feeling one, and also provides us with a constructive impetus for incorporating a more inclusive consideration of life. He provides this by understanding all life as valuable and necessary within the pursuit of the constructive aim of a greater, more diverse whole. In the next section I will explore Braidotti's notions of nomadic and posthuman subjectivity as a means to emphasize the immanence we've been in the process of formulating, as well as to ensure that we account for non-humans within our present state of interdependency as well. The ethical principle of precarity is predicated on an understanding that all life is vulnerable. To provide a slight anthropocentrism would be a disservice to this vision, and it is for this reason that discussing Braidotti's vision is warranted to fulfill the more ethical frame of recognition I'm seeking to uphold.

MAKING CONSIDERATIONS FOR A POSTHUMAN, ZOE-CENTERED IMMANENT VISION

The philosophical endeavors of Butler, Whitehead, and Braidotti each convey a prizing of interdependency, as opposed to substance-oriented modalities where lives are understood as closed-off from one another. Appreciating interdependence is useful in providing an analysis of the subject that may hold our Administration accountable for failing to ensure the well-being of Syrian refugees. Within an immanent cosmology there is no sense in which one life can be made sustainable all on its own, rather it conveys the need for us to be held accountable for the protection and sustainability of others on a global scale.

In our discussion thus far, Butler has provided us with a principle to utilize in making considerations of the other. By identifying all lives as precarious this helps us to think of lives as equally at-risk, as well as mutually requiring certain conditions that will enable our survival. Whitehead adds a framework that reflects how we are porous to one another through his notion of prehension and process of concrescence. Feeling others in our immanence also contributes to greater novelty and beauty if we incorporate more variety and difference, and this is helpful for critically probing the systemic marginalization of Syrian life. Braidotti also values immanence in her work, but she is distinctly interested in thinking of the subject as related to non-human others.[11]

Braidotti's work is helpful because she is interested in our current Anthropocene period, where humans are now the most dominant influence on the sustainability of our species as well as the planet. Remaining sensitive to this as well as the pitfalls of neoliberalism, advanced capitalism, and necropolitics, Braidotti argues that these are all contributing factors to our "posthuman predicament," where technology mediates how we experience the world and ourselves (Braidotti 2013, 1).

In her appropriately entitled *The Posthuman*, Braidotti builds upon her work on nomadic subjectivity to critically address the problem of anthropocentrism in the Life Sciences and the Humanities. In the opening lines of this text, she states that "not all of us can say, with any degree of certainty, that we have always been human, or that we are only that" (Herbrechter 2013, 6). She seeks to debunk the myth that there is a universal humanity to which we all correspond and shines a light on the gradations that exist within the category of the human insofar as gender, race, class, citizenship, and sexuality are concerned. We speak about the fundamental rights of humans, but the very term "human" is not a given (although philosophers of the Enlightenment suggest otherwise). Braidotti reveals how humanism has been bound up with a certain, exceptional vision of the human to which minorities fail to have any sense of belonging. This fact is what so many post-colonial, feminist, and post-structuralist philosophers have shown us. There are always exclusions taking place, and this requires that we affirm a subjectivity that is more inclusive and intersectional in its determination.

Braidotti argues that our world has become so technologically mediated that we must make considerations for the non-human, inhuman, anti-human, and inhumane when we think about the most basic unit of reference for "our species, our polity and our relationship to the other inhabitants of this planet" (Braidotti 2013, 2). She utilizes *zoe* as a means for traversing political discourse that remains centered on the *anthropos,* as opposed to "vitalistic, prehuman, and generative life" (Braidotti 2011, 326). Humanity is not the focal point of her work, nor does she pose humans as the measure of all things. *Zoe* is an animating life force belonging not to an individual or particular species, but to the "dynamic, self-organizing structure of life itself" (Braidotti 2013, 60). Such a grounding force is impartial to life, and functions as a means to affirm an egalitarianism where no one species monopolizes the notion of life, rather all of the iterations of generic life are valued as interactive, in process, and co-related participants in *zoe.*

This *zoe*-centered approach is rooted in the vitalist and monist philosophies of Deleuze and Spinoza, and prioritizes immanence and radical inclusivity. Braidotti describes her work as making a "post-anthropocentric turn," and utilizes "generative vitality" as a "transversal force that cuts across and reconnects previously segregated species, categories and domains" (Braidotti 2013, 60). These are the traditional categories of the subject that are genderized, racialized, and sexualized in dichotomous ways. She exposes the unitary vision of the subject as being constructed by way of certain entitlements, be they masculine, white, heterosexual, property-owning or otherwise, and pushes for its dismantling. Such a notion of the subject is constructed through making exclusions, which serve to marginalize women, non-citizens, racial and sexual minorities, as well as animals. Nomadic thought challenges essentializations of the subject by emphasizing a Deleuzian rhizomatic subjectivity, which thinks of life in accordance with an ontology of becoming. Braidotti describes that:

> the key elements of this conceptual operation are the notion of a deep vitalist interrelation between ourselves and the world, in an ecophilosophical move that binds us to the living organism that is the cosmos as a whole. (Braidotti 2011, 213)

Her immanent vision is one of solidarity, and sees the world as entwined in an amalgamation of affirmative affects, where subjects are open-ended assemblages as opposed to autonomous isolated agents.

Life within the nomadic, vitalist account Braidotti provides is not an overarching concept, rather it becomes and immanently abides among heterogeneous relations and virtual multiplicities. Subjects are knowable insofar as they are perceived as singularities that are relational in their essence, and consequently we must think of them as existing in codependence. Braidotti seeks to cope with how subjects are located in space and time, and also longs for a future whereby alternative "schemes of representation" and power dynamics may be pursued that will both empower and speak to ethical accountability (Braidotti 2011, 216). Subjects are understood as figurations, where they are constantly in flux and live among binaries such as "nature/technology, male/female, black/white, local/global, [and] present/past" (Braidotti 2011, 217). The point here is that we think of life not as static or easily theorized, but instead in a more slippery sense, as actively in-between, hybrid, and nomadic. Subjects are nonlinear and live in transition among a variety of factors that are not isolated from one another, but rather intersect and flow into a complex genesis, an assemblage of life.

The universalist account of life must be done away with, for it seeks to provide a claim to knowledge that is limited in its recognition of who—or what—counts as life in the first place. Nomadic consciousness is about making us aware of the limitations of discursive representation, to address the subject in terms of figurations and counterimages that are becoming-other, and thus have radical consequences for making considerations for our specific geopolitical- and historical-locatedness. Braidotti understands subjects as involved in patterns of different becomings, such as becoming-animal, becoming-earth, and becoming-machine. Life remains central among these becomings, and each serve as a means to critique the dangerous practices of advanced capitalism which fail to recognize this.

In the example of becoming-animal, Braidotti argues that we must recognize animals as embodying *zoe* along with us, and correspondingly we should be held accountable when their lives are unjustly commodified for our benefit.[12] The same principle of *zoe*-egalitarianism applies when making considerations for the planet as well, as one can recognize when she discusses the posthuman becoming-earth where humans are understood as biological *as well as* geological agents. Such a geo-centered perspective is grounded in a naturalistic foundationalism whereby humans can no longer consider themselves as somehow above or beyond nature, nor can we disregard the geological force we wield on the planet itself.[13] Also, her discussion of the posthuman as becoming-machine takes issue with what has now evolved into an intimate relationship with the inorganic, manufactured, electronic devices of our time.

Through her deep understanding of human entanglements with the nonhuman, Braidotti implores us to incorporate an understanding of interrelationality that is more open-ended, where life is not strictly delineated within the human, but the nonhuman as well. Such an immanence requires that we preserve our mutual interdependence, and respect *zoe* by making ourselves more accountable to the other on a planetary scale. Butler, Whitehead, and Braidotti each recognize the need for a more immanent vision of reality to emerge, such that we may be held more accountable toward enacting greater compassion and inclusivity of the other. Now that much effort has been given to invoke an alternative vision of immanence as opposed to the nationalist power-over paradigm being upheld by the current Administration, it is time to speak more overtly such that we may hold systems accountable for systemically denying Syrians life.

EMBRACING PRECARIOUS SYRIAN LIFE

It may seem as though I have digressed from my original aim, but invoking Braidotti's posthuman sensibility to the "transversality of relations" and connections among multiple relations and forces speaks to our need to invoke a greater recognition not only to Syrian life, but to our nonhuman others we are affecting in this Anthropocene era. Such a consideration of immanence is not foreclosed by Whitehead's cosmology and his notion of prehension. But, having lived in the beginning of the twentieth century, he couldn't possibly account for the extent to which things have changed. We are living in a technological milieu which requires a different understanding of self and are polluting the earth to such an extent that we pose the greatest risk to its survival. Sensitivity to these essential factors is needed when making considerations of precarity and mutual codependency. When considered in conjunction with Butler and Whitehead, Braidotti's *zoe*-centered egalitarianism serves as a beneficial means to recognize our deep entanglement with others, whether they be of a human, animal, earth, or technological kind.

Braidotti speaks to an "ecosophical sense of community" that is relevant in our current task that longs for a greater inclusivity of Syrian life (Braidotti 2011, 210). To achieve this aim, the parameters and modes of recognition imparted by the nation-state need to be pried open. Butler achieves this through her critical provocations that address mutual grievability, precarity, and vulnerability. Whitehead also serves us well by elucidating our intimate relations with others through his notion of prehension. He also incites us to appreciate differences more broadly, which if applied to the interests of the present discussion, welcoming Syrians will produce greater novelty and beauty in our nation, as opposed to simply posing a threat. Braidotti's immanent vision is comprised of mutual co-becomings where we are all on this earth together, whether we are human or not. By employing a filter to exclude Syrians to seek asylum here, the Administration is prioritizing some lives as more precarious than others. Such a stance requires a rationale that can only be pursued by understanding lives as isolated from one another, rather than codependent through a mutual prehension of the other. For lives to go unrecognized in this way is significant, for in its failure to value Syrian life it also serves as a means to justify their disposability.

We are living in a time where nationalist agendas are at the forefront of global apparatuses of power, and with this comes a resurgence of xenophobia (Baker and Rubin 2018). President Trump and his policies of exclusion are leading the Islamophobic and nationalist disregard for Syrian life. Such a stance cannot hold based on any predilections of morality or making strides toward ensuring our national security. No data has been given to suggest that Syrians are any more dangerous than citizens of countries who haven't been included on the ban list, or even U.S. citizens who have actually enacted acts of terrorism on our shores. Syrian lives need to be deemed just as grievable as our own, and our policies should recognize this and provide them with conditions that will ensure their survival. By thinking of ourselves as mutually vulnerable subjects who prehend others, and live in an immanence that values *zoe*, this poses an affirmative means to prod the current policies of this Administration. These policies are legitimized through an exclusionary vision that perceives American lives as precious and fails to allow for the viability of Syrian life. This is unethical, for we are all precarious and live in a mutual state of vulnerability. Our policies that allow for refugees to seek political asylum here should reflect this.

We all require basic conditions for living, and this shared vulnerability can function as a principle for us to see others as our equal. The fact that we are codependent and beholden to others in this way also makes the Administration accountable for its denial of ensuring basic conditions of living for Syrian refugees. They are not citizens of this country, but they need our support because they have no means to protect themselves or survive in their own land. By closing our borders as the travel ban does, the Administration is systematically precluding Syrians from enacting their own persistence, which cannot stand. Now is the time that we deem these policies unethical and turn to an alternative mode of recognition that employs a *zoe*-centered egalitarian vision, as opposed to nationalist visions of exclusion.

NOTES

1. This assessment is according to Finnish Prime Minister Juha Sipila at an aid conference in Helsinki, as reported in Huuhtanen 2017.
2. See how more than half of U.S. governors chose to close their borders after the terrorist attacks in Paris in Lennard 2015. See President Trump making erroneous statements in regards to Sweden suffering from increasing crime and terrorism after admitting Syrian refugees in Valverde 2017. See Senator Ted Cruz's degrading comments about Syrians as "jihadists" during his presidential campaign as documented in Jilani 2015.
3. See statistics provided in "Over the Decades, American Public Generally Hasn't Welcomed Refugees," Pew Research Center 2015.
4. The executive order can be read at "Full Text of Trump's Executive Order on 7-Nation Ban, Refugee Suspension," CNN, last modified January 28, 2017, http://www.cnn.com/2017/01/28/politics/text-of-trump-executive-order-nation-ban-refugees/index.html.
5. See Bier 2017. In this article he specifically lists the origin countries of the radicalized Muslims who have "carried out deadly attacks in the U.S. . . . [as] Saudi Arabia, Egypt, Lebanon, United Arab Emirates, Pakistan, Russia, and Kyrgystan."
6. See statement by Chris Woods, Director of Airwars, in an interview in Hussain 2017b.
7. See statement by Jay Morse, Senior Military Advisor at the Center for Civilians in Conflict, in Hussain 2017b.

8. See *Frames of War: When Is Life Grievable?* (Brooklyn: Verso, 2009); *Dispossession: The Performative in the Political,* written with Athena Athanasiou (Malden, MA: Polity Press, 2013); and *Notes toward a Performative Theory of Assembly* (Cambridge, MA: Harvard University Press, 2015).

9. Braidotti, for instance, goes at length to criticize Butler's work as lacking constructive aims, and classifies her work as residing in melancholia, negativity and lack. See Braidotti 2002.

10. Butler exposes the problematic aspects of the neoliberalist mindset that informs our nation's policies, such that they increasingly subject a variety of populations to "precaritization" (Butler 2015, 15). She argues that neoliberalism requires that subjects be self-reliant in order to have value or be recognized. If one cannot afford certain services that will ensure basic conditions of life such as food, shelter, health care, and so forth, then they are deemed irresponsible within the eyes of the law. One can certainly see a certain prioritization of paying your own way among the current policy choices being made on behalf of the conservatives in congress as well as the Trump White House, where we see a consistent push to eliminate services and institutions that will ensure public welfare and basic conditions for living.

11. To be clear, to utilize Braidotti in a chapter emerging from a Butlerian framework is not without its problems, for Braidotti is explicit in her negative assessments of Butler's critical work (see Butler 2013, 136). She characterizes Butler as residing in melancholia and lack, while arguing that her work is an affirmative politics. I disagree with these negative assessments of Butler, for as I have mentioned thus far in this exploration, her attention to what is lacking recognition within the normalized frame is done in an effort to *promote an ethic of care* towards those who go unaccounted for. Pointing to the lack of recognition maintained by the state apparatus functions as *a means for us to be attentive to real discrepancies of power and accountability that exist*. To do so does not focus on what isn't there, such that we simply abide in lack, melancholia, or the negative. Rather, this critical stance is an enabling force such we may begin to see the marginalization of life that takes place in the construction of hegemonic matrices of intelligibility and recognition.

12. See her discussion of the posthuman becoming-animal in Braidotti 2013, 67–76.

13. See her discussion of the posthuman becoming-earth in Braidotti 2013, 81–89.

REFERENCES

Baker, Peter, and Alissa J. Rubin. 2018. "Trump's Nationalism, Rebuked at World War I Ceremony, Is Reshaping Much of Europe." *New York Times*, November 11. https://www.nytimes.com/2018/11/11/us/politics/macron-trump-paris-wwi.html.

Bier, David J. 2017. "Trump's Immigration Ban Is Illegal." *New York Times*, January 27. https://www.nytimes.com/2017/01/27/opinion/trumps-immigration-ban-is-illegal.html.

Braidotti, Rosi. 2002. *Metamorphosis: Towards a Materialist Theory of Becoming.* Malden, MA: Polity Press.

———. 2011. *Nomadic Theory: The Portable Rosi Braidotti.* New York: Columbia University Press.

———. 2013. *The Posthuman.* Malden, MA: Polity Press.

Butler, Judith. 2009. *Frames of War: When Is Life Grievable?* Brooklyn: Verso.

———. 2015. *Notes Toward a Performative Theory of Assembly.* Cambridge, MA: Harvard University Press.

Butler, Judith, and Athena Athanasiou. 2013. *Dispossession: The Performative in the Political.* Malden, MA: Polity Press.

CNN. 2017. "Full Text of Trump's Executive Order on 7-Nation Ban, Refugee Suspension." Last modified January 28, 2017. http://www.cnn.com/2017/01/28/politics/text-of-trump-executive-order-nation-ban-refugees/index.html.

Dalai Lama, Desmond Tutu, and Douglas Abrams. 2016. *The Book of Joy: Lasting Happiness in a Changing World.* New York: Penguin Random House.

Herbrechter, Stefan. 2013. "Rosi Braidotti (2013) *The Posthuman.*" *Culture Machine* 14 (April): 1–13.

Hussain, Murtaza. 2017a. "Trump Prepares to Shut Door on Refugees, Ending Long U.S. Tradition." *The Intercept,* January 25. https://theintercept.com/2017/01/25/trump-prepares-to-shut-door-on-refugees-ending-long-u-s-tradition/.

———. 2017b. "The U.S. Has Ramped Up Airstrikes against ISIS in Raqqa, and Syrian Civilians Are Paying the Price." *The Intercept,* May 30. https://theintercept.com/2017/05/30/the-u-s-has-ramped-up-airstrikes-against-isis-in-raqqa-and-syrian-civilians-are-paying-the-price/.

Huuhtanen, Matti. 2017. "The UN Refugee Agency Is Asking for Nearly $8 Billion to Help Displaced Syrians." *Business Insider,* January 24. http://www.businessinsider.com/ap-syrian-aid-conference-appeals-for-8-billion-in-aid-2017-1.

Jilani, Zaid. 2015. "Cruz's Swearing of Syrian Refugees Echoes Attacks on Cuban Refugees During His Father's Era." *The Intercept,* December 24. https://theintercept.com/2015/12/24/cruzs-smearing-of-syrian-refugees-echoes-his-fathers-attacks-on-cuban-refugees/.

Johnson, Jenna, and Abigail Hauslohner. 2017. "'I Think Islam Hates Us': A Timeline of Trump's Comments about Islam and Muslims." *The Washington Post,* May 20. https://www.washingtonpost.com/news/post-politics/wp/2017/05/20/i-think-islam-hates-us-a-timeline-of-trumps-comments-about-islam-and-muslims/?utm_term=.59724d61a675.

Leclerc, Ivor. 1983. "Being and Becoming in Whitehead's Philosophy." In *Explorations in Whitehead's Philosophy,* edited by Lewis S. Ford and George L. Kline. New York: Fordham University Press.

Lennard, Natasha. 2015. "Tragic Farce of Anti-Refugee Threats: U.S. Was No Sanctuary for Syrians in the First Place." *The Intercept,* November 20. https://theintercept.com/2015/11/20/tragic-farce-of-anti-refugee-threats-us-was-no-sanctuary-for-syrians-in-the-first-place/.

Lin, Deena M. 2012. "Prehending Precarity: Presenting a Social Ontology That Feels Beyond the Frame." In *Butler on Whitehead: On the Occasion,* edited by Roland Faber, Michael Halewood, and Deena M. Lin. Lanham, MD: Lexington Books.

Lowe, Victor. 1990. *Alfred North Whitehead: The Man and His Work, Volume II: 1920–1947,* edited by J. B. Schneewind. Baltimore: Johns Hopkins University Press.

Pew Research Center. 2015. "Over the Decades, American Public Generally Hasn't Welcomed Refugees," November 18. http://www.pewresearch.org/fact-tank/2015/11/19/u-s-public-seldom-has-welcomed-refugees-into-country/ft_15–11–18_refugeepublicopinion/.

Sommerfeldt, Chris. 2017. "President Trump's Muslim Ban Excludes Countries Linked to His Sprawling Business Empire." *NY Daily News,* February 1. http://www.nydailynews.com/news/politics/trump-muslim-ban-excludes-countries-linked-businesses-article-1.2957956.

The UN Refugee Agency. "Syria Regional Refugee Response," accessed October 21, 2018. http://data.unhcr.org/syrianrefugees/regional.php.

Valverde, Mariam. 2017. "What the Statistics Say about Sweden, Immigration, and Crime." *Politifact,* February 20. http://www.politifact.com/truth-o-meter/article/2017/feb/20/what-statistics-say-about-immigration-and-sweden/.

Vogue, Ariane de, Jeremy Diamond, and Kevin Liptak. 2017. "US President Donald Trump Signs New Travel Ban, Exempts Iraq." *CNN,* last modified March 7, 2017. http://www.cnn.com/2017/03/06/politics/trump-travel-ban-iraq/index.html.

White House, Office of the Press Secretary. 2017. "Executive Order: Protecting the Nation from Foreign Terrorist Entry into the United States." Issued January 27. https://www.whitehouse.gov/the-press-office/2017/01/27/executive-order-protecting-nation-foreign-terrorist-entry-united-states.

Whitehead, Alfred North. 1933. *Adventures of Ideas.* New York: The Free Press.

———. 1938. *Modes of Thought.* New York: The Free Press.

———. 1978. *Process and Reality: An Essay in Cosmology.* Corrected ed. Edited by David Ray Griffin and Donald W. Sherburne. New York: The Free Press.

World Economic Forum. 2017. "The Global Risks Report 2016—Frequently Asked Questions (FAQ)." Accessed January 28. http://reports.weforum.org/global-risks-2016/faqs/.

World Vision. 2017. "Syrian refugee crisis: Facts, FAQs, and how to help." Last modified July 13, 2017. http://worldvision.org/refugees-news-stories/Syria-refugee-crisis-war-facts.

Chapter Six

Conceptual Prehensions, Worlds of Experience

Whitehead and Uexküll on the Nonhuman Subject

Tano Posteraro

This chapter finds its motivation in the provocation that concepts have for too long been conceived canonically under the aegis of an essentially human linguisticism, confined to the offices of conscious judgment, refused to the diversely fluorescent realms of other modes of organic experience. So claims Alva Noë, whose own work has argued convincingly against the dominant trend of the first set of restrictions—that concepts need be linguistic, that they are species of judgment, and that they are therefore necessarily conscious.[1] Noë's work is encouraging, but does not go far enough. For that, I contend that we need Whitehead, whose own metaphysical scheme liberates conceptual activity from the human realm completely. Concepts, for him, are ways of feeling the world. And all experience—whether vegetative, animal, or otherwise—is, on Whitehead's account, a kind of feeling. This chapter endeavours to construct out of Whitehead's insight, in conversation with Jakob von Uexküll, a world in which the relations between a diverse array of nonhuman organisms and their subjective environments are mediated conceptually, and so no longer foreclosed to philosophical speculation. I begin by reconstructing a relevant network of Whitehead's concepts with an aim toward illuminating what he calls "conceptual prehensions." Then I turn, in the chapter's second section, to Uexküll's biosemiotic account of animal experience. My ambition, in staging this encounter, is to demonstrate the way Whitehead's ontologization of conceptual activity provides a fruitful ground from which to think, with Uexküll, the experiential worlds of other subjects. And in the process, we might even lend some weight to Nietzsche's claim—

sarcastic though it is—that if only we could communicate with the gnat, we would learn that it too feels itself the center of its own world (Nietzsche 1997, 42–46). We humans are just such beings, swooning under an illusory exceptionalism, overlooking at every step the anarchic subjectivities of billions of other organisms and the flashing zones of their own ecologies of experience.

WHITEHEAD

Whitehead's account of conceptual activity is radical enough that we need to begin first with an explicatory tour (selective though it must be) through his metaphysical scheme.[2] Consider, to start, the provocation that "apart from the experiences of subjects there is nothing, nothing, nothing, bare nothingness" (Whitehead 1978, 167). This statement might seem to entail at first, and in orthodox phenomenological fashion, a reduction of the natural world to the content of experience. But read correctly it proffers precisely the opposite suggestion—that the concept of subjective experience, appropriately enlarged, can be made to capture the whole of nature, albeit to varying degrees of relevance or intensity. Indeed, "nature is," for Whitehead, "that which we observe in perception through the senses" (Whitehead 1920, 3). We observe the entire world under a certain form of relation, thus spoke Leibniz (see Leibniz 1989, 42). Whitehead agrees, though experience is, for him, emphatically not cognitive; it's emotional, felt (Whitehead 1925, 176). Whitehead's subject is an "occasion" of feeling, a pulse of emotion constituted by its relations to the actual world.[3] That world is a composite of actual particulars and the universal patterns of relation that structure them.[4] What we observe is always simultaneously concrete, the mark of a singular experience, as well as universal and abstract. Color, shape, number, sensation: all endlessly iterable, transcendent over the particularity of any one of their manifestations. But those manifestations are each singularities, unrepeatable. The brown, smoothly tapered surface of the desk beneath my fingers is particular to my experience of it, even if the qualities realized in it are not.

Whitehead, for his part, prefers to speak of "pure potentials" or "eternal objects."[5] He defines the eternal object thus: "Any entity whose conceptual recognition does not involve a necessary reference to any definite actual entities of the temporal world" (Whitehead 1978, 44). Which makes sensory qualities, colors, conceptual abstractions, moral virtues, and physical forces like gravitational attraction all eternal objects.[6] Eternal objects shape the way an experience is felt (Whitehead 1978, 291). They mediate the actual world, structure and inform it—but without thereby determining it totally. In fact, the eternal objects do precisely the opposite, opening in the actual world the space required for metaphysical novelty. These potentials are eternal in that they are not exhausted by their real manifestations or what Whitehead calls their "ingressions" into actuality. Cerulean is not at risk of depletion, no matter how many blue skies one enjoys. The very possibility, in fact, of new and different skies depends in part on a reserve of inexhaustible potentials—of, for example, the patterns and intensities that possibilize different cloud formations—from which the actual world can draw in the course of its becoming, lest it lapse into a purely mechanical repetition or endless reorganization of what already exists. Pure potentials are therefore best conceived in terms of multiplicity, irreducible to a definite set. "Although they seem to be 'complete,'" to take a line from Roland Faber, "their completion is not finite (countable or uncountable) but comprises an *infinity* (of possibilities) which per definition cannot be circumscribed" (Faber 2014, 196). Every actual event is mediated and therefore differentiated by its relation to the eternal objects. In this resides the possibility for novelty, for "precisely insofar as the becoming of any actual event includes the '(infinite, chaotic) whole' of this pure multiplicity without unity, it offers *infinite differentiation* of actual events and, hence, the sought creativeness of unprecedented novelty" (Faber 2014, 196). So we begin to see the way experience opens onto a vast and natural creativity by integrating or synthesizing processes that exceed the perspective of any one subject.

Whitehead credits Kant for having introduced into philosophy for the first time "the concept of an act of experience as a constructive functioning" (Whitehead 1978, 156). Experience is, for Kant (as for Whitehead), the inverse of a noetic mimesis of intrinsic nature; it is formative of the world, inseparable from the objects it observes. "For our observation of the world, or of anything in the world, is," to speak with Steven Shaviro, "a process that interacts with, intervenes in, and changes the nature of, whatever it is that we are observing" (Shaviro 2009, 48). It is here, however, that Whitehead departs from Kant. For Kant's subject forms the world in terms of its transcendental categories while Whitehead's subject is *formed by* the world and informs that world only in the processes of emerging out of and settling back into it.[7] Kant's is a world conditioned by a subject whose categories of understanding constitute its intelligibility; Whitehead's, a world capable of generating the intelligibility of subjective experience. So the subjective unity of an act of experience is not, for Whitehead, a *condition* for the possibility of a world, but rather precisely the opposite—it is conditioned by the world and produced in the course of its unfolding (see the "Category of Subjectivity Unity," Whitehead 1978, 26 and 223–25).

Whitehead's subject is not a structure of possible experience, but an event or pulse of actual experience, a quantum. He prefers to speak of "actual occasions." These are the "final real things of which the world is made up," its atoms (Whitehead 1978, 18). Every actual occasion is precisely that—an *occasion*, a coming-to-be and a passing-away. The occasion is a processual integration of a multiplicity of experiential data, a response and reaction to—as well as a variation of—the settled, objectified past. Whitehead speaks instead of "prehensions," both to foreground the fact that the subject *feels* its world (prehensions are visceral, bodily), as well as "to avoid the anthropomorphic—or at least cognitive and rationalistic—connotations of words like 'mentality' and 'perception'" (Shaviro 2009, 28). Prehensions are primarily nonconscious forms of experience. Basic causal relationships are as prehensive as acts of conscious contemplation.[8] The subject, no matter its compositional complexity, is constituted (and so exhausted) by what and how it prehends.[9] But it does not for that reason merely repeat the world to which it is related. It emerges out of that world on the basis of a fundamental *decision* regarding *how* to feel it. No subject can feel all the world equally; it must instead *feel it out*, smooth some differences over, reject others, intensify others still. "Call it what you will," writes Didier Debaise, "a feeling is above all a capture, a particular way of possessing, an activity through which something 'appropriates the datum so as to make it its own'" (Debaise 2014, 303).[10] Subjectivity indexes the movement through which the objective actuality of the world is taken into account, privatized and felt. The completed occasion is a satisfaction of these feelings, the final realization of the decisional process. The world advances creatively as each subject emerges out of and—satisfied—perishes back into it, adding to the objective data available for new experience. Each subject therefore plays a role both in its own constitution as well as in the constitution of the world, for this is a world whose rhythmic oscillations between feeling and being felt intensify with each pulse the complexity of actuality.

But the actual, as we've seen, tells only half the story. Feelings are haunted by what they could have been, by what was negated or denied in the decisional processes that subtend their attainment. An experience, by virtue of its singularity, has to select among possibilities; it has to exclude. And what it excludes plays a positive role in its composition. "A feeling bears on itself the scars of its birth," as Whitehead so nicely puts the point; "it recollects as a subjective emotion its struggle for existence; it retains the impress of what it might have been, but is not" (Whitehead 1978, 226–47). The actual is therefore tied inseparably to the potential, what is felt to what is not. The subject can, moving beyond what is present for physical feeling, prehend unrealized possibilities as well. Whitehead calls this form of prehension conceptual: "the feeling of an unqualified negation; that is to say, it is the feeling of a definite eternal object with the definite extrusion of any particular realization" (Whitehead 1978, 243). Every physical feeling involves eternal objects, but only immanently, "as determined," to borrow a line from Donald Sherburne, "to specific actualities, namely, those actual entities being prehended" (Sherburne 1981, 211). Conceptual prehension is, on the other hand, the prehension of undetermined, unactualized eternal objects, the feeling of—to restate Whitehead—what might have been, but is not; the feeling too of what might still be.[11]

Conceptual feelings also evaluate the physical feelings out of which they arise. This is their primary role. Later phases of experience integrate the two, intensifying in the physical what is valued adversely in the conceptual.[12] Whitehead calls this the first phase of the mental pole of experience, that category through which the world is captured, felt, subjectivized.[13] For the subjectivity of the subject resides in the fact that it evaluates and so modifies in feeling the world to which it responds. This first phase is succeeded by a second in which arise conceptual feelings "with data which are partially identical with, and partially diverse from, the eternal objects forming the data in the first phase of the mental pole" (Whitehead 1978, 26). Whitehead calls this conceptual reversion (Whitehead 1978, 249). If the first phase of mental experience accounts for the subjectivization of the world, then the second accounts for the introduction of novelty, for reversion frees the subject from a limitation to only those eternal objects that are realized in its physical feelings. "Even if everything that it sees is blue," Shaviro explains, "it is also able to imagine red" (Shaviro 2009, 137). Which is to say that the subject is therefore capable of forming feelings "which are partially identical with, and partially diverse from, the eternal objects forming the data in the primary phase of [its] mental pole" (Whitehead 1978, 249). It is not bound to the actual.

Subjects aim at the attainment of a maximum of experiential depth or intensity. These aims activate processes of feeling; they are at the origin of valuation and reversion (Stengers 2011, 361). Faced with a gradient of colors, we are adept at imagining missing shades.[14] "And the very experience of the person who, faced by the 'lack of a shade,' imagines the missing shade, is," in the words of Isabelle Stengers, "an abstract example of a properly cosmic event" (Stengers 2011, 361). An example of the process through which initially unrealized potentials are brought into contrast with what is given in physical feeling. Reversion produces contrast; contrasts introduce novelty and deepen experiential intensity.[15] Whitehead sets this concept of contrast against incompatibility. I cannot, for example, feel at once both the desk beneath my fingers as well as the cool metal of the room's door handle. The two feelings are incompatible. It's one or the other. To contrast is, then, to render compatible. And compatibility implies experiential depth. Consider my ability to feel at once the desk beneath my fingers, the carpet under my feet, a windowed draft on my arms that relieves an otherwise oppressive humidity, all while I inhale the ozone in the rain, taste its faintly metallic effects, and slouch into the resistant solidity of a hard chair—not to mention at all the array of digitized audiovisual phenomena by which I'm also stimulated. "The more an actual entity can hold the items of its experience in contrasts, and contrasts of contrasts," as Sherburne puts the point, "the more it elicits depth and intensity for its satisfaction" (Sherburne 1981, 216). Conversely, less sophisticated subjects, "unable to hold the items of their experience in contrasts are forced, because of the resulting incompatibilities," he continues, "to dismiss some items as irrelevant, with the result that their experience is relatively shallow and trivial" (Sherburne 1981, 216).[16]

This process works by what Whitehead calls transmutation. Recall that the qualities and sensations characteristic of experience are each eternal objects, ingressed into actuality. Transmutation indexes the fact that, in the processes of conceptual valuation and reversion, irrelevant physical feelings are neglected, incompatibilities dismissed, contrasts introduced, and certain qualities made to stand forth, in focus. We are, in experience, confronted initially with a multitude of physical data—a crashing wave's overwhelming assortment of individual auditory impressions, to take from Leibniz. Perception is, however, marked not by an incoherent chaos of sensory information, but by the prehension of particular qualities, the roar of the wave, a spatter of rain. We are capable even of distinguishing that roar and that spatter from other qualities of the experience, the growl, say, of a distant highway. Transmutation resolves a problem of perceptual mereology articulated first by Leibniz—how it is that infinitely many microperceptions, or physical feelings, coalesce to constitute a simplified, qualified sensation. If every perception consists of infinitely many microperceptions, it is because every subject "is like," in Leibniz's own words, "a complete world and like a mirror . . . of the whole universe, which each one expresses in its own way, somewhat as the same city is variously represented depending upon the different positions from which it is viewed" (Leibniz 1989, 42). If each subject expresses the world in its own way, from its own point of view, and if each expression nonetheless implicates the whole world, it is only because a particular zone of that expression is clear in experience, prehended positively. Everything else is obscure. Clear perception is not by virtue of its clarity distinct. In fact, for Leibniz, just the opposite: the clear perception of a pang of hunger confuses—literally, *fuses together*—an infinity of microscopic bodily sensations (see Deleuze 1993, 88). And if one were able to isolate a distinct set of those minute perceptions (a lack of protein, say), the larger feeling of hunger would be lost, obscured. Microperceptions are therefore distinct to the extent that they disclose a set of the genetic elements of perception, but obscure insofar as these elements are not yet actualized in clear, qualified terms (Voss 2013, 120; cf. Smith 1996, 39). Every zone of clarity, every positive feeling is therefore relative to a field of obscurity that surrounds it, an infinite plane of minute perceptions out of which it is constituted. It emerges out of this field genetically, "as it were through a series of filters, a series of successive integrations or syntheses" (Voss 2013, 120). This is Leibniz.

Whitehead is unconvinced. The theory of perceptual confusion names a problem without adequately resolving it.[17] Prehensions of the qualities that mark the qualified perception are, on Whitehead's account, integrated with the physical data out of which they emerged. That physical data—the microperceptions alone—is incapable of constituting a qualified macroscopic feeling; required for that result is the integration of an eternal object, the datum of a conceptual feeling (see Stengers 2011, 345–46). The object qualifies the multiplicity of physical feelings at a primary phase of experience so that successive phases need only prehend the objectified sensation.[18] Confusion isn't the right word for this process. Minute perceptions are not so much fused or obscured as they are integrated with a definite conceptual prehension; the result of that integration is not so much emergent out of a differential relation among minute perceptions as it is objectified and transmuted along each successive phase of subjective experience. This is Whitehead's solution to the Leibnizian problematic and so the condition for qualified, spatialized perception as such. "Only if it has issued from a transmutation," to speak with Stengers, "can what is felt be felt 'there,' that blue stain entering into contrast with other colors in the midst of a colored world, or the great roar of that wave crashing, there, against that rock" (Stengers 2011, 346). Conceptual prehensions condition, as a result, the very mechanisms of perceptual experience. "The experience, and the conceptualizing, are," to take a line from Alva Noë, "*one and the same activity*" (Noë 2004, 194; emphasis in original). The coextensivity of concepts and experience thus elucidated, and with Whitehead's metaphysics of the subject in mind, let's turn now to Uexküll and his "foray" into the worlds of other animals.

UEXKÜLL

In 1934, Jakob von Uexküll, an Estonian biologist, implored his contemporaries by way of an eccentric picture book to stroll with him through a series of the distinct perceptual environments of other animals. For all its whimsy, *A Foray into the Worlds of Animals and Humans* introduced into philosophical circulation a radical new idea: that ours is not the only environment available to thought, that a sea anemone, a grizzly bear, a tick, might each spin out of itself a web of meaningful relations constitutive of a subjective world all its own.[19] Uexküll called these worlds *Umwelten*. Translators routinely render the word in its original German—although it is just as often translated as "environments"—to denote the fact that a world (or environment) is always a world for a particular organism, always therefore subjective, relative, circumscribed.[20] We should hear in this proposition its Kantian overtones; indeed, Kant's "idea that 'all reality is subjective appearance' informs all of Uexküll's thought" (Buchanan 2008, 21). Like Whitehead, Uexküll champions the Kantian insight that experience functions constructively. And like Whitehead, Uexküll frees this claim from an explicitly anthropocentric bias. "If it is agreed that the world is constituted through each individual subject," explains Buchanan, "then it becomes necessary to ask how the world appears to each organism as a subjective appearance" (Buchanan 2008, 21–22). Uexküll suggests, in response, that "every animal is a subject, which, in virtue of the structure peculiar to it, selects stimuli from the general influences of the outer world, and to these it responds in a certain way" (Uexküll 1926, 126). This play between selection and response forms the organism's *Umwelt.* Uexküll locates its mechanism in the animal body and conceptualizes its function in fundamentally semiotic terms.

In the composition of a given *Umwelt,* different elements of the surrounding ecology are rendered present, but present only in the form of a specific mode of relation, present relative to the constitution of a specific animal, in accordance with a constellation of meanings unique to the structure of its subjective experience. The architecture of this presence is, first and foremost, essentially nervous, physiological: indeed, "outside the animal under observation, numerous influences proceed from the object that are not taken up, because a certain intensity of the external influence is required if a nerve is to be excited" (Uexküll 1926, 134). This is a fact of anatomy. Every animal is, by virtue of the configuration of its perceptual organs, "cut off from a great number of physical and chemical influences coming from the outer world" (Uexküll 1926, 134). But the opposite is just as true, for it is only by means of its body that an animal gains access to the world at all. Bats can echolocate and are therefore sensitive to a cascade of perceptual cues silent and invisible to other organisms. This point is perhaps best made by the autopoietic systems-theorists, for whom the nervous system communicates changes of state to the organism of which it is a part only by interacting with an environment external to it. The nervous system is structurally open to an outside, but it is operationally closed, "for in each interaction it is the nervous system's structural state that specifies what perturbations are possible and what changes trigger them" (Maturana and Varela 1992, 169). That with which the nervous system relates does not actually precede its relation with the nervous system, at least not in terms of the way it can affect the system. It is the nervous system's own structure that specifies the nature of the relation.

Closure is self-reference, recursivity. The system's network of processes is set into motion by a perturbation from the outside (it is structurally receptive), but the referents of its activity remain internal to the system itself (it is operationally recursive).[21] In the human perception of color, for example, an optical image is formed by the machinery of the eye and projected onto a thin layer of photosensitive neurons, the retina. These cells are part of the central nervous system. The visual apparatus—its photoreceptors, rods, cones, and corresponding circuitry—works first by transforming the initially optical image into chemical and electrical information, and then by transmitting those signals to the brain through the optic nerve (Fairchild 2005, 4). If the system as a whole is, however, only structurally receptive to its environment, if the system is operationally self-referential, then the consequences are inescapable: the images we form of the world outside us do not precede the process of their formation.[22] We constitute them in terms of our bodily capacities. The same patterns of light and reflectance "lend themselves," in Varela's words, "to a wide variety of color spaces, depending on the nervous system involved in that encounter" (Varela 1992, 12). There can be no accurate, representational correspondence between the perception of color and the physical properties of one's environment. "Color is," on the other hand, "a dimension that shows up only in the phylogenetic dialogue between an environment and the history of an active autonomous self which partly defines what counts as an environment" (Varela 1992, 12). Patterns of light and reflectance provide an occasion for perturbation. It is to these elements that the nervous system is structurally receptive. But once it is set into motion, the system itself forms the image of a color that in no way preceded the processes of that formation, a color that in no way corresponds to the external patterns that initiated the process. Indeed, "it is only after all this has happened, after a mode of coupling becomes regular and repetitive . . . that we observers, for ease of language, say color corresponds to or represents an aspect of the world" (Varela 1992, 12). So to speak at all of images or visual information prior to its digestion in the body is misguided, a classically mistaken cart placed in front of the horse meant to pull it. "'Information,' as Varela, Thompson, and Rosch put it in *The Embodied Mind*, is not 'a prespecified quantity, one that exists independently in the world and can act as the input to a cognitive system'" (Wolfe 1998, 60–61). It must be constituted, composed, or enacted. And it is in this composition that Uexküll locates a decidedly active role for the organism in the organization and configuration of its *Umwelt*.

Body and sign are, however, experientially inseparable; physiological stimulation—even autopoietically nuanced—cannot on its own account for the qualitative organization of subjective experience. "Anything and everything that comes under the spell of an environment is," in Uexkull's own words, "either redirected and re-formed until it becomes a *useful carrier of meaning* or it is completely neglected" (Uexküll 2010, 144; emphasis added). In his *Theoretical Biology*, Uexküll distinguishes nervous excitation from relations of indication, stimulus from meaning (Uexküll 1926, 135). Every stimulus undergoes a conversion, as we saw above, through the nervous system of the animal body in question; the result is a patterned excitation indicative of different aspects of the animal's environment (Uexküll 1926, 137). The same stimulus can indicate different things for different animals, the way butyric acid activates the tick but tends to repel human olfactory receptors, while different stimuli can carry the same meaning and invoke the same response across different subjects. External stimuli must therefore be taken always alongside their indications in the analysis of experience. But indications, too, are double: "part of their qualities serves the subject as carriers of perception marks, another part as carriers of effect marks" (Uexküll 2010, 144).

Perception marks are best understood in terms of what James J. Gibson called environmental affordances. The way an organism's environment gives itself over to that organism is an affordance. "The *affordances* of the environment are," in Gibson's words, "what it *offers* the animal, what it *provides* or *furnishes*, either for good or ill" (Gibson 1986, 127). This computer affords me the ability to render digitized and coherent a stream of thoughts. The floor affords me a surface on which to walk, the door a means by which to isolate myself. Affordances are tied inextricably to animal ability. They are co-defining, which "implies the complementarity of the animal and the environment" (Gibson 1986, 127). Word-processing is a computational affordance only for organisms capable of operating a keyboard. An airplane can only offer itself as a means for transportation to organisms capable of purchasing tickets and reserving seats. These latter capacities determine the airplane's set of affordances. An airplane affords humans a means for transportation, but only because they are, in the first place, capable of operating airplanes. It might afford birds the potential for high-altitude collisions. Its affordances vary relative to the bodily capacities of whichever organisms relate with it. Ability and affordance are like sound and auditory system. One hears only the sounds one's ears are capable of registering. Affordances are tied to animal abilities, in other words, the way sounds are tied to their perceptual reception. In fact, perception marks are, for Uexküll, relative always to a given perceptual capacity—for humans, they are aural, visual, tactile, olfactory, gustatory, or they are nothing at all.

If perception marks are afforded the animal by aspects of its environment, "effect marks are generally impressed by the subject on other properties of the carrier of meaning" (Uexküll 2010, 145). Consider the tick, an organism capable of no more than a few simple sensations and a now classic Uexküllian example (Uexküll 2010, 44–47).[23] The tick has only three perception marks: sunlight, butyric acid, and temperatures indicative of warm blood. Sunlight is a perception mark that guides the tick upward, off the ground, toward a suitable lookout from which to drop onto passing prey. Butyric acid is a perception mark indicating the possible presence of a worthy host, a warm-blooded mammal. And warmth is a perception mark confirming for the tick that its prey is in fact suitable, that it has not missed or misjudged. Successful, the tick bores its head through the skin tissue of its host and feeds. Perched, the tick releases its legs and drops only on cue, when confronted with the right perception mark. Uexküll calls the activation of this release an "effect mark." It is the culmination of a perception mark and so erases the mark that set it off. The relation between the two is therefore distributed temporally, even if they are unified behaviorally. The termination of a perception mark in an effect mark indexes the transformation undergone by an otherwise insignificant object into a carrier of meaning through the exercise of an animal ability, the way the tick's leap transforms a passing animal into the potential for nourishment.

The animal relates to its world through a web of semiotic intermediaries. "All creatures . . . *interpret* perceptual *signs*," as Franklin Ginn puts the point; they do not enter "into any direct relationship with an object" (Ginn 2014, 132). Every animal action finds its genesis in the production of a perception mark and its satisfaction in the impression of an effect mark. These rhythms of perception and effectuation constitute "functional cycles" that relate carriers of meaning to their animal subjects (Uexküll 2010, 145). Most *Umwelten* are composed of cycles of nourishment, predation, and sex. Higher organisms may, of course, bring into being cycles that relate them to carriers more sophisticated, subtle, complex. But content aside, the cycle's guiding mechanism, "insofar as it runs through the animal's body, is the nervous system, which, beginning with the receptors (sense organs), guides the current of stimulation through the central perception and effect organs to the effectors" (Uexküll 2010, 146). The animal receives a certain stimulus through its organs of perception and transposes its corresponding sign outward onto its world. That sign becomes a property of the carrier of meaning. This is the perception mark. Butyric acid, for the tick, is the sign of a host, a property of its body. The excitation of a given perception organ, the presence of that sign, induces a corresponding excitation in the relevant effect organs—the coxa, trochanter, femur, patella, tibia, and tarsus of the tick's legs. Flexion and extension of those organs results in the execution of the effector—the tick's leap—and the impression of an effect mark. The object or carrier of meaning is meaningful, a part of the animal's *Umwelt*, "only insofar as it connects the qualities carrying operational cues [or effect marks] with the qualities carrying perception cues" (quoted in Luure 2001, 313).[24] This connection runs through the animal's own body and so forms the relevant functional cycle out of an organism-sign-action complex. Ginn is right to labor the point, "meaning is crucial to all beings" (Ginn 2014, 132).

The subject spatializes the meanings it attributes to cues in its environment through the behavioral possibilities that belong to its organic constitution. "These possibilities derive," explains Carlo Brentari, author of a recent monograph on the topic, "from 'hints' of muscular movement based on self-produced directional signs, which on a subjective plane, however, are experienced as qualities of the environment" (Brentari 2015, 111). What the subject experiences as qualities of its environment are describable equally as triggers for possible lines of action. As the subject explores its environment, it develops a sense for what it can do; as the subject explores what it can do, so does it develop a sense for the qualities of its environment. Abilities and affordances are, after all, co-constitutive phenomena. Deleuze and Guattari are famous for having proclaimed, in *A Thousand Plateaus*, that "we know nothing about a body until we know what it can do" (Deleuze and Guattari 1987, 257). I hasten to add that we know nothing about its world until we know what it can offer, and that we misunderstand both if we fail to think them together. But animal bodies are, for Uexküll, always primary. Such is the way he stylizes Kant's Transcendental Aesthetic: the body as condition for the possibility of a meaningful world, the structure of that meaning subtended by the abilities of its animal-subject. Brentari calls it a "true *transcendental biosemiotics*" (Brentari 2015, 111).

REPRISE

Reading Whitehead into Uexküll, we can, I think, claim for the semiotic web through which the animal senses its environment a conceptual status. We can claim of functional cycles and of their meaning carriers that they are concepts, that in constituting them the animal is engaged in a form of mental prehension. We can see, then, in the Uexküllian Aesthetic a fundamental role played by conceptual activity. But only if we allow from the outset that Uexküll is not Whitehead, that Uexküll's theoretical biology does not a Whiteheadian metaphysic make. My aim is, accordingly, not to translate the conceptual resources of one into the vocabulary of the other. With Nietzsche, my preference is for difference: "seeing things as similar and making things the same is the sign of weak eyes" (Nietzsche 1974, 228). But I do want to suggest that reading Whitehead together with Uexküll affords us possibilities previously unavailable, that their respective systems do resonate on a number of frequencies, and that the encounter between them is indeed a productive one. Let me explain what I mean.

Uexküll's semiotics recapitulates the Kantian distinction between what appears for the subject and what does not, and what is therefore unknowable. Experience is always of a world, and worlds are made meaningful, for Uexküll, on the bases of their subjects' sensorimotor capacities. We saw above how it is for him only in being able to interact with an object that the subject can transform it into a carrier of meaning. Sense is enacted, brought forth in activity. This works according to an order of operations: the excitation of a perceptual organ, the transposition of a sign onto the stimulus, a correlative excitation in the relevant effect organs, and the culmination of the process in the execution of an action and the impression of an effect mark that erases the perceptual cue that triggered the process. Signs are bound up at almost every stage in the processes of experience. But in bringing Whitehead to bear on this account, we can, I think, go still further. For Uexküll, it is the body that undergirds subjective experience. The sensory organs transpose signs onto the objects that stimulate them; those signs trigger responses; the functional cycles that result structure and articulate an *Umwelt*. But we should take care not to move too quickly, not to allow biological analysis to pass too easily for metaphysical pronouncement. How, we might ask, does the transposition of a perception mark onto a carrier of meaning correspond to the external world so signified? The perception mark originates in the reception of a stimulus from that unknowable world, and the resultant sign is supposed to allow the animal to navigate it. How do the organs alone spatialize their data, and how does that spatialization map onto a world unknowable at every step, Kant's noumenon? Brentari formulates the problem in terms of agreement. "How do we explain," he asks, "that a self-produced directional sign, once it has been re-transposed in the environment, comes to 'agree' with the unelaborated, 'bare' stimuli which come from the extra-organic reality" (Brentari 2015, 113). The agreement "seems to lie in the fact that both the perceptive sphere and the operative one derive from the subject's activity," the animal's sensorimotor capacities as transcendental determinant of its *Umwelt*; but Brentari is right to insist that "this only shifts our problem from one place to another," from the question of how signs agree with the world to the question of how the animal's body alone is capable of grounding their agreement (Brentari 2015, 113).

I want to suggest, with Whitehead, that it is emphatically not the animal body *alone* that grounds the meaningful experience of a subjective world. The animal feels the world both physically as well as conceptually; subjective experience is a complex of both types of activity. Uexküll's transcendental biosemiotics fails to take account of the concept, and assumes for that reason the metaphysical baggage of a noumenal realm, the problem of how the subject's production of perceptual signs is supposed to map onto it, and the question of how it is that the animal body itself, its organic structure, is supposed to ground this noumenal-phenomenal relation. Whitehead's Category of Transmutation relieves the difficulty. Experience, on the account of that category, does not face the problem of having to map itself onto an inscrutable reality; it is instead emergent out of a process of feeling that physical reality. The subject is constituted by a succession of phases of concrescence or integration; at its most primary, it is in communion—as if directly—with a world that will, from the perspective of the later phases of its experience, appear noumenal. Uexküll's *Umwelt* is the meaningful world only of a completed occasion, a satisfied subject. The processes of feeling capture that world, bring it under a certain relation, determined by a number of concepts, and in so doing transform it, render it phenomenal. Noumenon and phenomenon are, on this account, better understood as two poles of a spectrum traversed through the successive phases of subjective experience. The question, then, is not one of agreement or correspondence, but rather of processual emergence, transformation, capture. The order of operations does not run from phenomenal to noumenal—and so one need not ask how the former accords with the latter—but precisely the inverse, for the subject arises out of the noumenal world and in feeling it, in *digesting* it, experiences it phenomenally. One may as well ask how bat guano is supposed to correspond to mosquitoes, or how the finished statue agrees with the bronze out of which it was formed. It is fitting, then, that Whitehead describes his system as an inverted Kantianism, for while Kant's "world emerges from the subject," Whitehead's "subject emerges from the world" (Whitehead 1978, 88). If Whitehead sets Kant on his feet, then Uexküll acts as if he hasn't all this time been standing on his head.

Concomitant with this inversion is a shift from transposition to simplification. Which is to say that the subject does not transpose internal signs onto an unintelligible external reality so much as it progressively simplifies the data of that world, qualifying it in accordance with a relevant set of conceptual determinations—the salty frigidity of an ocean breeze, a distant crack of thunder. "Perceptual experience is," to speak again with Mays, "an immensely simplified version of physical reality" (Mays 1959, 105). Simplification means abstraction and qualification. Experience is abstract to the extent that it cannot feel every minutiae of the physical world to the same degree of intensity: the cost of intelligibility is complexity. Experience is qualified to the extent that it involves concepts, eternal objects, qualities.[25] The difference between an incoherent chaos of physical data and a specific perceptual experience, the difference between a multiplicity of aural stimuli and the sound of that bird pecking curiously at that window there, is a difference precisely in conceptual feeling. Thus is the world spatialized, *worlded*, even. Thus does reality become *Umwelt*. Not by way of transposition—which is in any case just a name for the fantastical transformation undergone by inner sensations into meaningful signs and the leap made subsequently from animal viscera onto external objects. But by way of conceptual prehensions, which qualify the physical data of experience and thereby facilitate the processes through which the world is prehended and progressively simplified, privatized, in terms unique to the experiential subject. "Mere sensory stimulation does not add up to experience," to return now to Alva Noë, with whose words this chapter began (Noë 2004, 194). We don't apply conceptual feeling *to* experience, but rather "bring it to bear *in* experience; bringing it to bear in this way enables what would otherwise be mere sensory stimulation without world-presenting content *to be* experience."[26]

Concepts, on Noë's account, are understood best as styles of access, forms of grasping, tools that allow us to make present the world, to differentiate, articulate, even to prehend it (Noë 2012, 112). These connotations come through clearer in the German, *Begriff*—which means, quite literally, "to grasp." To conceive is not to name; it is to prehend, to feel. The more sophisticated the conceptual activity, the more complex the ability to discern environmental differences; they are two forms of describing the same operation, for the felt world is articulated conceptually. We see this quite clearly in forms of higher observation:

> Take science. Here you observe things, of course, but you can't see them properly unless you have the right concepts. If you just look through a microscope with no guidance on how to look at what you see, you have no clue what you're looking at. Even if you're doing high school biology, you need to have concepts like "cell wall" or "organelle." . . . So observation is happening there, of course. But also a *lot* of conceptualizing. (Heuman 2014)

The thought of scientific observation without concepts is incoherent. In order to bring out the right contrasts, one needs the right concepts. Concepts are not extrinsic to experience, not added to it; the two are at every stage entangled inextricably. Perception is a kind of conceptualization, and conceptualization is a kind of prehension, a mode through which the world is made present, captured. Perception involves concepts because it is always from a perspective; it captures the world under some specific form. Conceptual prehensions determine, as we've seen, the contrasts of a complex datum. The distinction between contrast and incompatibility is, to speak again with Whitehead, the very hallmark of conceptual activity. Without concepts, no contrasts; and without contrasts, no experience. Concepts are, as such—this is my claim—complexifications of the process of feeling. To experience the world such that a change in environment passes unregistered is just to lack concepts.[27] Higher intensities of experience emerge correlative with a higher grade of conceptual activity. Higher grades of conceptual activity generate an experience more complex, refined.

"The more contrasts you add," in Bruno Latour's words, "*the more differences and mediations you become sensible to*" (Latour 2004, 211). Latour has in mind what he calls the "acquisition of a nose" (2004, 207). It takes training if one is to develop one's nose, one's capacity to discern finer and finer a set of contrasts between different chemical odors. And as one's nose develops, it's as if a whole hidden dimension of the world begins to open up; the development "is thus a progressive enterprise that produces at once a sensory medium [the olfactory apparatus] *and* a sensitive world [a newly articulated field of differences]," for one learns to discern contrasts in smells that had seemed previously homogeneous, undifferentiated. It is a mistake to speak as if those differences were there already, covered over by an unlearned nose. They are neither discovered nor projected, neither pre-existent nor strictly produced; they are *articulated*. And this means that one acquires an environment in the same way that one acquires a nose—for no one thinks that its acquisition implies transplant; and yet, we know better than to suggest that those "noses" among us are simply hallucinating their discernments. The content of an articulation corresponds to the way one is affected by it; "learning to be affected means exactly that: the more you learn, the more differences exist" (Latour 2004, 213). Concepts ought to be understood in exactly this sense, as affective tools, forms of articulation.

I hope it is clear that we need not, even after a remedial tour through this account of the concept, renounce the insights won by the Uexküllian semiotic. I hope it is clear that Uexküll's construction of a world that fluoresces with animal subjects and their cycles of meaning, whose experiences spin out of themselves an unfathomable diversity of distinct perceptual environments, an array of *Umwelten* each shot through with semiotic activity and emergent out of nested sensorimotor relationships, I hope it is clear that this is a world not supplanted, diminished, or circumscribed, but rather supplemented, grounded, even expanded and complexified by Whitehead's metaphysic of the subject and theory of (conceptual) feeling. I have sought, in this paper, to bring these two thinkers together as fellow travellers, intent as they both are on developing a rich and nuanced account adequate to the experiences of other subjects and the worlds they inhabit. I have sought to provide for Uexküll's theoretical biology a foundation in Whitehead's metaphysical scheme, one that thinks the Whiteheadian account outward, opening it onto new expanses of nonhuman analysis while it thinks the Uexküllian project downward, into a robust metaphysical account of subjective experience that alleviates its tensions while providing it a number of new resources. This project, finally, was animated by the desire to refigure the concept, or more precisely to push a refiguration that is currently well underway in the work of Alva Noë even further, freeing it not only from what Deleuze and Guattari might call the "imperialism of language," but from an anthropocentric metaphysic entirely. Conceptual activity is, to conclude, not the mark of a distinctly human agency, but of the subject defined by it. And if the subject is nothing other than its experience of the world, then the ability to prehend new and different concepts is at the same time the ability to become otherwise. "No thinker thinks twice," as Whitehead so famously put the point (Whitehead 1978, 29). I hope to have suggested how this insight might be as revelatory of the dazzlingly diverse nonhuman ecologies of subjective experience and of experient becoming to which we have for too long refused the concept as it is of the imbrication of knower and known, perceiver and perceived, and indeed—and perhaps above all—of subject and world, human or otherwise.

NOTES

1. See, for his best work on the topic, *Action in Perception* (Cambridge: MIT Press, 2004), and *Varieties of Presence* (Cambridge: Harvard UP, 2012). Some of that work will be addressed in the sections to follow.

2. I should say at the outset that the aim of this chapter is not to reproduce or otherwise faithfully represent what Whitehead has already written. I take only those concepts from him

that are necessary to the present project. I will, in particular, neglect the otherwise important (if contentious) role played in his system by God.

3. More technically, the occasion prehends only its immediate past—contemporaries are causally independent on Whitehead's account—but since that past in some sense involves the rest of the actual world, the distinction is, for our purposes, a negligible one. See Whitehead 1933, 219.

4. Experience is thus decomposable, in theory, "into actual things of the actual world and into abstract attributes, qualities, and relations, which express how those other actual things contribute themselves as components to our individual experience" (Whitehead 1927, 17).

5. See, for the relation (or equivalence) between the two terms, Whitehead 1978, 129. Cf. Shaviro 2009, 39.

6. I take this list from Shaviro 2009, 39.

7. By placing the subject at a remove from the world, and by insisting on the primarily cognitive, transcendental basis of its "constructive functioning," Shaviro argues that "Kant's subject both monopolizes experience, and exempts itself from immersion in that experience" (Shaviro 2009, 50).

8. Even fundamental causal relationships obtaining among molecules are forms of prehension. Consciousness marks one phase among several of the simplification of a datum, but it does not define the activity of experience; far from it. See Whitehead 1933, 213. Consider also Nietzsche's claim, in support of his polemic against "fact," that "everything of which we become conscious is arranged, simplified, schematized, interpreted through and through" (Nietzsche 1967, § 477). This line captures well Whitehead's own position on consciousness.

9. This means that what differs across traditional metaphysical divides—an/organic, human/animal—is not the presence of prehension (or perception, relation, feeling, and so on), but rather its form and complexity: "it is the *how*, not the *if*," to speak with Melanie Sehgal (2014, 168).

10. The quote concludes with a line from Whitehead, *Process and Reality*, 164.

11. The ability to feel unactualized potentials works on a spectrum, so while no actual feeling can be divorced from the potentials to which it refers, some feelings (as in, for example, human imaginational experience) can orient themselves toward incredibly distant objects while others can do little more than feel the fact of actual selection.

12. Adversion is, for Whitehead, a positive valuation; aversion, a negative one. That aside, it is perhaps worth reiterating the fact that each actual occasion is an indivisible drop of experience, a singular pulse of feeling—even if we can articulate it along a succession of phases. That conceptual feelings arise out of physical feelings does not, therefore, indicate that a stunted experience might feel only physically, and that the conceptual belongs only to more highly developed subjects.

13. This is the Category of Conceptual Valuation (Whitehead 1978, 248). While the mental can be distinguished analytically from the physical, they are, in actual experience, essentially inextricable. So much so that Whitehead claims it a matter of "pure convention" which aspects of experience we call mental and which physical. Indeed, "there is no proper line to be drawn between the physical and the mental constitution of experience" (Whitehead 1927, 20).

14. Whitehead takes this example from Hume, who allowed—as an exception—that the *idea* of the missing shade might in some circumstances arise in the absence of a corresponding *impression*. This is reversion. Over the course of *Process and Reality*, Whitehead comes to realize that the role played in his system by God ameliorates the necessity of the category, and he abandons it. But as this is less a paper on Whitehead's completed metaphysics than it is on the way those metaphysics might aid us in thinking differently about concepts, this point need not concern us here. For a succinct summary of the issue, see Shaviro 2009, 138–39; cf. Stengers 2011, 361–63. On the difficulties surrounding the issue, cf. Ford 1984, 235–38. It is worth noting, too, that Whitehead's abandonment of the *category* of conceptual reversion need not entail a rejection of reversion altogether. For this argument, see Nobo 1986, 89–91.

15. "This is," in Whitehead's own words, "the process by which the subsequent enrichment of subjective forms, both in qualitative pattern, and in intensity through contrast, is made possible by the positive conceptual prehension of physical incompatibles" (Whitehead 1978, 249).

16. This point—that a subject's world of experience is shaped by its conceptual activity—is crucial for the present account, and we will return to it in more detail in the chapter's next section.

17. "He solves the problem," to be more precise, "by an *unanalysed* doctrine of 'confusion'" (Whitehead 1978, 251). Emphasis mine.

18. On Wolfe Mays' account, transmutation functions to "bridge the gap between the autonomous physical activities and the passive perceptual qualities. Whitehead believes that the forms of energy impinging on the animal body from the external world undergo, when transmitted along the nerve routes, a process of simplification, and finally appear in our perceptual field as clear cut sensa in definite regions of space" (Mays 1959, 171; cf. Whitehead 1933, 314–15).

19. This claim needs qualifying. We find in other thinkers the suggestion that other forms of life may belong to their own worlds, but it is not until Uexküll that this line of thinking gets thematized and explored as such.

20. See "Translator's Introduction" (Uexküll 2010, 35–36). An *Umwelt* is alternatively understood as the "appearance-world," "surrounding-world," "world-picture," or "dwelling-world" of a given organism.

21. "The qualification 'operational' emphasizes that closure is used in its mathematical sense of recursivity, and not in the sense of closeness or isolation from interaction, which would be, of course, nonsense" (Varela 1992, 10).

22. Although this problematic does not figure significantly into the present discussion, it is worth making clear that operational closure does not necessitate a solipsism. We perceive only what we are capable of perceiving, but the perceptual process still involves interaction with an outside world. It is a world made meaningful to us on our own terms, but a world nevertheless external. Operational closure seems to invalidate a (directly) realist metaphysic, but structural receptivity counts just as much against a thoroughgoing idealism. We are therefore left to negotiate a path somewhere between the two. For more on this middle way, see Varela et al. 1991, 172.

23. The example was most recently taken up at length by Agamben in *The Open: Man and Animal* (2004), though it was popularized by both Merleau-Ponty and Deleuze before him.

24. Jakob von Uexküll, *Kompositionslehre der Natur: Biologie als undogmatische Naturwissenschaft: Ausgewählte Schriften* (Frankfurt: Ullstein, 1980), 371–72, quoted in Andres Luure, "Lessons from Uexkull's Antireductionism and Reductionism: A Pansemiotic View," *Semiotica: Journal of the International Association for Semiotic Studies* 134 – 1/4, Special Issue: Jakob von Uexküll: A Paradigm for Biology and Semiotics (2001): 313.

25. I am glossing concepts developed in more detail in the previous section of this chapter. For a more complete account of transmutation, see above.

26. Noë has in mind here sensorimotor knowledge, though he elsewhere identifies knowing how to navigate the world skillfully with conceptual knowledge. See, for example, his claim that "we should think of sensorimotor skills as themselves conceptual" (Noë 2004, 183).

27. Though experience never lacks concepts completely. Consider Whitehead's characterization of "the simplest grade of actual occasions," which experience only a few sensa, "with the minimum of patterned contrast" (Whitehead 1978, 115).

REFERENCES

Agamben, Giorgio. 2004. *The Open: Man and Animal*. Trans. Kevin Attell. Stanford, CA: Stanford University Press.

Brentari, Carlo. 2015. *Jakob von Uexküll: The Discovery of the Umwelt between Biosemiotics and Theoretical Biology*. New York: Springer Dordrecht Heidelberg.

Buchanan, Brett. 2008. *Onto-Ethologies: The Animal Environments of Uexküll, Heidegger, Merleau-Ponty, and Deleuze*. Albany, NY: SUNY Press.

Debaise, Didier. 2014. "Possessive Subjects: A Speculative Interpretation of Nonhumans." Trans. Thomas Jellis. *The Lure of Whitehead*. Ed. Nicholas Gaskill and A. J. Nocek. Minneapolis: University of Minneapolis Press: 299–311.

Deleuze, Gilles. 1993. *The Fold: Leibniz and the Baroque*. Trans. Tom Conley. Minneapolis: University of Minnesota Press.
Deleuze, Gilles, and Félix Guattari. 1987. *A Thousand Plateaus: Capitalism and Schizophrenia*. Trans. Brian Massumi. Minneapolis: University of Minnesota Press.
Faber, Roland. 2014. "Multiplicity and Mysticism: Toward a New Mystagogy of Becoming." *The Lure of Whitehead*. Ed. Nicholas Gaskill and A. J. Nocek. Minneapolis: University of Minneapolis Press: 187–206.
Fairchild, Mark. 2005. "Human Color Vision." *Color Appearance Models*. Chichester: Wiley & Sons.
Ford, Lewis. 1984. *The Emergence of Whitehead's Metaphysics*. Albany, NY: SUNY Press.
Gibson, James J. 1986. *The Ecological Approach to Visual Perception*. Hillsdale: Erlbaum.
Ginn, Franklin. 2014. "Jakob von Uexküll Beyond Bubbles: On Umwelt and Biophilosophy." *Science as Culture* 23, no. 1: 129–34.
Heuman, Linda. 2014. "The Embodied Mind: An Interview with Philosopher Evan Thompson." *Tricycle Magazine*. Accessed April 18, 2015. http://www.tricycle.com/interview/embodied-mind.
Latour, Bruno. 2004. "How to Talk about the Body? The Normative Dimension of Science Studies." *Body & Society* 10, no. 2: 205–29.
Leibniz, G. W. 1989. *Philosophical Essays*. Trans. Roger Ariew and Daniel Garber. Indianapolis: Hackett.
Luure, Andres. 2001. "Lessons from Uexküll's Antireductionism and Reductionism: A Pansemiotic View." *Semiotica: Journal of the International Association for Semiotic Studies* 134 – 1/4, Special Issue: Jakob von Uexküll: A Paradigm for Biology and Semiotics: 311–22.
Maturana, Humberto, and Francisco Varela. 1992. *The Tree of Knowledge: The Biological Roots of Human Understanding*. Boston: Shambhala.
Mays, Wolfe. 1959. *The Philosophy of Whitehead*. London: Allen & Unwin.
———. 1977. *Whitehead's Philosophy of Science and Metaphysics: An Introduction to His Thought*. The Hague: M. Nijhoff.
Nietzsche, Friedrich. 1967. *The Will to Power*. Trans. Walter Kaufmann and R. J. Hollingdale. New York: Vintage Books.
———. 1974. *The Gay Science*. Trans. Walter Kaufmann. New York: Vintage Books.
———. 1997. "Truth and Lie in the Extra-Moral Sense." *The Portable Nietzsche*. Trans. and ed. Walter Kaufmann. New York: Penguin Books: 42–46.
Nobo, Jorge Luis. 1986. *Whitehead's Metaphysics of Extension and Solidarity*. Albany, NY: SUNY Press.
Noë, Alva. 2004. *Action in Perception*. Cambridge: MIT Press.
———. 2012. *Varieties of Presence*. Cambridge: Harvard UP.
Sehgal, Melanie. 2014. "Situated Metaphysics: Things, History, and Pragmatic Speculation in A. N. Whitehead." *The Allure of Things*. Ed. Roland Faber and Andrew Goffey. New York: Bloomsbury Academic: 162–87.
Shaviro, Steven. 2009. *Without Criteria: Kant, Whitehead, Deleuze, and Aesthetics*. Cambridge: MIT Press.
Sherburne, Donald W. 1981. *A Key to Whitehead's* Process and Reality. Chicago: The University of Chicago Press.
Smith, Daniel W. 1996. "Deleuze's Theory of Sensation: Overcoming the Kantian Duality." *Deleuze: A Critical Reader*. Ed. Paul Patton. Oxford: Blackwell: 29–56.
Stengers, Isabelle. 2011. *Thinking with Whitehead: A Free and Wild Creation of Concepts*. Trans. Michael Chase. Cambridge: Harvard UP.
Uexküll, Jakob von. 1926. *Theoretical Biology*. Trans. D. L. Mackinnon. New York: Harcourt, Brace.
———. 2010. *A Foray into the Worlds of Animals and Humans: with A Theory of Meaning*. Trans. Joseph D. O'Neil. Minneapolis: University of Minnesota Press.
Varela, Francisco. 1992. "Autopoiesis and a Biology of Intentionality." Paper presented at *Autopoiesis and Perception*. Dublin City University. Dublin, Ireland. August 25–26.

Varela, Francisco, Evan Thompson, and Eleanor Rosch. 1991. *The Embodied Mind: Cognitive Science and Human Experience*. Cambridge: MIT.
Voss, Daniela. 2013. *Conditions of Thought: Deleuze and Transcendental Ideas.* Edinburgh: Edinburgh UP.
Whitehead, Alfred North. 1920. *The Concept of Nature.* Cambridge: Cambridge UP.
———. 1925. *Science and the Modern World.* New York: The Free Press.
———. 1933. *Adventures of Ideas.* New York: The Free Press.
———. 1978. *Process and Reality*. Corrected Edition. Ed. David Ray Griffin and Donald W. Sherburne. New York: The Free Press.
———. 1985. *Symbolism: Its Meaning and Effect.* Cambridge: Cambridge UP.
Wolfe, Cary. 1998. *Critical Environments: Postmodern Theory and the Pragmatics of the "Outside."* Minneapolis: University of Minnesota Press.

Part III

Time, the World, and Abstraction

Chapter Seven

Philosophy against Abstraction

On the Social Thought of Whitehead and Deleuze

Kris Klotz

Alfred North Whitehead never tired of saying that every occasion of experience can be viewed not only as it is, or as what it becomes, but also in terms of what might be or what might have been. In this case, alternatives—alternative possibilities—are built into the nature of things. Nonetheless, it is not immediately clear how philosophy ought to relate to the idea of alternatives. Is it philosophy's role to frame, pursue, or formulate alternatives? And how would Whitehead address this question?

From the many definitions of philosophy that Whitehead gives us, two in particular stand out on this question. The first comes from his lecture at the Harvard Business School (published in *Adventures of Ideas*). Lecturing on the topic of foresight, Whitehead writes that philosophy "is a survey of possibilities and their comparison with actualities. In philosophy, the fact, the theory, the alternatives, and the ideal, are weighed together. Its gifts are insight and foresight, and a sense of the worth of life, in short, that sense of importance which nerves all civilized effort" (Whitehead 1933, 98). This passage suggests that philosophy is in the business of considering alternatives. But this passage might also be misleading. The language of ideality in the quote might suggest, for example, that philosophy has access to some ideal social arrangement or paradigm, against which it can judge or measure the present state of affairs. I do not believe this is what Whitehead has in mind. The comparison of actuality and possibility is not about judging the actual according to the standard of a single ideal of a best possible world. Philosophy is not ideological in this sense. There are numerous passages in Whitehead's work that support this claim. As an example, consider Whitehead's opposition to "universal moral ideals" or universal codifications in

Modes of Thought: "The notion of the unqualified stability of particular laws of nature and of particular moral codes is a primary illusion which has vitiated much philosophy. . . . There is no one behavior system belonging to the essential character of the universe, as the universal moral ideal" (Whitehead 1938, 13–14).

Readers of Whitehead will be familiar with the second definition of philosophy, which comes from *Science and the Modern World*. There Whitehead claims, "Philosophy is the critic of abstractions" (Whitehead 1925, 87). The question for me is how do these two activities relate to one another? What does the critique of abstractions have to do with the survey of alternatives?

This brings me to Gilles Deleuze, the other philosopher with whom I will be occupied in this paper. In the preface to *Dialogues*, Deleuze writes:

> I have always felt that I am an empiricist, that is, a pluralist. But what does this equivalence between empiricism and pluralism mean? It derives from the two characteristics by which Whitehead defined empiricism: the abstract does not explain, but must itself be explained; and the aim is not to rediscover the eternal or the universal, but to find the conditions under which something new is produced (*creativeness* [sic]). (Deleuze 1987, vii)[1]

Here is the passage in *Process and Reality* to which Deleuze is probably referring, at least regarding the first of these two characteristics:

> The explanatory purpose of philosophy is often misunderstood. Its business is to explain the emergence of the more abstract things from the more concrete things. It is a complete mistake to ask how the concrete particular fact can be built up out of universals. That answer is, "In no way." The true philosophic question is, How can concrete fact exhibit entities abstract from itself and yet participated in by its own nature? In other words, philosophy is explanatory of abstraction, and not of concreteness. (Whitehead 1978, 20)

Deleuze's expression of his indebtedness to Whitehead suggests an important connection between philosophy as the critic of abstractions and the conditions of novelty. That is, when we give up looking to abstractions as explanatory, we can begin to look at the real conditions of novelty. Moreover, insofar as novelty is related to the pursuit of alternatives, the critique of abstractions will also have a lot to do with these alternatives.

I'll return to this connection in the conclusion. But first my aim will be to discuss how the critique of abstractions operates in the work of Whitehead and in the work of Deleuze and Félix Guattari. Regarding Whitehead, I will argue that the critique of abstractions and the recovery of concrete reality entails more than the mere recovery of what our abstractions prevent us from experiencing (as though it were just a matter of each individual having a more comprehensive experience). It also involves a responsibility towards those who are excluded by our abstractions. Regarding Deleuze and Guattari, I will suggest that their critique of opinions—as abstractions—and their concept of "becoming-minoritarian" has a function similar to the critique of abstractions in Whitehead's work. After this, I will turn to the question of how the first characteristic of empiricism relates to the second. At this point, I will also return to the question of how philosophy might approach the problem of alternatives.

WHITEHEAD: ABSTRACTION AND RATIONALITY

I am going to begin not with Whitehead's account of abstraction—though I will get to it shortly, but with a brief rehearsal of his metaphysics. If abstractions need to be explained, as Whitehead and Deleuze tell us, then it is only appropriate to build up from Whitehead's general metaphysics in order to isolate and identify the genesis or appearance of abstractions. This will also help us to understand how human beings should relate to their abstractions.

For Whitehead, the world is composed of "actual entities," or "actual occasions." Actual occasions—or quanta of experience—are the final agents of reality (Whitehead 1978, 18). An actual occasion is a "concrescence," or a "growing together," of "prehensions," or feelings or experiences, of its immediate past. This means that actual occasions are constituted by their relations to the world. Every occasion begins as a relation or reaction to its past. In this sense, it must conform to the past, at least at first. But this reaction to the past does not imply determination. The past is a condition, not a determination (Whitehead 1978, 108). The necessity of reacting to the past requires self-determination on the part of the actual occasion. According to Whitehead, every actual occasion is "the autonomous master of its own concrescence" (Whitehead 1978, 245). An actual occasion determines for itself how it will react to its given world. Because it is more than a passive recipient, it is to some extent "causa sui."

Regarding this self-creation, Whitehead writes, "In its self-creation the actual entity is guided by its ideal of itself as individual satisfaction and as transcendent creator" (Whitehead 1978, 85). The ideal that guides the actual occasion, which Whitehead mentions here, refers to the way in which each actual entity responds to its immediate past. Whitehead often refers to this ideal as a final cause, or a subjective aim. In its initial stages, the actual occasion is confronted with certain indeterminate, or incompatible, ways of responding to its past (Whitehead 1938, 54). Every occasion makes a decision about the world—really, an actual occasion is its decision (cf. Shaviro 2014, 39). An occasion must make a decision about the world because it cannot incorporate everything in its world into a coherent experience. "Such exclusions belong to the finitude of circumstance," Whitehead claims (Whitehead 1938, 54). There are mutually exclusive possibilities for how an occasion can react. The ideal, or subjective aim, expresses a particular solution or determinate outcome to this indeterminacy. Self-creation is transcendent because the actual occasion is not reducible to or determined by the world out of which it emerges. However, this transcendence is not absolute. Self-creation is momentary and fleeting. Every actual occasion "perishes." The term "satisfaction" refers to this perishing, or moment of completion. Having completed its self-creation, the actual occasion becomes an object for future occasions.

While strictly speaking every actual occasion is self-creative or autonomous, self-creation is often negligible. Often occasions merely conform to the past without making a noticeable difference. While there may be no difference in kind between human and non-human occasions of experience, there is a noticeable difference in degree when it comes to our capacity for novelty. Whitehead writes, "When we come to mankind, nature seems to have burst through another of its boundaries. . . . The conceptual entertainment of unrealized possibility becomes a major factor in human mentality. In this way outrageous novelty is introduced" (Whitehead 1938, 26). An increased capacity for novelty is joined by an increased capacity for abstraction. As I said, every process of concrescence, every actual occasion, is a selection of, or a decision about, its actual world. In other words, every selection is an abstraction. With the development of consciousness among more complex species, this ability to abstract becomes more intense: "The growth of consciousness is the uprise of abstractions. It is the growth of emphasis. The totality is characterized by a selection from its details. That selection claims attention, enjoyment, action, and purpose, all relative to itself" (Whitehead 1938, 123). In looking here rather than there, in making this choice rather than that, I make decisions about the world that necessarily leave something out. Attention emphasizes, but it also excludes. Our experience of the forms or defining characteristics of enduring objects, for example, is an abstraction from the actual occasions that constitute these objects.

But "abstraction" does not mean "illusory." Abstractions are real and efficacious. Decisions are abstractions, or a selective perspective on the past. The past itself was a determination of the abstractions that come to condition our lives or decisions. Moreover, our decisions bequeath abstractions to the future. They are something the future will have to deal with. If these abstractions are repeated often enough, they become defining characteristics. A "society"—and for now I mean this term in Whitehead's technical sense—is a group of actual occasions with such a defining characteristic (Whitehead 1978, 34–35). This defining characteristic, that which makes the society what it is, must be continually reaffirmed by the future occasions in order for this defining characteristic to endure. Moreover, every society belongs to a larger environment, with its own defining characteristics and these characteristics condition the experience of occasions within this environment. The laws of nature would be an example. Yet, even these—Whitehead believes—are abstractions from the activity of actual occasions (Whitehead 1978, 90–92).

While we do not have control over many of the defining characteristics or abstractions that condition our lives, human beings—as a species—have had and continue to have incredible control over their environments. As individuals, we often have some say in what ideals guide our lives, or how our lives are structured. This is evident in many of our habits and value-commitments, for example. Put simply, the ends we pursue order our lives. Of course, we belong to a larger environment, just like any other society of actual occasions. This means that the ends we pursue are in part conditioned by the societies to which we belong—and here I mean "society" in both its technical and in its more common sense.

Of course, the ability to form and criticize ends might seem like an obvious feature of our lives, so what does the Whiteheadian account add? If we see the defining characteristics, or the abstractions, that condition our lives as the result of decisions, we emphasize the contingency of these abstractions. Though the past is necessary insofar as we cannot change what happened, Whitehead often encourages us to envision the past in terms of what might have been and what may be (cf. Whitehead 1938, 98). Often, the defining characteristics of our lives seem all too rigid. For example, I live in a democracy, but it is not always clear that I have much say in the formation of laws. I will not claim that the recognition of abstractions as contingent will necessarily obviate these cases of rigidity. At the very least, though, the recognition of contingency has a genealogical and critical function. The recognition that any given order is contingent opens that order to critique or evaluation. Of course, Whitehead is not alone in embracing a genealogical critique of social contingencies. Rousseau's *Second Discourse* and Nietzsche's *Genealogy* are notable examples. But, for Whitehead, contingency is much more pervasive, insofar as it is not unique to human social order.

I will admit, though, that there are many aspects of our lives that we would not want to change, even if we could. For this reason, the title of this chapter is somewhat misleading. To criticize abstractions is not necessarily to disown them. As Isabelle Stengers notes:

> For Whitehead, abstractions as such were never the enemy. We cannot think without abstractions: they cause us to think, they lure our feelings and affects. But our duty is to take care of our abstractions, never to bow down in front of what they are doing to us—especially when they demand that we heroically accept the sacrifices they entail, the insuperable dilemmas and contradictions in which they trap us. (Stengers 2008, 50)

Taking care of our abstractions is a responsibility. Because actual occasions determine themselves, they are ultimately responsible for what they are or what they become (Whitehead 1978, 88).[2] Strictly speaking, this is not unique to human beings. However, since we are capable of recognizing the contingency of abstractions, the sense of responsibility is heightened for us. We can recognize that the stance we take toward inherited abstractions has consequences for the future. For this reason, when we recognize the contingency of what we inherit, we are responsible for its evaluation. I would argue, therefore, that the recognition of contingency entails the responsibility to evaluate inherited abstractions, to consider their worth for present and future occasions of experience.

This notion of responsibility is, I believe, further evident in Whitehead's account of rationality. Whitehead identifies rationality with the recovery of "concrete reality." As I have said, consciousness necessitates abstraction. By emphasizing, it excludes. Yet, for Whitehead, "the process of rationalization" is a return to that from which we abstract: "This process is the recognition of essential connection within the apparent isolation of abstracted details. Thus rationalization is the reverse of abstraction, so far as abstraction can be reversed within the area of consciousness" (Whitehead 1938, 124). Abstraction is a selection or a choice about the way in which we inherit the immediate past. But the past is composed of other occasions of experience. This means that abstraction excludes other occasions of experience. In this case, rationality aims at the recovery of the excluded.

Here we begin to see the importance of Deleuze's comment on empiricism. If we maintain that abstractions are not what explain but what need to be explained, then it is only by returning to that from which we abstract that we can notice what our abstractions exclude or what they are incapable of explaining. And, of course, these two are related because if an explanation does not take into account some x, then that explanation has excluded this x.

Whitehead refers to the process of rationalization as an ideal: "rationalization is the partial fulfillment of the ideal to recover concrete reality within the disjunction of abstraction" (Whitehead 1938, 124). I think "ideal" is meant here in two ways. First, the recovery of concrete reality is ideal because it can never be fully accomplished. As I have insisted throughout this chapter, experience is inevitably selective. As an experience, the attempt to recover what is lost can only ever be another such selection. This is not to suggest that these attempts are futile, only that they must remain incomplete. Secondly, "ideal" suggests something that we should pursue. In this sense, the ideal to recover concrete reality is moral or ethical (Whitehead 1978, 15). On this point, I need to add to my earlier discussion of responsibility.

I argued that the recognition of the contingency of inherited abstractions entails the responsibility to evaluate, or take a stance toward, these abstractions. We can now see that a criterion of this evaluation will be a consideration of what these abstractions exclude. Since rationality aims to recover that which is obscured, or lost, because of abstraction, it encourages us to discover what (or who) is not recognized by inherited abstractions, what evades them, and what could have been or could still be if it were not for these abstractions. If I am correct to include responsibility within this conception of rationality, then this would mean that to be engaged in this process of rationalization, or the recovery of the concrete, requires taking responsibility for that which is excluded by abstraction.

I should note that this regard for what is excluded would not be the only criterion of evaluation. According to Whitehead, every occasion of experience is a value experience. An actual occasion is an evaluation of the past, insofar as it makes some determinate selection of the past, but it also has value for itself. Experience is fundamentally valuable or worthy. He contends, therefore, that "[w]e have no right to deface the value experience which is the very essence of the universe" (Whitehead 1938, 111). Accordingly, our responsibility to that which is excluded by our abstractions is a responsibility to promote the value experience of the excluded. This means not only that we should "take care of" or be responsible for the abstractions that we use or affirm, insofar as they affect our value experience, but also insofar as they might inhibit the value experience of others.

Let me repeat and highlight one more element of the quote from *Modes of Thought*: "[R]ationalization is the partial fulfillment of the ideal to recover concrete reality within the disjunction of abstraction. This disjunction is the appearance which has been introduced as price of finite conscious discrimination" (Whitehead 1938, 124–25). While this disjunction is an inevitable part of experience, it is also potentially dangerous or harmful. In *Adventures of Ideas*, Whitehead writes, "A feeling of dislocation of Appearance from Reality is the final destructive force, robbing life of its zest for adventure. It spells the decadence of civilization, by stripping from it the very reason for its existence" (Whitehead 1933, 293). In other words, if our abstractions become so disconnected from reality (which would include what our abstractions exclude), decadence ensues. I take this to be an example of the consequences of the "bifurcation of nature."

I believe that Deleuze (with Guattari) is particularly sensitive to the kinds of suffering that can arise from such dislocations, or from the disjunction of abstraction. I'll turn, then, to Deleuze and Guattari's work in order to show how the criticism of abstractions operates in their work.

DELEUZE: ABSTRACTION AND OPINION

In *What Is Philosophy?* Deleuze and Guattari return to the first characteristic of empiricism (this time without reference to Whitehead): "The first principle of philosophy is that Universals explain nothing but must themselves be explained" (Deleuze and Guattari 1994, 7). In this work, they identify and criticize three philosophical universals in particular, corresponding to "three philosophical eras," namely, the eidetic, critical, and phenomenological (Deleuze and Guattari 1994, 47). All three eras share the tendency to make immanence immanent to something, thereby reinstituting transcendence: first, "the great Object of *contemplation*" (from eidetic or Platonic philosophy); second, "the Subject of *reflection*" (from critical or Kantian philosophy); and third, "the Other subject of *communication*" (from phenomenological or Husserlian philosophy) (Deleuze and Guattari 1994, 51). The introduction of transcendence by these three "universals"—contemplation, reflection, and communication—halts or inhibits the movement of immanence.

The third universal (communication) is especially relevant to us today. Deleuze and Guattari identify phenomenology, or more generally what they call the philosophy of communication, as the philosophy of our era (Deleuze and Guattari 1994, 146). However, this claim is not limited to the domain of philosophy, since Deleuze and Guattari view this philosophy of communication as proper to modern democratic states. They interpret the importance given to consensus, for example, as an expression of a philosophy of communication.

Why is communication a universal or abstraction? In the first place, this follows from how Deleuze and Guattari understand philosophy, which they famously define as "concept creation," although this definition is a bit of an oversimplification of their developed view. More specifically, philosophy is one way of responding to what they call chaos (or what I would say is what is "real" beneath or before all abstractions or sedimentations). They write, "Chaos is defined not so much by its disorder as by the infinite speed with which every form taking shape in it vanishes" (Deleuze and Guattari 1994, 118). Philosophy responds to chaos through the "laying out" of a "plane of immanence," which is "like a section of chaos and acts like a sieve" (Deleuze and Guattari 1994, 42). Philosophy must establish a plane of immanence—its presuppositions or its "image of thought"—so that the concepts it creates can gain a consistency not found within chaos (Deleuze and Guattari 1994, 19–20 and 40–42). In other words, philosophy—through its creation of concepts—gives order to reality. Transcendence enters the picture when philosophy makes the plane of immanence—this selection of chaos or reality—immanent to some kind of universal or abstraction. Transcendence is negative in such cases because it *subordinates* reality to some universal. In the case of communication, the plane of immanence is made immanent to an intersubjective activity. For Deleuze and Guattari, what is unique to communication or intersubjectivity is the exchange of opinions.

Opinions represent a third risk for philosophy, in addition to chaos, on the one hand, and transcendence, on the other, so that philosophy must also struggle against opinion.³ Deleuze and Guattari write that we form opinions in order to protect ourselves from chaos (Deleuze and Guattari 1994, 202). Opinions protect us from chaos because they halt the movement of chaos, introducing a stability into our experience, even if this stability is illusory (cf. Deleuze and Guattari 1994, 49). Despite the similarity between the formation of a plane of immanence—as a response to chaos—and opinion-formation, Deleuze and Guattari contend that "the struggle with chaos is only the instrument of a more profound struggle against opinion, for the misfortune of people (*hommes*) comes from opinion" (Deleuze and Guattari 1994, 206).⁴ In the remainder of this section, I'll try to elucidate this claim.

Opinion refers to a "particular relationship between an external perception as state of a subject and an internal affection as passage from one state to another" (hence its connection to phenomenology, understood as a philosophy of communication) (Deleuze and Guattari 1994, 144). However, an opinion is not the mere relationship of a single subject and a single object. It requires a quality, or perception, common to several objects and an affection common to several subjects. Opinion "is the rule of the correspondence" between these common perceptions and common affections. In other words, opinions are abstracted from our perceptions and affections.

Because opinions refer to common affections, they are political by nature: "[A]ll opinion is already political" (Deleuze and Guattari 1994, 145).⁵ Opinions are shared by societies or communities. When they are reified, opinions can develop into orthodoxy. In this case, opinions can become the "condition of a group's constitution," that is, they determine that group's identity (Deleuze and Guattari 1994, 146). For this reason, opinions are also abstractions insofar as they come to define a group or community. Deleuze and Guattari maintain that the "essence of opinion is will to majority and already speaks in the name of a majority." Finally, they argue "opinion triumphs when the quality chosen ceases to be the condition of a group's constitution but is now only the image or 'badge' of the constituted group that itself determines the perceptive and affective model, the quality and affection, that each must acquire" (Deleuze and Guattari 1994, 146).

Because of the alliance between opinion and majority, the struggle against opinion is also a struggle against the majority. We should recall from *A Thousand Plateaus* that "majority" is used primarily in a qualitative, not a quantitative, sense. A majority is a standard of domination or evaluation (Deleuze and Guattari 1987, 105 and 291). Deleuze and Guattari identify "man"—in particular, the "average adult-white-heterosexual-European-male-speaking a standard language"—as the majoritarian paradigm.⁶

Nonetheless, everyone is related to this majority because it functions as a standard of calculation, even though it is not primarily quantitative (Deleuze and Guattari 1987, 469–70). That is, the majority determines who counts, or who belongs to the majority, and what counts, or what opinions or beliefs conform to the dominant standard. At the same time, Deleuze and Guattari claim that the majority is "always nobody," even though it is the dominant standard. The majority is nobody, because no one can perfectly live up to this standard. We are all irreducible to the majority, even those of us who most obviously fit its standard (cf. Deleuze 1997, 253).

Since the majority is a dominant, or dominating, standard, we can begin to see why "the misfortune of people comes from opinion." It is within the nature of opinion to become a majority and it is within the nature of a majority to impose standards, inclusive and exclusive, by which we judge ourselves. Even though it is an empty standard inhabited by no one, some of us are certainly closer to this standard and therefore less likely to notice it or to notice how our opinions are a function of this standard.

In opposition to the majority, Deleuze and Guattari claim that "[a]ll becoming is minoritarian" (Deleuze and Guattari 1987, 106).[7] But this should not be heard as a mere opposition between majority and minority groups, because the latter can function according to the terms of the majority. That is, it can risk reinstating a mode of domination. In place of this opposition of majority and minority, Deleuze and Guattari propose a becoming-minoritarian of everybody/everything (*tout le monde*). Instead of a minority *group*, becoming-minoritarian implicates everybody. Becoming-minoritarian involves a variation of the majority, to which we are all related. Just as absolute deterritorialization is always accompanied by reterritorialization, becoming-minoritarian is "nothing" if it does not "reshuffle," or bring itself to bear, on the majority (cf. Deleuze and Guattari 1987, 216–17 and 470–71).[8] It's important to note that becoming-minoritarian is not merely about overcoming an illusory abstraction (such as the majority), it's also creative—and that's what this language of variation indicates.

This movement from the majority to becoming-minoritarian in Deleuze and Guattari's work parallels the movement from abstractions to the concrete via the process of rationalization in Whitehead's work. And we could say that, for Whitehead, the recovery of concrete reality can also have this effect of introducing novelty or variety into our abstractions. This is not to say that these two movements are strictly equivalent, but my hope is at the very least that this explication of Deleuze and Guattari's work demonstrates how they are committed to the first characteristic of empiricism, to refer back to the quote from Deleuze that I mentioned in the introduction. One difference might be that becoming-minoritarian is more explicitly collective or social than Whitehead's process of rationalization, though I have tried to suggest how this process has broader social implications, namely, in terms of a responsibility to the excluded.

SEEKING ALTERNATIVES

Let's return to the quote from which we began, where Deleuze identifies the two Whiteheadian characteristics of empiricism:

> I have always felt that I am an empiricist, that is, a pluralist. But what does this equivalence between empiricism and pluralism mean? It derives from the two characteristics by which Whitehead defined empiricism: the abstract does not explain, but must itself be explained; and that aim is not to rediscover the eternal or the universal, but to find the conditions under which something new is produced (*creativeness*). (Deleuze and Parnet 2007, vii)

I have spent a good deal of time considering the first of these characteristics, abstraction, but have not yet emphasized its connection to the second characteristic, the conditions of novelty. But the two are intimately related, as I suggested in the introduction.

For Whitehead, the critique of abstractions and the recovery of concrete reality (the process of rationalization) is not just about uncovering a fixed and given world that preexists our abstractions. Whitehead refers to philosophy in terms of disclosure frequently throughout *Modes of Thought*, but disclosure is much more than bringing to light what is already in the world. Disclosure, or the critique of abstractions, also involves creativity and novelty. Certain abstractions are inhibitive—not only because they prevent those who affirm such abstractions from seeing what these abstractions occlude, but also because these abstractions inhibit that which they exclude. If, for example, I take it as natural for human beings to be characterized by certain modes of production (*homo economicus*) not only am I believing in a false abstraction, I am also harming those who are victims of the market economy by reinforcing the beliefs and practices that underwrite such an economy. In this case, the critique or the overcoming of such abstractions can act as a counter to the inhibitions that follow from such abstractions and therefore allow for novelty on the part of those inhibited and those excluded. In other words, *the critique of abstractions makes room for the activity of the concrete*.

Of course, it often seems that when we talk about novelty in Whitehead and Deleuze, we think that they are concerned with novelty for its own sake. Fred Evans has referred to this as the "fascism of the new" (Evans 2016, 85–99). But a concern for the conditions of novelty is not necessarily limited to the new as such. The production of novelty (or the transformation of the present) is not concerned with novelty merely for the sake of novelty. Instead, we have to have some reason or reasons why the new would be desirable in some particular context. If we are seeking an alternative, then there must be something about present conditions that lead us to do so. And, to reiterate what I said in the introduction to this chapter, these reasons will be immanent and contextual since philosophy does not have access to the best possible social arrangement.

Throughout this chapter, I have suggested some reasons that might guide our critique of abstractions. For example, with Whitehead, I said we are responsible for who and what our abstractions exclude. And with Deleuze and Guattari, I suggested that the very nature of opinion can be exclusionary. But to end this chapter it might be useful to quickly look at some of these thinkers' more concrete assessments or diagnoses of their respective eras in order to try to think about how the critique of abstractions relates to such concrete conditions. My examples will be economic in nature.

Although economic conditions have changed since Whitehead's time, some of his comments about the economy of his era are very relevant to that of our own. In a 1933 article for the *Harvard Business Review*, he identified three economic ages—feudalism, individualism, and ugliness, each one replacing the other in turn. He suggests that the form of industrialism that had arisen in the beginning of the twentieth century had led to the end of a vibrant individualism and to the rise of an ugliness, characterized by a loss of freedom and the homogenization (or canalization) of aesthetic interests and tastes. He identified the growth of "great commercial corporations" and of mass production as particularly responsible for this decline into ugliness. Consider this passage: "In any large city, almost everyone is an employee, employing his working hours in exact ways predetermined by others. Even his manners may be prescribed. So far as sheer individual freedom is concerned, there was more diffused freedom in the City of London in the year 1633, when Charles the First was King, than there is today in any industrial city of the world" (Whitehead 1947, 157).

Deleuze and Guattari share some of these concerns. Throughout *What Is Philosophy?* they frequently oppose philosophy to marketing, which they see as a sort of vulgarization of thought. But Deleuze and Guattari also note the inequality that accompanies a homogenizing economy. They draw attention to the "determinate inequalities of development" presupposed and produced by global capitalism. For Deleuze and Guattari, this is not only an economic problem but also a political one, because they view modern democratic states as complicit in these determinate inequalities of development. They also suggest that we are compromised by such inequalities.

I find this notion of compromise or complicity to be quite useful for further specifying what might motivate our critique of abstractions. For Deleuze and Guattari, a particular affect follows from this kind of complicity, namely, what they call "the shame of being human." They take this phrase from Primo Levi's reflections on Auschwitz, but they extend it to include anything that inhibits the becoming of a people—such as the suffering and inequality (or the ugliness, to use Whitehead's term) produced by global capitalism. This gives an affective dimension to the critique of abstractions, or what Whitehead refers to as the process of rationalization (though Whitehead was very aware of the affective dimension of reason and thought). In other words, when we consider which abstractions need to be critiqued or when we talk about seizing an alternative, we might follow Deleuze and Guattari by trying to identify those abstractions or sedimented practices that occasion this "shame of being human." Or we might simply ask what are we compromised by today? For my part, this is another way of asking, following Whitehead, who and/or what are excluded by our abstractions. That is, we might interpret this kind of compromise or this shame of being human in terms of a lure for feeling that is related to our contemporary abstractions.

I have one final consideration I'd like to close with. Once we've identified the conditions or abstractions that contribute to this shame of being human. Or—more generally—once we've identified our exclusionary and inhibitive abstractions, how should we respond? How does philosophy, as critic of abstractions, relate to such problems? At this point, I'm back to the question with which I began. When it comes to the survey of alternatives or even formulations of alternatives, how should philosophy proceed? I think Deleuze and Whitehead diverge on this question, at least at times. Consider again Whitehead's claim that philosophy is "a survey of possibilities and their comparison with actualities. . . . Its gifts are insight and foresight, and a sense of the worth of life, in short, that sense of importance which nerves all civilized effort" (Whitehead 1933, 98). It's important to note, first, that Whitehead is addressing the Harvard Business School with these words. This is in keeping with what he says in this passage: philosophy needs to be immanent in the community.

Now let's consider the following passage from Deleuze: "I think there's a public for philosophy and ways of reaching it, but it's a clandestine sort of thinking, a sort of nomadic thinking. The only form of communication one can envisage as perfectly adapted to the modern world is Adorno's message in a bottle, or the Nietzschean model of an arrow shot by one thinker and picked up by another" (Deleuze 1995, 154). For my part, this passage indicates a very different, and perhaps more individualistic and pessimistic, approach. To be clear, I don't want to claim that this is necessarily Deleuze's definitive position and perhaps the many decades between these two thinkers can help explain this divergence. Nonetheless, I think the comparison of these two passages raises the question of how philosophy should think about addressing the public or how or if it should communicate an alternative vision of the world. At the very least, the contrast suggests that Whitehead's approach is more amenable to the stated aims and ideals of higher public education (such as the collective pursuit of the common good). This is not to say that Deleuze—who was a professional philosopher and educator—opposes such education, but that if such education is to offer an alternative then it must proceed in a subterranean manner, hidden from or in opposition to the stated mission of the university. These final remarks are no doubt preliminary. My hope, however, is that they indicate the divergent paths of two philosophers who otherwise have much in common.

NOTES

1. For an account of why "creativeness" does not capture the meaning of Whitehead's neologism "creativity," see Meyer, 2005, 1–33.
2. Whitehead also notes that the capacity for self-determination is the root of irresponsibility (1933, 195).
3. Despite Deleuze and Guattari's opposition to Platonism, this aspect of their work indicates its resonance with Socratic philosophical practice, which takes *doxa* as its immediate object of critique.
4. Philosophy's struggle against opinion does not mean that philosophy's creation of concepts can bypass opinion. As Rodolphe Gasché notes, the liberation of opinion from its use as a standard of truth is a condition of concept creation (cf. Deleuze and Guattari 1994, 79 and 150). See Gasché 2014, 65–81.
5. Paul Patton misses this point in his defense of Deleuze against Philippe Mengue's charge that Deleuze's opposition to opinion makes democracy impossible. See Mengue 2003, and "People and Fabulation," Mengue 2008. Patton contends that for political philosophy we should distinguish between "everyday" opinions and opinions that are the product of reflection and deliberation. The latter, he claims, are the object of Deleuze's criticism of opinion and should become the locus of political transformation. See Patton 2010, 161–84. As the cited passage suggests, Deleuze and Guattari make no such distinction. Their account of opinion is general and includes both everyday and more refined opinions.
6. We might more commonly refer to the majority in terms of ideology, though Deleuze and Guattari are reluctant to use the latter term due to its connection to Louis Althusser's work.
7. Paolo Marrati sketches the relation between opinion and becoming-minoritarian. See Marrati 2001, 205–20.
8. Deleuze and Guattari frequently refer to women's movements on this point (cf. Deleuze and Guattari 1987, 276 and 471).

REFERENCES

Deleuze, Gilles. 1987. *Dialogues.* New York: Columbia University Press.
———. 1995. *Negotiations.* Trans. Martin Joughin. New York: Columbia University Press.
———. 1997. "One Less Manifesto." Trans. Eliane dal Molin and Timothy Murray, in *Mimesis, Masochism, and Mime.* Ed. Timothy Murray. Ann Arbor: University of Michigan Press.
Deleuze, Gilles, and Felix Guattari. 1987. *A Thousand Plateaus: Capitalism and Schizophrenia.* Trans. Brian Massumi. Minneapolis: University of Minnesota Press.
———. 1994. *What Is Philosophy?* Trans. Hugh Tomlinson and Graham Burchell. New York: Columbia University Press.
Deleuze, Gilles, and Claire Parnet. 2007. *Dialogues II.* Rev. ed. Trans. High Tomlinson and Barbara Habberjam. New York: Columbia University Press.
Evans, Fred. 2016. "Deleuze's Political Ethics: A Fascism of the New?" *Deleuze Studies* 10, no. 1: 85–99.
Gasché, Rodolphe. 2014. *Geophilosophy: On Gilles Deleuze and Félix Guattari's* What Is Philosophy? Evanston, IL: Northwestern University Press.
Marrati, Paola. 2001. "Against the Doxa: Politics of Immanence and Becoming-Minoritarian." *Micropolitics of Media and Culture: Reading the Rhizomes of Deleuze and Guattari.* Ed. Patricia Pisters and Catherine M. Lord. Amsterdam: Amsterdam University Press.
Mengue, Philippe. 2003. *Deleuze et la question de la démocratie.* Paris: L'Harmattan.

———. 2008. "People and Fabulation." *Deleuze and Politics*. Ed. Ian Buchanan and Nicholas Thoburn. Edinburgh: Edinburgh University Press.
Meyer, Steven. 2005. "Introduction" *Configurations* 13, no. 1 (Winter): 1–33.
Patton, Paul. 2010. *Deleuzian Concepts: Philosophy, Colonization, Politics*. Stanford: Stanford University Press.
Shaviro, Steven. 2014. *The Universe of Things*. Minneapolis: University of Minnesota Press.
Stengers, Isabelle. 2008. "Experimenting with Refrains: Subjectivity and the Challenge of Escaping Modern Dualism." *Subjectivity* 22.
Whitehead, Alfred North. 1925. *Science and the Modern World*. New York: The Free Press.
———. 1933. *Adventures of Ideas*. New York: The Free Press.
———. 1938. *Modes of Thought*. New York: The Free Press.
———. 1947. *Essays in Science and Philosophy*. New York: Philosophical Library.
———. 1978. *Process and Reality*. Corrected Edition. Ed. David Ray Griffin and Donald W. Sherburne. New York: The Free Press.

Chapter Eight

The Charge of Resistance

The Influence of Whitehead on Deleuze's Concept of Power

Elijah Prewitt-Davis

In the season six finale of *Buffy the Vampire Slayer*, Willow—the shy, disconnected, nerdy comrade to Buffy in her never-ending, counter-apocalyptic struggles—becomes the most powerful mortal witch of all time. Her newfound potency emerges when her girlfriend, Tara, is killed by the comically inept arch nemesis of the season. Having previously given up "the magics" at Tara's pleading due to her dark potential, Willow once again takes up the magics to seek revenge for Tara's death. "Dark Willow"—as she comes to be called in the Buffyverse—becomes unstoppable, even for Buffy, and her quest for revenge becomes ever more destructive. After defeating the last person capable of stopping her, she absorbs his magical virility. Endowed now with an overwhelming power, she falls to the floor in a head rush of entangled energy. Stammering, she explains, "It's like no mortal person has had this much power—ever. It's like I'm connected to . . . everything. I can feel . . . and it feels like . . . I can feel . . . everyone." The power she feels comes from her interconnectedness and simultaneously enhances the awareness of her own entanglement; it gives her intimate knowledge of our cosmic and earthly relations. Where Dark Willow was only previously concerned with her private relation to Tara, she finds herself now affected by the pain of the world. Her entangled rapture thus quickly becomes entangled despair as she becomes cognizant of the ghoulish nightmares of evil and pain in the world. She stammers on, "I can feel . . . everyone . . . oh, oh my God . . . emotion . . . and the pain. It's too much. Oh, it's just too much. . . . I have to stop this. I'll make it go way. All you poor bastards; your suffering has to end." The one who helped Buffy save the world—a lot—rushes off to destroy it. As she explains to Buffy, "it's the only way to stop the pain" (Fury 2002).

Might we imagine this scene as the hyperbolic expression of the complications inherent to process relationalism? Here, the excess of the world in all its force reveals an apocalyptic entanglement as the very test of relationalism. The paradox at the heart of this argument is on full display: our radical connection to the world is the very thing that disassociates, disconnects, and alienates us from it. For Whitehead and Deleuze, the world of interconnected becoming events is epistemologically *descriptive* of the world before it is *evaluative.* If it is the case that those committed to process—or Whiteheadian or Deleuzian—relationalism give too much honor to our relations, we can see that that honorific role is directly challenged by Willow's intense reaction against her own feelings of the pain of the world. It brings to mind precisely what Judith Butler has asked of Whitehead: "Even if we are restored to our animality, our interdependency, and even our natural connections, are we in any sense relieved of our precarity or our apprehension of the precarity of living processes?" (Butler 2012, 14). Might we say that what Willow prehends in her moment of conscious relationality is the precarity of the world, her animality restored to the *nth* degree, precisely there where on "this occasion of loss, the sun is too bright, the world is too loud, and all efforts at communication are too arduous"—that is to say precisely where the world is too much? (Butler 2012, 13). But might we imagine that what happens to Willow in her moment of interconnectedness is not a denial of the singularity of loss, as Butler rightly fears. It represents, rather, an overwhelming incarnation of all those singularities simultaneously, revealing a precarious vulnerability *par excellance*, where every event is *felt* in a virtually transcendental explosion?

This scene both affirms the fact that we are radically interconnected while simultaneously challenging the claim that relational becoming is a positive concept upon which we might ground meaning. It highlights the sad irony of relations: our interactions cause the most pain because they cause the most joy. Of course, it must be noted that within the frame of a world of interrelated events, meaning is posited as if in consequence. Apart from these processes there would be nothing. It is Willow's love for Tara, her loss of the joys that can no longer be, the loss of relation, and an actual refusal and failure to grieve—what Butler calls "the vexations of memory, desire, and regret" inherent to life—that launches her into a despair that ends in an apocalyptic desire for total destruction (Butler 2012, 13). It is precisely Willow's deep connection to Tara (a homophone for *"terra*," the Latin for "land" which can also mean "earth") that brings her into a mode of existence in which the force of her own power struggles between the pain of a loss and the joy of a memory. Interconnectedness is the source of her power, but it is also the cause of her agony.

As Deleuze writes in *On Nietzsche*, "The history of a thing, in general, is the succession of forces which take possession of it and the co-existence of forces which struggle for the possession" (Deleuze 1983, 5). He is referring to Nietzsche's insistence, later developed by Michel Foucault, that there is a struggle for power at the heart of every relation. The history of a thing is the history of its power, of its struggle to maintain its own force amidst a multiplicity of contending forces and to exert force over them in order to evince its own vitality. Likewise, for Whitehead, the history of a thing—an actual entity—is a succession of forces. These forces do not struggle in the Greek sense of *agon*, but instead interact in a co-constitutive becoming that is a folding and unfolding of power. The forces prehended in any specific occasion may well form a contrast that produces struggle, though such contrast is not essential, the implication being that the unfolding of power is not necessarily a domineering exertion of power. There are thus striking similarities between Nietzsche's and Foucault's thoughts on relationality and becoming, but also key differences.

While not wanting to overstate the case, my contention is that Deleuze's engagement with Whitehead in this specific period (*Cinema 2, Foucault, The Fold*) might be key to his navigation of these similarities and differences, as well as his creative reading of Foucault. For instance, in his 1986 *Foucault* the problematic of the outside/inside is central to his understanding of control society. Here, the thought of the outside and its relation to the inside is explained in terms of folding, leading to his next publication, *The Fold* (1988a), where Deleuze devotes a small, but central and pivotal chapter, to the process philosophy of Alfred North Whitehead titled "What Is an Event?" This makes a more detailed dialogue between Whitehead, Nietzsche, Foucault and Deleuze, a promising place to pursue the questions to which Willow's experience alludes.

GENEALOGY AND PROCESS

Entangled events unfold into a multiplicity of interpretations. For genealogy as for process thought, the world is entangled in a variety of perspectives. These perspectives become in relation to each other. Substance is undone by becoming otherwise than before. If the genealogist interrogates a "value"—specifically as it is produced by power/knowledge—she brings to light the historico-political factors and forces that allowed it to emerge in relation to a specific context or environment. For each mode of thought, there is no such thing as an objective "view from nowhere": the perspective of the inquirer, just as the perspective of the actual entity, necessarily shapes the outcome of any and all interactions and interpretations.[1] In their very different vocabularies, genealogy and process both insist on a radical interconnectivity between the subject and the environment, and this has both ontological and epistemological significance. As Brian Lightbody has written about genealogy, "There must always be a relationship between the epistemic agent and the object claimed to be known. A non-relationship between subject and object is nonsensical" (Lightbody 2010, x). Whitehead's ontological principle finds itself expressed in genealogy.

For Foucault as for Nietzsche, substance is undone when genealogy reveals the falsity of a pure origin. The search for a pure origin is what Nietzsche, in *Twilight of the Idols,* associates with the fourth great error—the *causa prima*.[2] The absolute cause is simultaneously an invention of "purpose." The concept of a pure origin allows humanity to imagine that we have been given—as a special gift—our substantial qualities. When historical analysis seeks a search for origins, this is "an attempt to capture the exact essence of things, their purest possibilities, and their carefully protected identities" (Foucault 1978, 78). It is based on the error that something was able to exist outside the flux of becoming, but as Nietzsche asserts, *"there is nothing outside the whole!"* Genealogy exposes these qualities as having become in relation to a specific regime of power.

The search for a pure origin is simply a "metaphysical extension, which arises from the belief that things are most precious and essential at the moment of birth" (Foucault 1978, 79). Origins then, are always ontotheological, the work of Gods, God, and Goddesses before the fall. But the genealogist, indeed science, always reveals the irony at the heart of our origins. "We wished to awaken the feeling of man's sovereignty by showing his divine birth: this path is now forbidden, since a monkey stands at its entrance" (Foucault 1978, 79). Such compromised origins also compromise the future, and Zarathustra—John the Baptist of the overman—is followed by a monkey throughout his journeys. Truth stands at the origin as the key to the future of knowledge—the origin is the "site of truth." The recovery of an origin is also a recovery of knowledge, and the possibility of finding an origin is synonymous with the possibility of recovering knowledge. Genealogy is a history of the notion of truth and the history of the value of truth, exposing the false pretense by which truth originated in its search for an absolute origin. "The origin lies at a place of inevitable loss, the point where the truth of things corresponds to a truthful discourse, the site of a fleeting articulation that discourse has obscured and finally lost" (Foucault 1978, 79). What genealogy reveals is the history of an error—"the history of an error we call truth" (Foucault 1978, 80). Being, Essence, Man [sic] dissipates as its origin fractures, for genealogy reveals that such concepts have been "fashioned in a piecemeal form" from a perspective that always already valued these very concepts.

The search for a pure origin is arbitrary because it is based on a value assumption that something—God, who endows being with substance—can exist outside the flux of becoming: "forms that precede the external world of accident and succession" (Foucault 1990, 79). Instead of uncovering something totally originary, genealogy reveals the descent and emergence of an infinity of beginnings. The body has descended into destruction through the imprints of historical subjugation. It retains the stigmata of the past inasmuch as those past stigmata form the present expression of its "desires, feelings, and errors" (Foucault 1990, 81). The descent of origin is, however, also the story of emergence in the sight of a non-place where bodies resist the descent. "The analysis of the *Entstehung* (emergence) must delineate this interaction, the struggle these forces wage against each other or against adverse circumstances, and the attempt to avoid degeneration and regain strength by dividing these forces against themselves" (Foucault 1978, 84). Emergence happens not merely when forces erupt in conflict, but rather, any time they interact. Emergence thus always designates a struggle and all things emerge within this struggle. The relation of forces, which is the relation to power, is the condition of emergence and of all becoming. It is this struggle that keeps the world moving, keeps the world becoming, producing the condition of creativity and the emergence of event.

Power is thus at the center of every relation and every emergence; saying this, however, requires a new understanding of power. Assumptions that sovereignty, rule of law, violence, and systems of domination are the source of power simply redouble the idea of an origin or a God who remains outside. Consequently, power "has nothing to do with a group of institutions and mechanisms that ensure the subservience of the citizens of a certain state." These are merely "the terminal forms power takes." In *History of Sexuality Vol. 1*, Foucault gives his most precise definition of power:

> It seems to me that power must be understood in the first instance as the multiplicity of force relations immanent in the sphere in which they operate and which constitutes their own organization; as the process which, through ceaseless struggles and confrontations, transforms, strengthens, or reverses them; as the support which these force relations find on one another, thus forming a chain or a system, or on the contrary, the disjunctions and contradictions which isolate them from one another; and lastly, as the strategies in which they take effect, whose general design or institutional crystallization is embodied in the state apparatus, in the formulation of the law, in the various social hegemonies. (Foucault 1990, 92)

As a multiplicity of forces, power is immanent in the sphere in which it operates. Power is everywhere. The state, the law, sovereignty, is not power's fixed center of emanation, but rather, power is the condition by which these institutions emerge. The struggle for power at the heart of relations gives rise to their terminal state. They are the result of the conflict of unequal forces confronting each other. Such confrontations between forces "constantly engender states of power" (Foucault 1990, 92–93).

Power does not have a body that can be represented institutionally or structurally, nor can one point to some aspect of strength when speaking of power. Power is something that happens to bodies and between bodies, it is the "simple over all effect all these mobilities, the concentration that rests on each of them and seeks to arrest their movement" (Foucault 1990, 92). For Foucault, as for Nietzsche, power is what emerges when two forces meet in relation, and it is this encounter that constitutes the becoming of the world. Power is thus produced at every moment and in every interaction between forces, which is to say that power is relation. In *Foucault,* Deleuze sums up this theory of power by writing, "Power has no essence; it is simply operational. It is not an attribute but a relation: the power-relation is the set of possible relations between forces, which passes through the dominated forces no less through the dominating, as both these forces constitute unique elements" (Deleuze 1988b, 27). What this implies is that power is a consequence of the interactions between forces, but not necessarily their essential component. His reading of Foucault thus hinges around a power of action for the individual who is more or less inundated by force. "Power is not essentially repressive (since it incites, it induces, it seduces); it is practiced before it is possessed (since it is possessed only in a determinable form, that of class, and a determined form, that of state); it passes through the hands of the mastered no less than through the hands of the masters (since it passes through every related force" (Deleuze 1988b, 27). This idea of power is similar to what Deleuze calls, in *Expressionism in Philosophy*, "the power to be affected." For now, we can call the power to be affected a power of openness to our relation with other forces—to believe in the events that happen to us. But it is likewise a power to not be completely overrun and undone by those forces. While Deleuze will call this concept of power a "profound Nietzscheanism" (Deleuze 1988b, 71), one wonders if his understanding of power might have also been inspired by that thinker whom he calls, just one year after the release of *Foucault,* "the last great Anglo-American American philosopher"—Alfred North Whitehead.

POWER AND CAPACITY

Whitehead, like Nietzsche and Foucault, finds it necessary to disavow the search for pure origins or a *causa prima.* "In the *Timaeus*, the origin of the present cosmic epic is traced back to an aboriginal disorder, chaotic according to our ideals. This is the evolutionary doctrine of the philosophy of organism" (Whitehead 1978, 95). For Whitehead, a pure origin or order would entail something that existed outside of relation, something that existed, as Nietzsche notes, outside the whole. Each thing that exists—each actual entity—becomes in relation to a vector of data that comprises it. But unlike Nietzsche and Foucault, who draw the connection of the final consequence of the lack of pure origin and the undoing of substance to the death of God and the death of the subject, Whitehead reformulates both substance and subjectivity. Interestingly, it is precisely the role power plays in the becoming of each actual entity that allows for his reformulation.

When Whitehead speaks of power, he continually draws the concept from other thinkers and reinterprets it in his own language. Power is thus operative in Whitehead, and in a central way, but it expresses something broader and more vital than struggle, namely, the internal subjective constitution of actual entities in their becoming. In *Process and Reality*, Whitehead claims, "Locke, in his *Essay*, rightly insists that the chief ingredient in the notion of 'substance' is the notion of 'power'" (Whitehead 1978, 56). He continues, "The philosophy of organism holds that, in order to understand 'power,' we must have a correct notion of how each individual actual entity contributes to the datum *from which* its successors arise and *to which* they must conform" (Whitehead 1978, 56). In other words, the power of the prehended past affects the emergent subject in a way that opens up the subject to outside forces (it is not just an internal constitution but a relation to the world).

For Whitehead, actual entities are the various monads that comprise the world, everything in the world is an actual entity, and the cosmos is composed of actual entities in relation. As they interact, actual entities "objectify" one another; in their becoming, other actual entities form the data from which all actual entities originate. But origination in this sense is more similar to Foucault's notion of emergence: there is no pure origin, no *ex nihilo*, in sight. Rather, the origin of an actual entity is a process by which an actual entity, through objectification, "*feels*" or is affected by the influence and the power of its data. It is precisely through affect that the actual entity retains an agential power, for it is in feeling that the objectified datum gets transformed into subjectivity, making the datum "its own." "A feeling appropriates elements of the universe, which in themselves are other than the actual entity, and absorbs these elements into the real internal constitution of its subject by synthesizing them into the unity of an emotional pattern expressive of its own subjectivity" (Whitehead 1978, 117). It is in "feeling," then, that the power of the actual entity is expressed. It is an affective process of subjectivation in which singularity is retained in relation to the determinate forces acting upon it. If *each* actual entity did not exhibit an agential power—that is, if it were not simultaneously subject and object—if it were not *both that which is appropriated and that which appropriates*, then singularity would dissolve into a neutral universe of cause and effect. The many would become one, but not increase by one. As "drops of experience, complex and interdependent," actual entities interact with other actual entities and perish perpetually all while retaining "objective immortality" through the interaction (Whitehead 1978, 18). This is the way they affect an influence (from which) and are affected by (to which) other actual entities.

The "from which" and "to which" action of the process is a prehension. Prehensions are the way an actual entity absorbs the data taken in and gives it subjective form in a moment of concrescence. Power is at play in every prehension inasmuch as the actual entity retains a certain amount of agency as it determines the subjective character of the variety of data felt. Power is the agential determination of its own subjective form in the act of concrescence, and it is in this act that the actual entity influences other actual entities. By expressing its power in relation to the past data that comprise it, it exerts a force over the actual entity that it will be datum to in the future.

As Whitehead explains, there are two types of prehensions: negative and positive. A positive prehension is the inclusion of a datum into the subjective form of an actual entity. It is the way a prehension is felt; it is feeling in the technical sense. A negative prehension is the exclusion of a given datum "from positive contribution to the subject's own internal constitution" (Whitehead 1978, 41). This, however, does not mean that the negative prehension is not "felt," it simply means that it was excluded in the final concrescence, a necessary exclusion in order for that actual entity to attain "satisfaction." Power is operative inasmuch as the actual entity is able to "cut off" the datum it wishes to exclude and is thus related to decision: "Decision expresses the relation of an actual thing, *for which* a decision is made, to an actual thing *by which* that decision is made" (Whitehead 1978, 43). In decision, actual entities express a power in the form of prehension: "thus, the problem of perception and the problem of power are one in the same, at least so far as perception is reduced to mere prehensions of actual entities" (Whitehead 1978, 58). Without this power to decide—especially at the human level where we get a conscious glimmer of the process—there would be no experience of freedom, responsibility, or emphasis.[3] To return to the example at the beginning of this chapter, it is precisely this power to decide that Willow is separated from.

The question that power answers is this: "How can other actual entities, each with its own formal existence, also enter into the perspective constitution of the actual entity in question?" The question remains untenable so long as thinking remains tied to the philosophical bifurcations of universal and particular, of subject and predicate, "of individual substances not present in other individual substances" (Whitehead 1978, 57). In his alternative, power becomes a constituent aspect of every prehension. It is necessary for an actual entity inasmuch as other entities are its origin, but it is not unidirectional because the prehended entity likewise exerts an influence, a power, over the prehending entity. Substance gets transformed in and through power, for it is power that allows the actual entity in its internal constitution to have a subjective say. Power is what disavows the substance of a static identity and allows for other entities to constitute it while still retaining agency. "To be actual must mean that all actual things are alike objects . . . and that all actual things are subjects, each prehending the universe from which it arises" (Whitehead 1978, 57). The "mastery" and "agency" of actual entities' own concrescence hinge on a profound irony—it lasts for but a moment and is always dependent on its prehended world.

"Power thus considered is twofold; viz. as able to make, or able to receive, any change: the one may be called 'active,' and the other 'passive,' power . . . I confess power includes in it some kind of relation,—a relation to action or change." (Whitehead 1978, 57–58). In his exegesis of this Lockean passage, Whitehead concludes that power is a principal ingredient in the process of becoming. The power of an actual entity is the way in which it "objectifies" another actual entity, thereby taking it into its own constitution. Such objectification is "causal" rather than oppressive: it is the condition of the relation between two entities.[4] When one entity encounters another entity, it objectifies that entity inasmuch as the encounter with the other changes the internal subjective character of the prehending subject. This is its active power, expressed simultaneously as the passive power of the prehended object. But that active power is still in play in the moment of passivity in both objects. It is what allows both entities to be affected without being dominated, to retain a degree of subjectivity within and through the power relation. Thus, for Whitehead, power is not necessarily struggle, let alone control, but rather an agency retained by every entity in moments of interaction. This idea, as we saw briefly, is central to the understanding of power Deleuze develops in *Foucault*. As he reminds us there, "violence is a concomitance or consequence of force, but not a constituent element" (Deleuze 1988b, 70).

In *Adventurers of Ideas*, Whitehead quotes Plato to introduce his discussion of power: "My suggestion would be, that anything which possesses any sort of power to affect another, or to be affected by another even for a moment, however trifling the cause and however slight and momentary the effect, has real existence; and I hold that the definition of being is simply power" (quoted in Whitehead 1933, 120). As Whitehead unfolds these statements it becomes clear that power is operative in every mode of relation, and it is precisely because of this that Whitehead's understanding of "being" and "substance" take on a radically new conceptual understanding more in line with the late modern critique of these very terms. Being, understood here, means to be in a state of constant becoming influenced and acted upon by other actual entities. "This means that the essence of being is to be implicated in causal action on other beings" (Whitehead 1933, 120). Following his ontological principle—where to be requires a being in relation to other beings—Whitehead dismantles a unilateral notion of power in which one being exerts power over another. Rather, the power relation is both active and reactive. In a being's relation with another being, both exert a force over the other and retain a certain amount of force in constituting how they will be affected: "Being is the agent of action, and the recipient of action" (Whitehead 1933, 120).

Whitehead explains that the suggestion that "the definition of being as power . . . is the charter of the doctrine of Immanent Law" (Whitehead 1933, 113). Like Foucault and Nietzsche, Whitehead does not identify power as an imposition or a force from above, God or its mimics—sovereignty, the state, and so forth. It is precisely this imposing definition of power that affirms a fixed and stable universe made up of existents "in complete disconnection from any other such existent" (Whitehead 1933, 113). Law imposed in this way—and we are talking about Laws of Nature—required a God to set them in motion and secure their fixity, and to not allow complete dissipation into chaos. Thus, Imposed Law, with its transcendent God monitoring it, is dependent on the "Cartesian notion of substance," where substance means being immune to the effects of power, which are the effects of relations with other existents. Immanent Law opposes the Cartesian notion of substance, as well as the transcendent imposition, by affirming the mutual relations between things as the nature of substance.[5] It is as if the laws of nature take on a genealogical character. Rather than having a firm and fixed order, laws of nature become in relation to the existents they govern and interact with. "In other words, some partial identity of pattern in the various characters of natural things issues in some partial identity of pattern in the mutual relations of those things" (Whitehead 1933, 112). Simplified descriptions of the laws fail to understand this development; they are seen as given or imposed in the same way that the value of morality or truth is given, and therefore never questioned. Description describes the laws, explanation gets behind them and reveals their becoming. In seeking this explanation, one must do to the laws precisely what Nietzsche did to morality—that is, understand that they, too, become, in relation to the interaction of various forces. "Thus the modern evolutionary view of the physical universe should conceive of the laws of nature as evolving concurrently with the things constituting the environment" (Whitehead 1933, 112–13). It is only by studying the existents of an environment that we come to understand the laws that govern that environment, and vice versa. The interconnections of things write the laws, even as they become; indeed, it is their interconnection that allows them to become. Such an idea corresponds directly to the concept of world I have developed elsewhere: the world, as it is, is immanent to the concept of world. The world is created by the events within it, and the events within it create the world.

In his call to abandon the idea of "fixed eternal law regulating all behavior," it is not surprising that Whitehead critiques "the modern scholar" with the exact phrasing Nietzsche used to describe the modern historian: Egyptianism. "The modern scholar, with his tinge of speculation, is an Egyptian employing his wisdom upon his Hellenic and Semitic heritage" (Whitehead 1933, 121). This critique of "Egyptianism" and the becoming it seeks to affirm will, for the early Nietzsche as for the early Foucault, remain relegated to the sphere of historical genealogy in such a way that the internal constitution of the individual remains "trapped" by the power relation of forces. But if Whitehead's immanent laws *become* in relation to their existents, and the existents in relation to the laws, then the outside and the inside curiously fold into each other. Here, cause moves beyond a procedure of mere effect and becomes affective and agential: the influence of actual entities retaining internal power in and through every relation, a process which itself, as an internal cause, unfolds as an outward influence. We affect the world and are affected by it.

POWER UNFOLDED

It is not merely an accident that Whitehead appears as if in the center of *The Fold*. Indeed, it is the concept of prehension that allows Deleuze to accomplish what could be seen as the primary aim of his study of Leibniz—to ply the monad, make it straddle several worlds, keep it "half open as by a set of pliers" (Deleuze 1988a, 137). For Leibniz, each monad expresses the entire world and "sings the glory of God" (cf. Deleuze 1995a, 75). "Conveying the entire world, all monads include it in the form of an infinity of tiny perceptions, little solicitations, little springs or bursts of force: the presence of the world within me, my-being-for-the-world, is an anxiousness (being on the lookout)" (Deleuze 1988a, 130). When Deleuze is done with the monads, that very expression opens outward, such that monads and the worlds they express "penetrate each other, are modified, inseparable from the groups of prehension that carry them along and make up as many transitory captures" (Deleuze 1988a, 137).

> Matter thus offers an infinitely porous, spongy, or cavernous texture without emptiness, caverns endlessly contained in other caverns: no matter how small, each body contains a world pierced with irregular passages, surrounded and penetrated by an increasingly vaporous fluid, the totality of the universe resembling a "pond of matter in which there exist different ponds and waves."
> (Deleuze 1988a, 45)

The Fold thus serves as a lesson in folding this fluid matter, such that worlds fold into worlds, for the world is a fold. "Then in every event this becoming is an elevation, an exaltation: a change of theatre, of rule, of level or of floors. The theatre of matter gives way to that of spirits or of God" (Deleuze

1988a, 45). In relation to this excessive matter that gives birth to spirits and God, the constitution of the problem remains the same: "The question always entails living in the world" (Deleuze 1988a, 137).

For Deleuze this problem is related directly to the nature of an event. Deleuze turns to Whitehead in order to answer a not so simple question: "What is an Event?" While power is not explicitly mentioned in his discussion of Whitehead, it is no less operative in the production of an event, even as it must be teased out, as it were. "An event does not just mean 'a man has been run over.' The Great Pyramid is an event, and its duration for a period of one hour, thirty minutes" (Deleuze 1988a, 76). There is something expressive in the very examples used, for as we have seen, one way we can think of power is precisely as the ability not to be run over and overrun by the forces we constantly experience—power gives me a "duration." Deleuze will say that "events are produced in a chaos, in a chaotic multiplicity." However, he is clear that, for Whitehead, a "sort of screen" intervenes so that "many become one." This one, however, always increases and is as such not "a pregiven unity but instead the indefinite article that designates a certain singularity" (Deleuze 1988a, 76). Might we imagine this "screen" as the power of decision at work in every prehension? "The vector of prehension moves from the world to the subject, from the prehended datum to the prehending one (a superject); thus the data of prehension are public elements, while the subject is the intimate or private element that expresses immediacy, individuality, and novelty." But as each prehension becomes a datum for another prehension "it becomes public ... it is at once public and private" (Deleuze 1988a, 78). Or, as Whitehead will put it in *Process and Reality*, "the actualities are moments of passage into a novel stage of publicity; and the coordination of prehensions express the publicity of the world" (Whitehead 1978, 290).

This notion of the "public" and the "private" corresponds to the folding of the internal and external, what Deleuze will call in *Foucault* the inside and the outside. "Force is what belongs to the outside, since it is essentially a relation between other forces: it is inseparable in itself from the power to affect other forces (spontaneity) and to be affected by others (receptivity). But what comes about as a result is *a relation which force has with itself, a power to affect itself, an affect of self on self*" (Deleuze 1988b, 101). While it is true that this form of subjectivation constitutes a move from a society of discipline to a society of control, where the inward life of the subject gets reshaped to become self-regulating, it is equally true that this very process also constitutes the means of resistance as the ability to precipitate events.[6] "As a force among forces man does not fold the forces that compose him without the outside folding itself, and creating a Self within man" (Deleuze 1988b, 101).

Foucault asserts, "where there is power, there is resistance," but this resistance never becomes a power in itself, because "resistance is never in a position of exteriority in relation to power" (Foucault 1990, 92). But Deleuze, reading Foucault as a philosopher of the fold, folds the resistance inward, where a relation within oneself becomes possible within the interaction of forces. What Deleuze is after is a sense of power as "force" or "lines of force" that remain politically and ethically open, inherent to relations of immanence and to the world one finds oneself in. As such, each subject retains a degree of power to relate to itself, not outside of the influence of biopower, but precisely as the resistance to it: "there will always be a relation to oneself which resists codes and power" (Deleuze 1988b, 103). Read in light of Whitehead, subjectivation depends on a degree of power as the very possibility of subjective intensity, what we might call a positive power that the subject retains as agency even as it creates and is recreated. "There never remains anything of the subject, since he is to be created on each occasion, like a focal point of resistance, on the basis of the folds which subjectivize knowledge and bend each power" (Deleuze 1988b, 104). Is this not precisely similar to Deleuze's understanding of Whitehead, where the power to affect oneself resonates with the agential power of every actual entity as they objectify data? For Deleuze, there is always a "power to affect self," and this corresponds to the power of an actual entity who always retains a private power to express novelty, that is, to precipitate events that elude control. Could it be, then, that Deleuze saw Whitehead's power as a means of thinking the will to power otherwise?

THE WILL TO POWER

It is a matter of saying the same or similar things in new ways, with new expressions and new inflections. In *Nietzsche and Philosophy* this very same force to affect is named will to power. "The will to power is thus added to force, but as the differential and genetic element, as the *internal element of its production*" (Deleuze 1983, 51). The struggle between forces, each seeking to dominate, is what keeps the world becoming. Nietzsche, however, does not simply succumb to a simplistic Darwinism in this account, for he is always clear that the struggle for power can never be reduced to a struggle to survive. (Think, for instance, of Nat Turner—and there are countless other examples—who could have survived quite well without his rebellion. Not content with mere survival, he gathers the power available within his world and risks his life to actualize it.) The will-to-power, as the internal element of both resistance and production, keeps each and every singularity from coming completely undone.

It is this understanding of the becoming of the world that leads to one of Nietzsche's most infamous sayings: "This world is will to power—and nothing besides!" It is precisely here that the greatest confluence of Nietzsche/

Foucault/Deleuze and Whitehead can be found, as William Connolly has also recently suggested (Connolly 2015). Nietzsche describes this world as "a monster of energy, without beginning, without end." This world that is a:

> play of forces and waves of forces, at the same time one and many ... a sea of forces flowing and rushing together, eternally changing, eternally flooding back, with tremendous years of recurrence, with an ebb and a flood of its forms; out of the simplest forms striving toward the most complex, out of the stillest, most rigid, coldest forms striving toward the hottest, most turbulent, most self-contradictory, and then again returning home to the simple out of this abundance, out of the play of contradictions back to the joy of concord, still affirming itself in this uniformity of its courses and its years, blessing itself as that which must return eternally, as a becoming that knows no satiety, no disgust, no weariness: this, my Dionysian world of the eternally self-creating, the eternally self-destroying. (Nietzsche 1967, 1067)

What the will to power thus represents is a sort of radical folding and unfolding of the world and the individual, for just as this world "is the will to power—and nothing besides," Nietzsche also reminds us that "you yourselves are also this will to power—and nothing besides" (Nietzsche 1967, 1067). Thus, Deleuze says that the most important explanation of what Nietzsche meant by will to power is the following: "The victorious concept of 'force,' by means of which our physicists have created God and the world, still needs to be completed: and *inner* will must be ascribed to it, which I designate 'will to power'" (Nietzsche 1967, 1067). In Deleuze's hands, this inner will that is the will to power becomes the differentiating element. And it is striking how similar his discussion of Nietzsche is to his discussion of Whitehead: "The will to power is the element *from which* both the quantitative difference of related forces and the quality that devolves into each force in this relation" (Deleuze 1983, 51). Thus, the will to power corresponds to the power that is operative in every prehension and as such serves as a sort of non-dialectical "synthesis" or screen that intervenes when the forces are too much, inundating, and overwhelming. This includes the tense, conflictual relations that result from Whitehead's own metaphysics of force, where the lure toward complexity creates contrasts so that difference does not collapse. Again, it comes down to becoming one while being increased by one—"the reproduction of diversity at the heart of synthesis" (Deleuze 1983, 51). The will to power thus becomes "the differential and genetic element of forces which directly confront one another" (Deleuze 1983, 52).

It is important to see, however, that that sort of power for Deleuze, Whitehead, and Nietzsche is not particular to human animals but is itself organic, as William Connolly has shown (Connolly 2015). As Connolly brings into relief in his comparison of Whitehead and Nietzsche, in the fragmented thoughts and notes that came to be known as *Will to Power*, Nietzsche points, with Whitehead, to the possibility that the will-to-power exists in organic and pre-organic processes well beyond "the human estate." The internal will is built into the excess of the world (Deleuze 1983, 51). Force itself is victorious, but never absolutely. As Connolly clearly sees, "The most fundamental dimension of 'will to power' is expressed in activities of creative relation and becoming" (Connolly 2015).[7]

We can conclude from this that for both Whitehead and Nietzsche, power is constitutive of the ongoing process of life. For Nietzsche, life is the will-to-power and nothing besides because it is life itself that wants to *exert* (unfold) and *retain* (enfold) power as it contends with other forces that want to *exert* and *retain* theirs. It is in this struggle that the world emerges into more complex moments of creation. While the will-to-power often takes on the language of domination or the will to domination, Nietzsche (almost) always has in mind the will-to-power as a necessary component of vital life. Force is not the will to power, but the internal possibility of remaining different, of subjectivizing or affecting oneself amidst a flux of forces that have the same end. As Deleuze explains in *On Nietzsche*, "Force is what can, will to power is what wills" (Deleuze 1983, 50). The will to power is necessary for every thing in the world if it is to retain its difference from other things, that is, if it is to not be overrun by the world that is always too much for it.[8] It is the will to power that assures nothing is finally dominated precisely because there is always resistance, such that the world can continue the process. Nietzsche is strikingly close to Whitehead at this point:

> My idea is that every specific body strives to become master over all space and to extend its force (—its will to power:) and to thrust back all that resists its extension. But it continually encounters similar efforts on the part of other bodies and ends by coming to an arrangement (a "union") with those of them that are sufficiently related to it: thus they then conspire together for power. And the process goes on. (Nietzsche 1967, #636)

Just as for Whitehead power as agency allows actual entities to retain subjectivity within determinate relations of emergence, so too does Nietzsche assert that the individual life that is will-to-power is never entirely dominated in the struggle. The process goes on because the struggle continues. Deleuze would agree, but given his understanding of power as the *power to be affected*, he does not relegate the desire to retain singularity to a narcissistic will to dominate, though it might at certain points require coming asymptotically close, especially in Nietzsche.

We can see, then, the similarities—but Whitehead would reduce neither power, nor relations, to struggle, and neither does Deleuze. Both power and relation express the agency at the heart of an actual entity and allow it to retain (enfold) a subjective force in its necessary interactions with other entities in a world of becoming, and it is precisely this subjective force—

retained in all interactions—that allows for novelty to emerge in the world.[9] Whitehead is able to honor the relation not because he denies struggle or conflict, but simply because struggle is not the driving force of all interactions and all life. Whereas for Nietzsche the power to affect or differentiate oneself requires both an *exertion* and *retention*, unfolding and enfolding, for Whitehead power has no need to unfold its force: it is enough to *retain* it as agency. Or rather, we should say that the enfolding is simultaneous with the unfolding inasmuch as the power an actual entity expresses in its subjective aim will affect the actual entity that prehends it as datum. To put it otherwise, resistance is always possible. In this way, struggle and the exertion of power are not absent in Whitehead, but neither are they primary. Rather, it is simply derivative of our relations. As he explains in *Modes of Thought*, the very multiplicity of actual entities, "each with its own experience, enjoying individuality, and yet requiring each other," necessitates "conflicts of finite realizations." The becoming of an actual entity out of the many data it prehends "involves the notion of disorder, of conflict, of frustration," but the philosopher who chooses to privilege the conflict and the disorder "shirks his task" (Whitehead 1938, 51–52). In sum, he recognizes the possibility of cooperation alongside and within the struggle and agonism of living existents, each enhancing and helping the life of the other emerge. The point to be taken is that resistance to forces becomes immanent to the play of force itself, for without such resistance, the play would dissolve into a benign unity. The existence of any singularity is an incarnation of various forces, and as such any material formation becomes an expression of power. For Whitehead this power functions as a retention of agency, and exertion is simply a side effect that need not entail struggle. For Nietzsche, on the other hand, power requires a corresponding assertion of power. But each concludes that subjectivity is not a static thing, but rather an emergence that requires power.[10] And it is this power that we need to persist in any struggle against the denizens of a control society that always appear as overwhelming, as too much.

POWER OTHERWISE

Back to the Buffyverse. As Willow attempts to bring about the apocalypse, to end the world in order to end the overwhelming pain, all hope seems lost. Even the mighty Buffy has been rendered impotent in the force-field of Willow's boundless power. The viewer is left with a sense of despair, for it seems impossible that the world will not end. But as Willow begins the apocalyptic procedure, Xander—the other member of Buffy's Scooby gang—suddenly appears: "Hey dark-eyed girl." As the only Buffy companion without supernatural powers or any special skills, he struggles throughout the series with his mundane inadequacy in the face of increasingly powerful evil forces. But now, the mortal and mundane Xander is left alone, face to face, with the most powerful being in the Buffyverse. He is, quite literally, the only thing that stands between Willow and the end of the world. With no physical or magical force to exert, all Xander can do is bodily disrupt the apocalyptic procedure. As he struggles to his feet after Willow initially knocks him away, he stands in front of her, disrupting the force of her spell once more. Willow explains to him: "You can't stop this." But Xander immediately rejoins: "Yeah, I get that, it's just where else am I gonna go? You've been my best friend my whole life . . . world gonna end, where else would I wanna be?" Willow laughs at the banality of his feeble gesturing: "Is this the master plan? You're gonna stop me by telling me you love me?" But what else can Xander do? What other power does he possess? He knows he cannot defeat her, so he simply explains that he has no intent to stop her, he simply wants to be there, with her, for the end. "I'm not joking, I know you are in pain. I can't imagine the pain you're in. And I know you're about to do something apocalyptically evil and stupid, but hey, I still want to hang. You're Willow." He continues his speech with a mundane story: "The first day of kindergarten, you cried because you broke the yellow crayon. And you were too afraid to tell anyone. You've come pretty far, while ending the world is not a terrific notion . . . but the thing is, yeah, I love you. I love crayon-breaky Willow and I love scary, veiny Willow. So if I am going out, it's here. If you wanna kill the world. Well then start with me." After Willow assures him that she will, Xander simply replies. "It doesn't matter, I'll still love you." But this only incites further rage, and Willow continually strikes him and yells at him to "shut up" and "stop." But Xander, hardly able to stand or even speak due to her blows, will not stop repeating "I love you." The powerful Willow finds herself incapable of resisting Xander's love and devotion. The scene ends as they fall together to ground. Willow returns to her former self as she violently weeps in Xander's arms. The seemingly mortal and mundane Xander has averted the apocalypse by affirming the positive aspect of their intimate relation in the face of the overwhelming power of pain.

What we can take from this scene is two things. Xander has no physical power; his only force is love. In other words, love is his power and is expressed in a way similar to how Hardt and Negri describe it: "Love . . . is joy, that is, the increase of our power to act and think." For Hardt and Negri then, love, when it stops being cliché, "is really oriented toward the embodiment . . . of everything, it applies to the world" (Hardt and Negri 2009, 182). So love is Xander's power and his joy, and while it is directed to Willow, it simultaneously expands outward, and it increases Willow's capacity to act and think. Knowing this, Xander does all that he can do, the only thing he can do: disrupt the force of the spell with the force of his body—even if he knows it will eventually overcome him. He performs two actions: stating his love and engaging in bodily disruption—because if he loves, Willow's dark force will not overcome him (even if it kills him). This is not at all profound, or it is profound because it is mundane; it is simply Xander believing in the powers available to him, doing what he can do given the situation.

Xander gives expression to power thought otherwise: the power of relation as it mindfully unfolds in an affirmation of relation. This is not only the power of love, but also the power of all the mundane aspects of life. Xander's story of the yellow crayon reminds me of Nietzsche's thoughts on benevolence, which rarely get cited in discussions of the will to power:

> Among the little but immeasurably frequent and thus very influential things to which science ought to pay more attention than to the great, rare things, benevolence too is to be reckoned; I mean those social expressions of a friendly disposition, those smiles of the eyes, those handclasps, that comfortable manner with which almost all human action is as a rule encompassed.... The sum of these of these small doses is nonetheless enormous; their collective force is among the mightiest of forces. (Nietzsche 1996, 38)

Is it too much to suggest that Xander retains his power of agency through a benevolence that refuses to allow Willow to forget their own intimate bond? Does he not allow her, as Nietzsche continues, to re-discover that there is "much more happiness in the world than clouded eyes can see: *one can do so if one only calculates correctly and does not overlook all those moments of pleasure in which every day of even the most afflicted human life is rich*" (Nietzsche 1996, 38).[11] Perhaps all Xander does is help Willow re-calculate. This does not relieve the precarity of her pain; the scene ends with them weeping together. The point is that they are—together. It is the power of their relation that restores the world to Willow, and in doing so saves the world.

THE CHARGE OF RESISTANCE

Everything thus depends on the world one finds oneself in. For Foucault, this world remains the strictly historical. Deleuze honors this sense of a historical world even while unfolding it beyond historical and anthropocentric specificity. It is a matter of understanding certain conditions, which are tied, but not reduced, to "a particular historical status" (Deleuze 1988b, 114). It is in this sense that we return to the notion of a "problem" that correlates to a decision: "*What can I do, what do I know, what am I?*" (Deleuze 1988b, 115). One asks these questions, in that order, within power—but also as a means to asserting power or of resisting power. As we saw with Whitehead, the power within decision works to exclude certain data from the prehensive process, such that the assertion of power coincides directly with resistance itself, *is* resistance. But, Deleuze warns, "On these three questions, the 'I' does not designate a universal but a set of particular positions occupied within a One speaks-One sees-One confronts-One lives" (Deleuze 1988b, 115). And what these particular conditions acknowledge is that this particular One is always already many, becoming one and being increased by one.

A singularity appears within the process of subjectivation, and this singularity will always be confronted by the three questions and their corresponding decisions. It is in this regard that Deleuze returns to an unmistakably Kierkegaardian formula: "No single solution can be transposed from one age to another, but we can penetrate or encroach on certain problematic fields, which means that the 'givens' of an old problem are reactivated in another" (Deleuze 1988b, 115).

The internal power of action and retention we have explored here is strictly virtual, and it must be practiced, directed, and rehearsed in order to become actual. It also must be vigilant—seeking out the powers of action within the specificity of our world, for "our ability to resist control, or our submission to it, must be assessed at every level" (Deleuze 1995b, 176). Deleuze will say that the events of 1968 were like the "rehearsal" of making this virtual power actual, for they correspond to the essential questions:

> What is our light and what is our language, that is to say, our truth, today? What powers must we confront, and what is our capacity for resistance, today when we can no longer be content to say that the old struggles are no longer worth anything? And do we not perhaps above all bear witness to and even participate in the "production of a new subjectivity"? Do not the changes in capitalism [control society] find an unexpected "encounter" in the slow emergence of a new Self as a centre of resistance? (Deleuze 1988b, 115)

To be sure, our disconnection from the world makes answering such questions extremely difficult, which is why belief in the world is something of a rehearsal aimed at actualization.

Despite the difficulty, we can point to certain instances of what it means to believe in the world, to assert our power of resistance, to rehearse these questions, today. Believing in the world is saying to the world, "World, you are not too much for me." It is the cry of the prisoner who demands access to books; it is the nocturnal emission of the celibate monk; it is the scribbling of "fuck this shit!" by a teenager on the bathroom door of a fundamentalist church that she has been dragged to all her life; it is the escape of the octopus from an aquarium through will, intellect, and strategy (Malik 2016); it is the final walk out the door of a woman in an abusive relationship; it is coming out of the closet to unaccepting parents; it is the flower that grows through the sidewalk and the weed that keeps coming back; it is #blacklivesmatter; it is #metoo; it is #fucktrump; it is "I am Trayvon Martin"; it is "I Can't Breathe"; it is Occupy Wall Street; it is rolling jubilee; it is Moral Mondays; it is black power; it is the baboons who through collective effort escape a research lab (Schmidt 2018); it is MLK's agapic love and nonviolence; it is Malcolm X's non-nonviolence; it is the immigrant or refugee crossing the border; it is the call of Christ from the cross, eternally repeated within the specificity of difference; it is, in short, every resistance, however small and inconspicuous, that eludes control, that refuses to allow a world to be limited and folds the outside into the means of unfolding.[12]

NOTES

1. "The final trait of effective history is knowledge as perspective." For more see Foucault 1978, 87. "The actual entity which is the initial datum is the actual entity perceived, the objective datum is the 'perspective' under which that actual entity is perceived, and the subject of the simple physical feeling" (Whitehead 1978, 236). "But throughout this history, it is Gibbon who speaks. He was the incarnation of the dominant spirit of his own times. In this way his volumes tell another tale. They are the record of the mentality of the eighteenth century" (Whitehead 1933, 5).

2. Another way to approach the relationship between Nietzsche and Whitehead would be to simply ask: Does Whitehead commit the four great errors—The error of confusing cause and effect, the error of false causation, the error of imaginary causes, and the error of free will. It would take an entire paper to answer this question, but, other than the nuanced way that Whitehead leaves "elbow room in the universe" that might conflict with error 4, my intuition is that Whitehead's thoughts on cause and effect, subject and predicate, avoid at least the first three errors.

3. "Further, in the case of those actualities whose immediate experience is most completely open to us, namely, human beings, the final decision of the immediate subject-superject, constituting the ultimate modification of subjective aim, is the foundation of our experience of responsibility . . . of freedom, of emphasis" (Whitehead 1978, 47).

4. And it certainly does not strip that data of its "subjectivity."

5. "It is evident that the doctrine involves the negation of 'absolute being.' It presupposes the essential interdependence of things" (Whitehead 1933, 113).

6. Deleuze certainly saw this potential within Foucault's own works, and it was Deleuze who first articulated the idea of a "society of control." Drawing on Deleuze's interpretation, Hardt and Negri take Foucault's idea of power one step further by showing how late-modern society has morphed from a society of discipline to a society of control. Whereas a society of discipline rules through structures that regulate forces, by "sanctioning or prescribing normal and/or deviant behaviors," in contrast the society of control has a more interior effect on the forces of struggle and the subjects who produce and are produced by these forces. "We should understand the society of control, in contrast, as that society in which mechanisms of command become ever more 'democratic,' ever more immanent to the social field, distributed throughout the brains and bodies of the citizens." Control becomes interiorized within subjects as they interact with new techniques of power such as communications systems, information networks, etc. The influence of power subjectivates such that we become self-regulating and power comes to "internally animate our common daily practices." In this way, the society of control is more of an exemplar of biopower than the disciplinary society. Within biopower, the production of life is brought into the realms of power, and life (bios) and power become inseparable—"power is the production of life itself." When power becomes productive in this way, it becomes all the more omnipresent precisely because it becomes ever more internalized. Life is produced inasmuch as subjectivities are produced. And what sort of life, what sort of subject does biopower now produce? "They produce needs, social relations, bodies, and minds—which is to say they produce producers." Relations are left in the realm of production precisely because that is where they emerge (Hardt and Negri 2000, 23 and 33).

7. While Connolly chooses to focus on other passages in his assessment, it is precisely here, as I read it, that I find the most resonance between Nietzsche and Whitehead. "The many

become one and are increased by one" gets expressed by Nietzsche as the "returning home to the simple of this abundance, out of the play of contradictions to the joy of concord." The fact that for Whitehead cosmos moves toward complexity through this process is expressed as "out of the simplest forms striving to the most complex." And finally, we find the basis of the ontological principle inasmuch as actual entities reach concrescence by prehending a vector of a datum and then, after satisfaction, perish into objective immortality, as the "sea of forces rushing together, eternally changing, eternally flooding back . . . blessing itself as that which must return eternally." This is in no way to suggest a complete confluence, but rather a striking resonance.

8. "What a will wants to affirm is its difference. In its essential relation with the other, a will makes its difference and object of affirmation" (Deleuze 1983, 9). Deleuze is here playing on the fact that, in German, the meaning of "will" is broader. In a sense it is vastly so: in everyday speech *"ich will"* is the way to say not "I will" but simply "I want." *Wille* is inseparable from desire, from wanting. The English utterly lacks that fold of this more encompassing meaning: to will is always already an act of intention, or more, of intent to force an outcome. In German *Wille* can carry that coercive edge but does not imply it. Though it could that *Wille Zur Macht* does. Such a nuance may be key to understanding how and why Deleuze and Guattari make desire "productive"—a move that confounds and annoys Foucault, who holds that desire is always lack. Thanks to Catherine Keller for helping me gain clarity on the translation issues.

9. "For the finite individual there is penetration to novelty in its own experience; and the selection of detail is subject to the causation from which that individual originates" (Whitehead 1938, 52).

10. As Connolly writes, "subjectivity and intersubjectivity are not only ineliminable, they find differential degrees of expression in numerous processes outside the human estate that are entangled with it. Every 'center of force' or 'actual entity' expresses a 'perspective' through which it receives and repels potential relations. It 'measures, feels, forms, according to its own force'" (Connolly 2015).

11. We might rightfully be squeamish about Nietzsche making such a claim—closed off as he was from individuals who live under oppressive conditions. Nietzsche, of course, suffered greatly throughout his life from various bodily inflictions. But what I am thinking of here are the pleasures that oppressed peoples create. For instance, Otto Maduro argues that "suffering, urgency, and fear at times invade our existence, thus making fiestas less easy but also more crucial than before." Likewise, James Cone has made clear that Churches and "Juke Joints" were ways that Black People asserted their somebody-ness in the face of slavery and Jim Crow. And Elie Weisel speaks of the celebration of Jewish holidays within the camps. The point that I am making is that life seeks joy within oppression, and the seeking out of such joy is itself a form of power and resistance. For more see, Maduro 2015 and Cone 1972.

12. Collective action is incredibly important. In my view, Hardt and Negri have said all that needs to be said in relation to collective action from a Deleuzian perspective. For more, see their *Empire Trilogy*.

REFERENCES

Butler, Judith. 2012. "On This Occasion." *Butler on Whitehead*. Ed. Roland Faber, Michael Halewood, and Deena Lin. Lanham, MD: Lexington Books.
Cone, James. *The Spirituals and the Blues: An Interpretation*. Maryknoll, NY: Orbis Books.
Connolly, William. 2015. "Process Philosophy and Planetary Politics." *Common Goods: Economy, Ecology, and Political Theology*. Ed. Melanie Johnson-DeBaufre, Catherine Keller, and Elias Ortega Aponte. New York: Fordham University Press.
Deleuze, Gilles. 1983. *Nietzsche and Philosophy*. Trans. Hugh Tomlinson. New York: Columbia University Press.
———. 1988a. *The Fold: Leibniz and the Baroque*. Trans. Tom Conley. Minneapolis: University of Minnesota Press.
———. 1988b. *Foucault*. Trans. Seán Hand. Minneapolis: University of Minnesota Press.

———. 1995a. *Difference and Repetition.* Trans. Paul Patton. New York: Columbia University Press.
———. 1995b. *Negotiations.* Trans. Martin Joughin. New York: Columbia University Press.
Foucault, Michel. 1978. "Nietzsche, Genealogy, History." *Nietzsche.* Ed. John Richardson and Brian Leiter. London: Oxford University Press.
———. 1990. *The History of Sexuality, Vol. 1.* Trans. Robert Hurley. New York: Vintage Books.
Fury, David. 2002. "Grave." *Buffy the Vampire Slayer.* Season 6, Episode 22. Dir. James A. Contner. Santa Monica, CA: Mutant Enemy. Accessed via Hulu April 21, 2018.
Hardt, Michael, and Antonio Negri. 2000. *Empire.* Cambridge, MA: Harvard University Press.
———. 2009. *Commonwealth.* Cambridge, MA: Harvard University Press.
Lightbody, Brian. 2010. *Philosophical Genealogy Volume II: An Epistemological Reconstruction of Nietzsche and Foucault's Genealogical Method.* New York: Peter Lang.
Maduro, Otto. 2015. *Maps for a Fiesta: A Latina/o Perspective on Knowledge and the Global Crisis.* New York: Fordham University Press.
Malik, Wajeeha. 2016. "Inky's Daring Escape Shows How Smart Octopuses Are." *National Geographic.* April 14. https://news.nationalgeographic.com/2016/04/160414-inky-octopus-escapes-intelligence/.
Nietzsche, Friedrich. 1967. *The Will to Power.* Trans. Walter Kaufman. New York: Vintage Books.
———. 1996. *Human, All Too Human: A Book for Free Sprits.* Trans. R. J. Hollingdale. Cambridge: Cambridge University Press.
Schmidt, Samantha. 2018. "Ingenious Baboons Escape Texas Biomedical Lab for Brief Taste of Freedom." *The Washington Post.* April 17. https://www.washingtonpost.com/news/morning-mix/wp/2018/04/17/ingenious-baboons-escape-texas-biomedical-lab-for-brief-taste-of-freedom/?noredirect=on&utm_term=.21acb588bf96.
Whitehead, Alfred North. 1933. *Adventures of Ideas.* New York: The Free Press.
———. 1938. *Modes of Thought.* New York: The Free Press.
———. 1978. *Process and Reality.* Corrected Edition. Ed. David Ray Griffin and Donald W. Sherburne. New York: The Free Press.

Chapter Nine

Whitehead, Continental Philosophy, and the Bifurcation of Nature

Keith Robinson

Several commentators have recently suggested that continental philosophy represents a unique tradition unified by a set of reflections on time and temporality (Lawlor, McCumber, Reynolds). Of course, the process philosophical tradition, and Whitehead in particular, are said to have "taken time seriously." One key problem that the deep interest in time in both traditions of thought converges around is the problem of the "bifurcation of nature," to use Whitehead's famous phrase. As Whitehead puts it, we must "reject the distinction between nature as it really is and experiences of it. . . . Our experiences of the apparent world are nature itself" (Whitehead 1920). A good deal of continental philosophy can be understood as a critical response to the Cartesian theater of representation in which perception is regarded as an internal representation of an external world: mind as the mirror of nature. In this chapter, insofar as the Cartesian theater or the bifurcation of nature undermine our efforts to conceive and develop an "ecological sensibility," I want to study the conceptions of time through which both traditions aim to overcome the bifurcation of nature.[1]

WHITEHEAD

To turn to Whitehead first, one place to begin is his theories of perception. By tracing out Whitehead's understanding of perception we follow one route through the problem of bifurcation. As is well known Whitehead responds to bifurcation in his later works with his "one genus" theory of "dipolar" actual occasions designed to circumvent or escape the difficulties associated with the various dualisms and materialisms of the tradition. Rather than "panpsychism," which Whitehead never fully subscribed to (at least if we define panpsychism as a generalization of psyche, mind or consciousness), Whiteheads's theory ascribes a "physical pole" to every occasion as well as a more or less recessive "mental pole." Thus experience or perception (and Whitehead will generalize and equate them) is a contrast—an integration and synthesis—of physical inheritance and a more or less conceptual reaction. Conceptual appetition here should not be identified with consciousness. For Whitehead, consciousness presupposes experience. Consciousness is contingent and derivative, an evolutionary later form of integration. Moreover, as a fully fledged "process theory" the Whiteheadian occasion doesn't just passively "have" or "undergo" experience, isn't just a static perceptual experience "of" the real in the manner of a substance qualified by predicates but *is itself* experience, an active experience of passage and becoming between interrelated processes that "influence each other, require each other and lead on to each other" (Whitehead 1938, 157). The world is in the occasion and the occasion is in the world. This is Whitehead's Leibnizian inspired doctrine of "mutual immanence" (Whitehead 1938, 157), the creative "reciprocal insistence" (Whitehead 1982, 14), as he says, between the occasion and the rest of nature.

Whitehead's accounts of perception are amongst his most important philosophical legacies because they challenge the bifurcation of nature and attempt to show the connectedness of occasions. Along with Bergson's "duration" and James' "stream of consciousness," Whitehead's notions of "causal efficacy," "presentational immediacy" and "symbolic reference" offer a direct challenge to the various schools of thought derived from Hume and Kant in which causation is seen as a pale derivation from the "sensationalist" vivid impressions of immediate atomic sense-data presented to consciousness. By focusing only on sense data we end up in what Whitehead, following Santayana, called the "solipsism of the present moment" (Whitehead 1927, 29). In causal efficacy, by contrast, "the presentations of sense fade away and we are left with vague feelings of influences from vague things around us" (Whitehead 1929, 176). These vague influences attest to the repetition of the obscure processes of the past in us out of which emerge the selective crisp immediacies of our present experience. Whitehead ties his account of perception to a conception of temporality. No perception can be absolutely present and immediate but is always divided by an internal time that preserves or "conforms" to the past and opens onto an indeterminate future. All perception is conditioned by a temporal moment which is always ceasing to be, or what Whitehead calls "perpetually perishing." But, in the perishing of the "now" something is preserved in the past that can be altered or destroyed in the future. There is no "simple occurrence" and no "simple location," only the bare or minimal sense in which an occasion always "references" something else. Perception is the power to affect or be affected, an exposure to what happens as the condition not just for language, experience, or even God in Whitehead's sense, but for all becoming and life.

Whitehead begins his account of perception with what he calls the "withness of the body" (Whitehead 1929, 64 and 81). In this mode of perception "we see the contemporary chair, but we see it *with* our eyes, and we touch the contemporary chair but we touch it *with* our hands" (Whitehead 1929, 62). These statements for Whitehead show direct knowledge, or "direct recognition" (7) as he says in *Symbolism*, of the antecedent functioning of the body and the presence of the world in our experience. Direct knowledge or recognition isn't hidden behind the appearances. By attending to what appears or what is given in experience direct knowledge shows itself. For Whitehead the witness of the body here is not simply the recognition of a material object extended in space. The witness of the body shows a *how I am in the world*, a situated and relational mode of being that precedes the various "bifurcations" of actuality and nature that characterizes much of modern philosophy. Rather than a "view from nowhere" we are always engaged in a particular embodied situation and related to other things in a structured whole. For Whitehead we don't simply "have" a body. Rather, our experience is always with our bodies since "the *how* of our present experience must conform to the *what* of the past within us" (Whitehead 1927, 58). In seeing, hearing and touching with our bodies we are already interconnected with perceptual relations that are woven into the body-world. Rather than an atomistic collection of bare sensations or pure impressions connected through "high grade" inferences or mental processes, what we perceive is a perspective on a unified whole.

Whitehead begins his enquiry into the symbolism or significance of experience much like Merleau-Ponty, with the perceptual phenomena of the lived body, a "primacy of perception," that functions as a unifying ground for experience. We are surrounded by our bodies, involved in the world and situated in the here and now. High-grade mentality, as Whitehead puts it, is not required for our lived experience of the world but is, as we will see, dependent upon it. The primary type of symbolism moves from sense perception to bodies and, by beginning with the primacy of perception and the body, Whitehead immediately indicates his intention to problematize those bifurcated models of experience that posit a self-contained subject of experience locked up in the private "inner" space of the mind trying to connect its experience to an external world. Whether empiricism, rationalism or idealism all view the problem of perception as a set of ideas in the mind and the question is how we can know that they accurately "mirror" nature or reflect the world. For Whitehead the most fundamental kind of perception precedes these bifurcations opening onto an "undiscriminated background" (Whitehead 1927, 43) or field that we "conform" to and create with, allowing us to make sense of things. In seeing, hearing or touching I make sense of things against this background without constitution or mediation by the mind. As

Whitehead famously puts it, we don't dance with sensations and then infer a dance partner. In perceptual relations perspectives merge into a unity and acquire their meaning. Whitehead would agree with Heidegger, and contra Kant, that the real scandal isn't the lack of proofs for the external world but that they are attempted over and over again and still expected (Heidegger 1929, 249). The colored shape is not a "projection" on the interior surface of the mind which then needs to be reconnected with a world outside but functions more as an abstraction, effect or objectification of a bodily intentional correlate that conveys or transfers the world into my experiences. As Whitehead puts it, "my process of 'being myself' is my origination from my possession of the world" (Whitehead 1929, 81).

Presentational Immediacy and Causal Efficacy

In the basic description given above of the withness of the body, Whitehead introduces and develops a distinction between "sense-perception"—what he will call "perception in the mode of presentational immediacy"—and "causal efficacy." It is the fusion of these two pure types of perception, the transfer or directedness between them, that Whitehead calls "symbolic reference." If causal efficacy gives us "direct experience" or immediate acquaintance with fact, then symbolic reference gives us a derivative experience that can be trusted if it satisfies certain criteria exemplified in causal efficacy.

Presentational immediacy is a type of perceptual content that give us the familiar presentations of the contemporary world. It is a snapshot of the world immediately before us, "a world decorated by sense data" (Whitehead 1927, 14) that expresses how "contemporary events are relevant to each other, and yet preserve a mutual independence" (Whitehead 1927, 16). Presentational immediacy is particularly attuned to the spatial characteristics and extensive regions of our experience. The "white wall" that I see is not the projection by mind or a filtering through concepts of primitive "sensations" or sense data. We don't clothe a bare datum with a symbol or throw a "meaning" over some naked thing that appears in front of us. Rather, the white wall appears as "given" but only out of an antecedent functioning of the body. What presentational immediacy gives is vividness and precision in terms of immediate spatial location, shape and color, but our experience doesn't give us disembodied color, shape or extensiveness. As Whitehead says "we perceive the *wall's* colour and extensiveness. The experienced fact is 'colour away on the wall for us'" (Whitehead 1927, 15). Thus, presentational immediacy gives abstract elements—the color and the spatial perspective—characterizing the way the white wall enters our experience. What presentational immediacy leaves out, and what causal efficacy provides, is the relation between the percipient and the wall in the immediate past and the immediate future. Presentational immediacy objectifies the contemporary world as bare extension with parts distinguished by colors, sounds, feelings, tastes, smells. It is then a spatial representation of a more or less static present or the "now" of our experience. Presentational immediacy is then a "spatialization" of time, to use Bergson's phrase.

Whitehead likes to say that presentational immediacy is "handy" (Whitehead 1927, 43 and 56) and we might say that it provides data as "present at hand" in Heidegger's sense. Presentational immediacy is present at hand in Heidegger's sense because it offers a derivative and abstract perception of entities in terms of shape, size, color or material composition. Their "handiness" is narrowly defined in terms of a theoretical cognition or scientific "understanding" of objects that makes them manageable and controllable: "all scientific observation, such as measurements, determinations of relative spatial position, determination of sense data such as colours, sounds, tastes, smells, temperature feelings, touch feelings, etc., are made in the perceptive mode of presentational immediacy" (Whitehead 1929, 169). Like Heidegger, Whitehead insists that this understanding and attitude to objects is only possible on the basis of a more primordial comportment that Heidegger calls the "ready to hand." Whitehead's example of the light making me blink wouldn't be out of place as an example of Heidegger's "ready to hand."

In its disclosure of abstract qualities and spatial relations in the present presentational immediacy is clear and distinct yet "comparatively empty." Apart from the knowledge of the contemporary world derived from its participation in a scheme of spatial extension presentational immediacy is more or less "barren" and "superficial" (Whitehead 1927, 44) and displays a world under an "adventitious show," a show of a thousand tints that are "passing and intrinsically meaningless" (Whitehead 1927, 47). In presentational immediacy percepta are distinct, controllable, definite and apt for immediate enjoyment and, although inherently "meaningless" they have profound pragmatic or use value. Indeed, from this perspective Whitehead says that presentational immediacy has "overwhelming significance" (Whitehead 1929, 327). The discovery of the relevance of the mathematical relations disclosed in presentational immediacy was the "first step in the intellectual conquest of nature" (Whitehead 1929, 327). Apart from presentational immediacy science is "a tale told by an idiot and credited by fools" (Whitehead 1929, 327).

Although it has played a key pragmatic role in the development and use of science, one of Whitehead's central claims here is that, whether as sensations or appearance or impressions or perceptual ideas, presentational immediacy is the form of perception or data that, treated on its own, has led modern philosophy astray: "the current accounts of perception are the stronghold of modern metaphysical difficulties" (Whitehead 1929, 117). Philosophers have misconstrued presentational immediacy as our exclusive or primary access to the world and any other mode of perception is regarded as derivative or delusory. We open our eyes and our other senses and survey the contemporary world and then with this information we draw conclusions about the world. Typically this process will be understood as a passive physical seeing followed by an active mental structuring of the physical data. But this gets things the wrong way round. Whitehead cites "the various schools of thought derived from Hume and Kant" as operating "under a misapprehension generated by an inversion of the true constitution of experience. The inversion was explicit in the writing of Hume and Kant: for both of them presentational immediacy was the primary fact of perception, and any apprehension of causation was, somehow or other, to be elicited from this primary fact" (Whitehead 1929, 173).

Whitehead's concept of causal efficacy emerges from his inversion of Hume and Kant. For Hume "(i) Presentational immediacy, and relations between presentationally immediate entities, constitute the only type of perceptive experience, and that (ii) presentational immediacy includes no demonstrative factors disclosing a contemporary world of extended things" (Whitehead 1927, 34). On this basis, only the private immediate attributes are disclosed and so, as a consequence, space, time, memory and identity cannot be grounded in a real world: "there remains only what Santayana calls 'Solipsism of the Present Moment'" (Whitehead 1927, 33). Mere sense perception in presentational immediacy doesn't account for the whole of our experience because it "gives no information as to the past and the future" (Whitehead 1929, 168). Beyond the simple present our experience includes temporal and spatial extension expressing the mutual immanence of all actualities. Perception in the mode of causal efficacy is particularly characteristic of temporal extension. As Whitehead puts it: "causal efficacy is the hand of the settled past in the formation of the present" (Whitehead 1927, 50). The present "conforms" to the past, or later events confirm the presence in them of earlier events, and this conformation of the present to the immediate past is experienced reality. Although Kant accepts that causal efficacy is a fact of the phenomenal world, it is not presupposed in the data of perception. Rather, "it belongs to our ways of thought about the data" (Whtehead 1927, 37). For Whitehead, Kant's claims here presuppose Hume's "simple occurrence" or momentary events which are based on "the extraordinarily naïve assumption of time as pure succession" (Whitehead 1927, 34). Pure succession is the notion of time as indivisible moments or units that succeed each other but without any relation to each other. Whitehead compares pure succession to color in that there is no "mere color" as such but always some particular color. Similarly, there is no pure succession but always some "particular relational ground" (Whitehead 1927, 35) in terms of which succession proceeds. Pure succession, for Whitehead, is an abstraction from the fundamental reality of conformation (Whitehead 1927, 38). Conformation divides the present and is at work in every moment from the beginning through causality. Causality is perceivable in the relation of conformation between present and past occasions and perhaps most prominent when the organism is "low-grade." As Whitehead puts it, "time in the concrete is the conformation of state to state, the later to the earlier; and the pure succession is an abstraction from the irreversible relationship of settled past to derivative present" (Whitehead 1927, 35). Underneath the adventitious show of presentational immediacy lies the more primitive causal efficacy of our bodily organs and the vague world beyond them. In causal efficacy all organisms are conditioned by the environment, whereas sense-perception is enjoyed by mainly "advanced organisms."

Symbolic Reference and Originary Symbolism

Presentational immediacy and causal efficacy are "pure" modes of perception, but experience synthesizes and combines them in the complex mode of symbolic reference. They both, in their differing modes, "objectify" things in the environment directly but their complete purity is unobtainable. Independently they are abstractions. As Whitehead says, "perception in the mode of causal efficacy discloses that the data in the mode of sense perception are provided by it" (Whitehead 1927, 53). Thus, in practice the two modes of perception are fused and interrelated through what Whitehead calls a "common ground" enabling symbolic reference to take place. For Whitehead the common ground that enables the "intersection" between the two modes of perception are "sense data" and "locality" (Whitehead 1927, 49). Sense data play a double role: on the one hand they exhibit the spatial relations in the present and on the other they show the immediate past of our body organs pressing in on the experience. If we see red, we see with our eyes and the experience also refers to, or is localized in, an "external space," say the red of a traffic light. The localization is clearly demarcated when reference from presentational immediacy is involved, but, beyond the bodily organs, reference to causal efficacy shades off into the vague and indefinite. Thus the common ground of the two modes of perception is a spatio-temporal system in which the past conditions the present and acts as a symbol for the near future.

Stripped back to its essentials, symbolism is a mode of experience that functions by being directed toward or related to another component or element in the experience. Whitehead sometimes talks about this as the "vector character" involved in the experience. In other words, the causal influences within the symbolizing process have a direction which is marked or felt more or less directly by the other elements. As Whitehead puts it, this time in relation to "feelings": "feelings are 'vectors'; for they feel what is *there* and transform it into what is *here*" (Whitehead 1929, 87). At the base of experience we find a symbolizing process that requires that a component refer to or be directed toward or feel another component for it to be itself or for it to convey "meaning." As Whitehead puts it, "considered by themselves the symbol and its meaning do not require *either* that there shall be a symbolic reference between the two, *or* that the symbolic reference between the members of the couple should be one way on rather than that other way on" (Whitehead 1927, 9–10, italics in text). In classical phenomenology concepts of intentionality function in terms of a directionality that is one-way and unidirectional, a directionality without turns or reciprocity that runs between the knower and the known. For Whitehead the symbolizing process is a relation where either term in the relation can play one of the roles, but the directionality remains. In relation to language Whitehead gives the example of the word "tree" and the tree itself and asks why the word "tree" is a symbol for trees. The tree itself could just as well function as a symbol for the word. Abstracting from human experience symbolism does not require consciousness, subjectivity or agency as such, only that one entity invoke, respond to or be "present in" another although the relation and the components will vary greatly. Each component enters into the experience as "equals" with no one component taking precedence over the others. Nothing is simply present or absent since each element presupposes syntheses or referrals which prevent any one element simply referring to itself.

This notion that an individual element is present in all of the others for it to have value and meaning I suggest is the temporal challenge to the present at the heart of Whitehead's metaphysics. No occasion is ever fully present to itself but refers to the spacing by means of which the elements are related to each other. No "thing" can be meaningful in and of itself but must be inscribed within a chain of referrals that bears the marks of all these others within itself. All that perception in Whitehead's sense requires is that there is something to be received, a transmission, passage or transference of the recepta and an act of reception or inheritance. However, although the radical implications of this chain of references and referrals provides the rationale for the "epochal" structure of temporal occasions that comes to the fore in *Process and Reality,* those implications will also, I suggest, provide a challenge to that rationale when viewed through the lens of some continental philosophers.

The structure of perception in Whitehead can be traced to the condition of time since the general function of perception is to mediate between past and future. For one element to "aim" at another it must conform to the immediate past and anticipate the immediate future. Perception necessarily occupies a duration in which the present is immediately divided by conforming with a past that is preserved in the present and a future that is anticipated, invoked or elicited. Whitehead is very close to William James' famous descriptions of a "specious present," albeit generalized beyond the stream of consciousness, to indicate that experience never captures the individual present moments of a "now" but only a present that stretches back into the past and forward into the future. The present is "specious" in that it is never immediately available in an instantaneous now-moment, "knife-edge" or atomic sensation as such but only in a block or epoch that stretches through a continuity of immediate past and future moments. However, like James the "block" or durational act itself for Whitehead is not a continuity; only the moments in the duration are felt continuously. Whitehead not only adopts the phrase "specious present" and the idea that individual units of experience come in epochs, but he also accepts James' view that, although the percipient event is temporally extended, the act of perceiving is itself a unity that is unextended and indivisible. In other words, the "content" of the units of experience or objects of symbolic reference undergo temporal extension but the "form" remains unextended. As we've seen for Whitehead perception combines a spatializing moment which retains the immediate past and anticipates the immediate future, but as a formal whole the experience is given as a unifying epoch or indivisible "living presence" that doesn't have temporal extension. This is Whitehead's (and James') response to Zeno. As Whitehead puts it, "If we admit that 'something becomes,' it is easy, by employing Zeno's method, to prove that there can be no continuity of becoming. There is becoming of continuity but no continuity of becoming" (Whitehead 1929, 35). Perceptual units or actual occasions become and they constitute together an extensive world in which only extensiveness becomes, "but 'becoming' is not extensive" (Whitehead 1929, 35). Becoming occurs within the occasion, but the formal act of the becoming in the occasion occurs all at once so that reality grows for Whitehead, just as it does for James, by "buds or drops of perception" (Whitehead 1929, 68; James 1911, 155). You can divide the experience analytically upon reflection but as it is immediately given it's all or nothing. Thus Whitehead writes, "the conclusion is that in every act of becoming there is the becoming of something with temporal extension; but that the act itself is not extensive in the sense that it is divisible into earlier and later acts of becoming which correspond to the extensive divisibility of what has become" (Whitehead 1929, 69). Whitehead distinguishes the "form" of becoming, the structure of the act of experience, from the content in which something becomes in order to shore up the infinite regress that Zeno's paradox threatens. The epochal structure of occasions is supposed to put an end to temporal regression by being constitutive of itself and providing a unity and synthesis to the becoming that mediates reference. The act of becoming, as a non-temporal unity, thereby ensures that the chain of references doesn't continue without origin or end. It is this move, in my view, that will be challenged by various continental philosophers.

CONTINENTAL PHILOSOPHY

There is now a large body of work (monographs, journal articles, textbooks and anthologies) on "continental" philosophy. In textbooks and anthologies (e.g., West, Daniel, etc.) much of this work accepts the term more or less without question and lays out surveys of the supposed key thinkers, themes and developments of the tradition. In work that treats the term as the subject of philosophical inquiry two basic positions are laid out. Either continental is regarded as essentially distinct from its "other": analytic philosophy; or, the distinction (between continental and analytic) is regarded as one without much of a difference and what distinguishes philosophers is their "style," or socio-political and historical factors. William Blattner's view represents a good example of the latter (Simon Glendinning is a qualified example of the latter) and Simon Critchley an example of the former (I say Glendinning is a "qualified" example of the latter because he seems to think that analytic philosophy really does have a unity that continental lacks).

I want to pursue another position. Contra the deflationary "differences of style" account, continental philosophy, at least certain twentieth-century strands of it, does provide unifying features that mark out a tradition, but this is not based on identifying any essentialist criteria or set of necessary and sufficient conditions but rather on overlapping patterns of resemblances in methodology rooted in a shared commitment to the importance of temporality. John McCumber in his book *Time and Philosophy* argues that continental philosophy begins with the idea that "everything has come to be from something else and will pass away into something else" (7). In contrast to what he calls "traditional" philosophy defined by an appeal to the eternal or the atemporal, continental philosophers according to McCumber accept that "everything philosophy can talk about at all is in time" (7). Interestingly, McCumber refers to Heraclitus as the "ancient ancestor of continental philosophy." On McCumber's description continental philosophy begins to look remarkably similar to process philosophy or at least entangled with it. Or, if we say that continental philosophy begins with Kant, as McCumber does, then we could say that continental philosophy is a modern variant of process philosophy in its reaction to Kant.

Let's try to be a bit more precise about temporality and narrow our scope to twentieth-century continental philosophy. Len Lawlor uses several formulas in his book *Early Twentieth Century Continental Philosophy* to describe continental philosophy. He says "the second formula, in order to define continental philosophy, concerns the experience of time. Continental philosophy wants a renewal of thinking because all thinking so far has been thought on the basis of the present, or it is a thinking that is non-temporal, like an eternal present" (Lawlor 2012, 5). So, continental philosophy in the twentieth century distinguishes itself by questioning the concept of the "present" or the "now" as a self-identical or indivisible moment of time. This is the well-known "metaphysics of presence" that Heidegger and Derrida have pointed to as characterizing the Western metaphysical tradition of thinking or what process philosophers will call the "substance" tradition.

Jack Reynolds has, in several books and articles, defended the idea that contemporary philosophy is suffering from various "chronopathologies"—literally sicknesses of time—whether it be a preoccupation with the present or the eternal. On this view continental philosophy is a diagnosis of and resistance to the present. In other words what unifies those twentieth-century philosophers in the tradition that we call "continental philosophy" is a suspicion over common sense understandings of the "now," a critical detachment or distancing from everyday "intuitions" about the nature of the present. This critical questioning of the present is one way in which Whitehead and twentieth-century continental philosophy are brought into close proximity. In the next section I want to home in on a specific "representative" of continental philosophy, Gilles Deleuze, in order to focus on this proximity with Whitehead and the temporal and, as we'll see, the differences between them.

Deleuze

The critique of the present and the generalization of an originary temporal structure is taken up and developed in great detail and complexity in the work of the French philosopher Gilles Deleuze. Contrasting Whitehead's account of becoming with Deleuze will enable us to draw out some of the radical innovations and variations of the process/continental view with regard to time and becoming and the implications these have for thinking beyond bifurcation.

For Deleuze we can think becoming as the synthesis of time (what he calls "disjunctive synthesis") without positing a non-temporal act of atomic unity. The now of immediacy is divided between its own becoming past, which is simultaneously pointing toward a future. Immediacy is a primal perception or "reference" that enables repetition across time and perception to take place. Like Whitehead, Deleuze describes experience as conditioned by time, but it is a time that "ungrounds" all temporal unities in a generalized "opening" of experience to difference and becoming. One can see this ungrounding in Deleuze's account of the structures of time in his *Difference and Repetition*. Here Deleuze lays out three syntheses of time and gives an account of how they perform this work. What I suggest here is that the conception of time that underpins Whitehead's notion of becoming is consistent with Deleuze's description of time given in the first synthesis but doesn't include anything like the second and third syntheses since these syntheses cannot be recognized within the successive "state to state" movements of Whitehead's epochal structure of time. Deleuze offers an account of time and becoming that is prior to and makes possible the modes of perception that Whitehead describes.

Each synthesis in Deleuze's account involves processes that function as a perspective from which to view the operations of the other syntheses. Although the syntheses each correspond to the modalities of time (past, present, future), no temporal process is independent of the other. There is no present that doesn't gather an element of the past and the future, no past in general that doesn't allow the present to pass and no future that doesn't open the present and the past to new events. Each synthesis is determined by a primary modality that directs the processes involved but each modality operates "intratemporally," as Deleuze says, such that the syntheses work through each other and upon each other in a moving complex structure of interactions.

In the first synthesis, what Deleuze calls the "living present," experience is inscribed through a process of "contraction." This is close in some respects to phenomenological accounts of the "living present," but, more importantly for us, it is close to Whitehead's epochal becoming and James' specious present. Contraction is a "passive" synthesis whereby the succession of instants are drawn into each other. In contraction instants or particular elements are pulled into one unified experience. The succession of instants do not in themselves constitute time but indicate "only its constantly aborted moment of birth" (Deleuze 1994, 70). This notion is close to Whitehead's own notion of time as a "perpetual perishing" of the present where "pure succession" is an abstraction from a relational ground "in respect to which the terms succeed each other" through conformation (Whitehead 1927, 35). There are two key points of comparison here that bring Deleuze's account of the first synthesis of time close to Whitehead. Firstly, contraction is passive. In other words, this operation takes place beneath the "active" functions of the intellect and points to temporal levels and layers of bodily experience that are constitutive. As Deleuze says, it is not a synthesis carried out *by* the mind, but *in* the mind (Deleuze 1994, 71). Secondly, the succession of instants are never self-identically present and indivisible amongst themselves. Rather, each living present is already divided into a past and a future so that the "now" as a "knife-edge" moment (to use William James' phrase) is aborted into the extended contraction of the living present. The instants that are contracted can have a greater or smaller duration depending on the individual, the organism and species. Again, we could talk about this point in relation to Whitehead or William James. In relation to the latter the point would be that the "fringe" or "halo" of the experiences is more or less extended even across the experiences of one individual and this extension is determined by the intensity of the contraction, the number, connection and resonance of the instants contracted and "the natural contractile range of the contemplative souls involved" (Deleuze 1994, 76). The contraction of the living present includes the past by retaining preceding instants and anticipates the future through an expectation of instants that are to come. Deleuze generalizes this structure to all living things as a condition for any living organism to have experience (at points Deleuze appears to go beyond what we usually consider "living" and asks whether it is "irony" to say that "everything is contemplation"). Within the living present Deleuze stresses that the "moments" of the past and the future are not separate and distinct but part of the contraction of the living present. Past and future are "dimensions," as Deleuze, says, of the living present. As Deleuze points out, the passive synthesis does not need to go "outside itself in order to pass from past to future" (Deleuze 1994, 71). The synthesis doesn't need to go "outside itself" to pass because it constitutes the dimensions of the past and the future in the contraction. In other words the living present is already "outside itself." The first synthesis is a primary or "originary" dimension of experience for Deleuze and it is originary because the subject of the synthesis affects itself and relates to itself as an other by incorporating the dimensions of past and future. In the first synthesis time is "asymmetrical" meaning that the spatial arrangement and placing of the dimensions (of past and future) is strictly directional, moving from past to future. This is the famous "arrow of time," vector, or succession of phases from earlier to later that, as we've seen, Whitehead insists on in the movement of perception and in his epochs of becoming.

This whole structure of the living present constitutes an originary time without itself being coextensive with the whole of time. The living present is "intratemporal" and therefore undergoes passage. This constitutes the paradox of the present: the present constitutes time even as it passes within the time constituted. What is it that enables the living present to pass? Here Deleuze moves to a second passive synthesis, this time deeper than the first. Habit, or the first synthesis, is grounded in memory. Not the memory of retention, an active memory that is dependent upon habit, but a deeper memory that constitutes the being of the past. This is not a past that has been present. Indeed, Deleuze suggests that it is "futile" to try to reconstitute the past from the present. The past is trapped between two presents: the present that it once was and the present that it is now the past of. In other words Deleuze says we cannot access or get to the past by thinking it in relation to any kind of present. Deleuze says he is "unable to believe that the past is constituted after it has been present" (Deleuze 1994, 81). This is a key point in the undoing of the "ordinary" conception of the present or what Whitehead calls "pure succession." The moment isn't first present and then passes. Rather, the passage of time is underway from the "beginning" so that the present is already in a state of passage having never been present in itself.

So, the present passes and its passage is conditional upon a past that enables the present to become past. However, the past cannot be a past formed from the present. Nor can a past be formed when a new present appears. If a new present were required for the past to be formed, the former present would never pass. There is, Deleuze argues, a second time in which the first synthesis can occur and receive a ground. The living present requires a second paradoxical dimension for it to pass, but it is a past that has never been present. Memory synthesizes a "pure past" that is contemporaneous with itself. Such a past or time as pure memory is not conceivable in Whitehead's metaphysics of time since becoming is governed by rules of seriality and succession where the present conforms to a past that was the living present. In addition, Whitehead tends to treat the immediate past as a "degree" of the present and not really a past at all (and much the same can be said of the future as a degree of the present). The relationship of settled past to derivative present is, Whitehead says, "irreversible" (Whitehead 1927, 35). For Whitehead the living or extended present perishes perpetually, and the process by which it becomes passes and is taken up into new occasions is coextensive with time. For Deleuze the living present is not coextensive with time but presupposes a pure past, an *a priori* past in general, for it to pass. But the pure past doesn't itself pass.

The coexistence of the living present of habit and pure past of memory are complemented by the third synthesis, which marks a radical departure still from what we might call Whitehead's "rationalization" of becoming. The third synthesis or the "empty form of time" functions as the structure of the continuity of becoming or the differentiator for the expression of the other syntheses (present and past). The empty form of time is the originary "caesura," as Deleuze calls it, a break or interruption that divides every moment even as it subsumes the syntheses of present and past. As Deleuze says "it must be called a symbol by virtue of the unequal parts which it subsumes and draws together, but draws together as unequal parts. . . . This symbolic image constitutes the totality of time to the extent that it draws together the caesura and the before and the after" (Deleuze 1994, 89). In other words, we can think of the third synthesis as integrating the past into the present in order to relate to the future, but this way of explicating the empty form of time—as an image concerning the totality of time—is still only "introductory" (Deleuze 1994, 90) Deleuze tell us. The third synthesis properly concerns the *eternal return*, which is the key concept that organizes the entire structure of Deleuze's *Difference and Repetition* and functions as the thought of the future which subordinates the other stages and leaves them behind. Rather than merely "drawing off" a difference as in the mode of habit in the living present or making difference a variant of a memorial pure past, the eternal return, as repetition of the future, is the "production of the absolutely different, making it so that repetition is, for itself, difference in itself" (Deleuze 1994, 94). Deleuze gives us an image of time without origin or end where difference in itself repeats and differentiates itself: "the eternal return has no other sense but this: the absence of any assignable origin, in other words the assignation of difference as the origin which then relates different to different" (Deleuze 1994, 125). The only "in-itself" is difference or pure becoming that functions to unground the other modalities of time summarized as succession and coexistence. The living present and memory of the pure past are conditioned by a deeper order which is not extensive but "intensive, purely intensive. In other words it is said of difference" (Deleuze 1994, 243).

BETWEEN DELEUZE AND WHITEHEAD — ON BECOMING AND TIME

Both Deleuze and Whitehead develop their views of time and becoming in relation to the broader problems that their work seeks to engage. For both, the problem of dualism understood as the bifurcation of nature or transcendence is one of the motivating problems of their work, and both find in the empiricist and rationalist traditions resources for their own ontological accounts of perception. For both Deleuze and Whitehead perception puts us directly in contact with the real; indeed perception *is* the real. Whitehead and Deleuze share a commitment to what we can call events of perception in which experience directly conditions, prehends or communicates with the thing itself. This more fundamental form of perception is a dynamic and constitutive relation between "prehensions," a temporal and affective relation of occasions, differences, becomings or "images" where one flow or series intersects with another, affects it and/or is affected by it. To reach this idea of a primary process or "pure perception" Whitehead generalizes from a human subjective point of view yet reaches beyond any individual consciousness. As we have seen, however, in Whitehead's metaphysical works the subject-object structure of this process is increasingly atomized, perhaps most especially in *Process and Reality*, at the expense of the "continuity of becoming." Deleuze, in contrast, appeals to the continuity of a non-human "pure perception," an "originary nowhere" or virtual plenitude and sees an atomized or individual "point of view," however extended, as a limitation of the virtual field of differences, a canalization of the becomings that traverse the non-organic flow of life.

The accounts of perception and experience in Whitehead and Deleuze are conditioned by their understanding of time and becoming. Whitehead insists in several texts, especially *Process and Reality*, that time is atomized and epochal. Like James, for Whitehead reality grows in drops and buds and so time cannot be thought as a continuity. As Whitehead says, "temporalization is not another continuous process. It is an atomic succession. Thus time is atomic (i.e, epochal), though what is temporalized is divisible" (Whitehead 1925, 126). Whitehead arrives at this position as a result of an analysis of

Zeno. If we analyze the act of becoming with the premises that something becomes, and that every act of becoming is divisible into earlier acts of becoming, then we end up in the contradiction of an infinite regress where nothing becomes. To use Whitehead's example, if we take an act of becoming during one second we can divide that act into two, namely, the act of becoming in the first half of the second and the act of becoming in the second half of the second. Operating with the above premises "that which becomes during the whole second presupposes that which becomes during the first half second. Analogously, that which becomes during the first half second presupposes that which becomes during the first quarter second, and so on indefinitely" (Whitehead 1929, 68). If we consider the process of becoming up to the beginning of the second in question and ask what becomes, Whitehead concludes that "no answer can be given" (Whitehead 1929, 68). Infinite regress leads to a contradiction in the notion of becoming because if the act of becoming is itself temporally divisible it cannot act as a synthetic unity for something to become but must itself be subject to further acts of becoming. Fundamentally, no symbolizing or perceptual process can be self-constituting if it is subject to the temporalization of pure becoming. Indeed, "these conclusions are required by the consideration of Zeno's arguments" (Whitehead 1929, 68).

For Whitehead contradiction and temporal becoming are incompatible. A contradiction already contains its other within itself and so it could, for example, never cease to be or not be. And yet becoming on this view is a never ceasing to be or something that cannot not be. For Whitehead the claim that the regress of becoming would make it impossible to think the nature of experience appears as a presupposition of his mature thought. What is distinctive of some of the thinkers within the continental tradition, particularly Deleuze and Derrida, is the idea that not only does life or experience not need a primal ground or non-temporal unity to perform the requisite synthesis but is constituted by a *pure* or *absolute becoming* that functions as a condition for the movement of temporalization. Infinite regress or "becoming unlimited" is the originary movement of time in Deleuze, a movement that ungrounds any origin or end. For Deleuze, out of the paradoxes of pure becoming emerges a conception of time consistent with infinite regress and indefinite divisibility.

CONCLUSION: WHITEHEAD, DELEUZE, AND THE PROCESS TRADITION

For Whitehead a symbolizing relation or actual occasion gives perceptual content unity and shows how a stretch of time holds that content together in experience. In other words, the specious present is made possible by a non-extended or momentary unit of becoming that explains an act of experience. Only if there is an actual occasion that holds it together can there be a sensed or perceptual content in time. As we've seen, if the act of becoming itself, not just the content, were temporally extended then nothing is held together or becomes, and a "rational" explanation of experience becomes impossible. For Whitehead symbolic reference is a solution to the problem of perception and the actual occasion is a speculative solution to the problem of temporal experience. Together they show how Whitehead approaches the solution to the problem of bifurcation.

The challenge of Deleuze's process thinking emerges out of a problematization of this solution. For Deleuze the living present (or the specious present) points to a problem that needs to be explained, a problem that in one way or another informs his work from beginning to end: how is "sense" made in experience? How is symbolization possible? If Whitehead's explanation "rationalizes" the problem by positing a non-temporal act (a form of transcendence for Deleuze), Deleuze wants to think the problem in terms of immanence and that means the thought of time as absolute becoming. In *Difference and Repetition* Deleuze pursues an answer in terms of syntheses of time, syntheses that are "intratemporal" and require explanation through each other. For example, the syntheses of the living present themselves need to be explained by and grounded in a synthesis of memory, a past that has never been present, which in turn is dependent upon a future that will never be present, the repetition of the empty form of time as difference. Deleuze embraces these structures of time because they are required by the thought of pure becoming or difference in itself, where every moment is already divided by a "caesura" or a "splitting" such that each moment can be no longer or not yet.

In their philosophical systems both Whitehead and Deleuze are responding to the Heraclitean "all things flow," that "ultimate generalization around which we must weave our philosophical system" (Whitehead 1929, 208). But each gives a different interpretation of *Panta Rhei*. For Whitehead the flux is temporally extensive but, adhering to the logic of some of Zeno's paradoxes, it cannot be absolute because nothing would become. The form or *logos* of the flux corresponds to a non-temporal act such that "the creature is extensive but that its act of becoming is not extensive" (Whitehead 1929, 69). In contrast Deleuze's interpretation distinguishes him within the modern process and continental traditions as the most recent proponent of flux understood as the affirmation of absolute becoming. As Deleuze remarks "we have to reflect for a long time to understand what it means to make an affirmation of becoming" (Deleuze 1983, 23). Deleuze says that Heraclitus affirms becoming and in two senses. Firstly, Heraclitus affirms that there is no being, only becoming. This is what Deleuze calls Heraclitus' "working thought" (Deleuze 1983, 23). This working thought is consistent with the more conventional understanding of Heraclitean becoming as the idea that both spatio-temporal location and qualities/predicates are subject to change and are perhaps always changing. The working thought is consistent with the idea that "things" are flows or processes, but flows or processes that are identifiable flows or processes. Secondly, Deleuze claims that Heraclitus affirms the idea that there is a being of becoming, that being is the being of becoming. In what he calls Heraclitus' "contemplative thought" (Deleuze 1983, 23) Deleuze argues that Heraclitus affirms that the being of becoming is return: "return is the being of that which becomes" (Deleuze 1983, 24). This "contemplative" or speculative thought is Deleuze's notion of absolute becoming where, as we saw earlier with the third synthesis of time, what returns is precisely the difference that doesn't allow a becoming to be identified. This is the only "being" that absolute becoming can have. As we've seen, in several of his books Deleuze gives the notion of absolute becoming the Nietzschean name "eternal return": "the eternal return is predicated only of becoming and the multiple. It is the law of a world without being, without unity, without identity. Far from *presupposing* the One and the Same, the eternal return constitutes the only unity of the multiple as such, the only identity of what differs: coming back is the only 'being' of becoming. Consequently, the function of the eternal return as Being is never to identify but to authenticate" (Deleuze 2004, 124). What is authenticated is the "superior" ever-changing form of what "is," the transformation of recognized and identifiable values by the flux of absolute becoming. Thus, the eternal return is Deleuze's Nietzschean and Heraclitean inspired "solution" to the problem of "transcendence," a solution which is never fixed or finalized. It presages a different relation to time, an ongoing, contingent disposition. Eternal return is the name that Deleuze gives to the movement of temporalization, the infinite return of the now as an originary splitting that in becoming past and, at the same time, being projected into a future becoming eliminates the need for a non-temporal synthesis.

Both Whitehead and Deleuze offer a challenge to substantive conceptions of the present but in different ways. For both thinkers an originary synthesis of time that displaces the present is the condition for anything to happen and, for both, by challenging the conceptions of time rooted in the present, we free our thinking from the bifurcation of nature and open up new modes of inhabiting time that presage an "ecological sensibility."

NOTE

1. Whitehead's relation to philosophy in general, and continental philosophy in particular, has once again become a topic of discussion as part of the ongoing reflection on Whitehead's unsettled place within twentieth- and now twenty-first-century philosophy. In part spurred on by Deleuze's interest, Whitehead's so-called migration to continental is now receiving attention. Of course the very idea of "continental philosophy" is itself question begging and proble-

matic. In this chapter I want to argue that one of the most widely recognized and significant aspects of Whitehead's work—its effort to "take time seriously"—brings it into close connection with what I take to be one of the distinguishing features of continental philosophy: its emphasis upon time and temporality. I want to argue that this shared interest in time provides a lens to evaluate how each tradition responds to the central problem of the bifurcation of nature, a problem that hinders the development of an ecological sensibility. Perhaps the key concept propping up the bifurcation of nature is a humanist or anthropocentric conception of temporality grounded in a conception of the "present," what continental philosophers have called a "metaphysics of presence." Whitehead and certain thinkers from the continental tradition, particularly Deleuze, attempt to give us concepts of time that are non-anthropocentric or go "beyond the human condition." Such conceptions of time, I argue, offer a critical challenge to the present and, in doing so, attempt to free our thinking from the bifurcation of nature and open up new modes of inhabiting time. Although I can't develop this argument here freeing up our modes of inhabiting time is important because I want to suggest that environmental degradation and the worst violence are derivative from a certain *ressentiment* to the present. Nietzsche talks about this in terms of a hatred for the idea of becoming. As he puts it, for those philosophers of the eternal "what is does not become," must not become. For Nietzsche this hatred for the passing of the present is a "revenge" against time's "it was." David Wood describes this ressentiment as a kind of "ground logic" for violence, a basis for violence against the other, an "ontological violence" that emerged out of an enlightenment that took on a "hysterical" form when characterized by this rage against time (Wood 2005, 33).

REFERENCES

Deleuze, Gilles. 1983. *Nietzsche*. New York: Columbia University Press.
———. 1988a. *Bergsonism*. New York: Zone Books.
———. 1988b. *Foucault*. London: Athlone Press.
———. 1989. *Cinema 2: The Time Image*. London: Athlone Books.
———. 1990. *Logic of Sense*. New York: Columbia University Press.
———. 1991. "A Philosophical Concept . . ." In *Who Comes After the Subject?* Ed. E. Cadava, P. Connor, and J. L. Nancy. New York: Routledge.
———. 1993. *The Fold: Leibniz and the Baroque*. London: Athlone Press.
———. 1994. *Difference and Repetition*. London: Athlone Press.
———. 2004. *Desert Islands and Other Texts 1953–1974*. New York: Semiotext(e).
Deleuze, Gilles, and Felix Guattari. 1984. *Anti-Oedipus*. London: Athlone Press.
———. 1988. *A Thousand Plateaus*. London: Athlone Press.
———. 1994. *What Is Philosophy?* London: Verso.
Heidegger, Martin. 1929/1962. *Being and Time*. Oxford: Basil Blackwell.
James, William. 1911/1996. *Some Problems of Philosophy*. Omaha: University of Nebraska Press.
Lawlor, Len. 2012. *Early Twentieth Century Continental Philosophy*. Bloomington: Indiana University Press.
McCumber, John. 2011. *Time and Philosophy: A History of Continental Thought*. Durham, UK: Acumen Publishing.
Meillassoux, Quentin. 2008. *After Finitude: An Essay on the Necessity of Contingency*. London: Continuum.
Reynolds, Jack. 2011. *Chronopathologies: Time and Politics in Deleuze, Derrida, Analytic Philosophy and Phenomenology*. Lanham, MD: Lexington Books.
Whitehead, Alfred North. 1920. *The Concept of Nature*. Cambridge: Cambridge University Press.
———. 1925. *Science and the Modern World*. New York: The Free Press.
———. 1927. *Symbolism: Its Meaning and Effect*. New York: Capricorn Books.
———. 1929. *Process and Reality*. New York: The Free Press.
———. 1933. *Adventures of Ideas*. New York: The Free Press
———. 1938. *Modes of Thought*. New York: The Free Press.

———. 1947. *Essays in Science and Philosophy*. New York: Philosophical Library.
———. 1982. *An Enquiry Concerning the Principles of Natural Knowledge*. New York: Dover Publications.
Wood, David. 2005. *The Step Back: Ethics and Politics after Deconstruction*. Albany: State University of New York Press.

Index

abstraction, 6, 100, 112, 124–127, 129, 130, 133, 162, 164–165, 170; critique of, 122–123, 125, 131, 132; and philosophy, 122, 125; and universals, 128
activism, 41, 42, 51, 54, 55n5, 83
actual entity, 6, 39, 68, 70–71, 88, 89, 100, 104, 123, 139, 142–145, 148, 151, 156n1, 157n10
actual occasion, 2, 3, 5, 17, 29, 55n3–55n4, 68, 69–70, 72, 74, 88, 100, 101, 115n3, 115n12, 116n27, 121, 123–125, 126, 127, 159, 166, 174. *See also* actual entity
actuality, 14, 16, 100, 102, 104, 121, 161
Adbusters, 51
Adorno, Theodor, 133
adventure, 4, 64, 127
adversion, 115n12
adversity, 12, 13, 14, 18
aesthetic, 4, 17, 27–28, 52, 109–110, 132
aesthetic naturalism, 5, 22
agency, 5, 6, 47, 49, 54, 56n14, 64, 78–79, 82, 114, 144, 144–145, 148, 151, 154, 166
agriculture, 18, 55n5
Allan, George, 51–52
alternative facts, 11
alternatives, 3, 41, 61, 63, 121, 122, 123, 131, 132–133
ancien régime syndrome, 48

animals, 55n11, 85, 93, 94, 96n12, 99, 105–106, 107–111, 114, 115n9, 116n18, 138, 150; and subjectivity, 92, 106, 109, 114; and sustainability, 19, 20; and value, 78
anthropocentrism, 5–6, 12, 28, 52–53, 61–62, 73, 90, 91, 92, 105–106, 114, 154, 176n1
apocalyptic, 137, 138, 152–153
appearance, 64, 67, 85, 105, 116n20, 123, 127
Apple, 30, 38, 63
art, 17, 23n15, 51, 64, 75
Athanasiou, Athena, 82, 83, 84
atomism, 47, 55n11, 101, 160–161, 166, 169, 173
aversion, 115n12

Barbour, Ian, 55n10
beauty, 3, 21, 64, 70, 74–75, 89–90, 91, 94
becoming, 3, 4, 5–6, 61, 63, 64, 65–67, 68–71, 88, 92, 93, 94, 100–101, 114, 138–139, 139–140, 141, 142, 143, 145, 146, 147, 149, 150, 151, 160, 166, 169, 170, 171–176, 176n1; animal, 93, 96n12; imperceptible, 5, 61, 71–75; minoritarian, 122–123, 130, 132, 134n7
Begriff, 112
being, 13–16, 20, 21, 22, 53, 65, 85–86, 88, 89, 132–133, 140–141, 145–146, 147, 156n5, 161, 162, 171, 175–176

Index

Bergson, Henri, 21, 24n31, 160, 163
Bestand, 14, 18–19, 19, 19–20, 21
bifurcation, 5, 6, 29, 127, 159, 160, 173, 176, 176n1. *See also* nature, bifurcation of
biology, 38, 107, 110, 113, 114
biopower, 148, 156n6
bios, 72, 156n6
biosemiotics, 109, 111
Blattner, William, 168
bodies, 15, 16, 19, 20, 27, 29, 30, 32, 37, 39, 51, 62, 69, 109, 141, 142, 151, 156n6, 161; organs of the, 30, 34, 38, 106, 109, 110, 164, 165
boundary, 4, 16, 85
Braidotti, Rosi, 5, 61, 62–64, 65–67, 68–69, 70–71, 71, 72–74, 74–75, 75n2, 78, 84, 85, 87, 90, 91–93, 93, 94, 96n9, 96n11
Brentari, Carlo, 109, 110
Buchanan, Brett, 105
Buffy the Vampire Slayer, 137
Butler, Judith, 5, 75n1, 78, 82–84, 84, 85–86, 86–87, 87, 90–91, 93, 94, 96n10–96n11, 138

California, 43, 52
Canguilhelm, Georges, 34–35
capitalism, 33, 38, 39, 55n8, 61, 62, 66, 67, 132, 155; advanced, 5, 62, 64, 67, 68, 74, 91, 93; and schizophrenia, 62, 63, 65, 67, 74–75
Cartesian, 12, 14, 15, 20, 23n16, 146, 159
causal efficacy, 5, 27, 29, 30, 32–33, 160, 162, 164, 165
causality, 30, 164
Center for Civilians in Conflict, 82
chaos, 56n17, 104, 112, 128, 146, 148
citizens, 11, 55n5, 78, 80, 81, 82, 85, 87, 91, 92, 94–95, 141, 156n6
civilization, 4, 41, 41–42, 61, 64, 67, 70, 127; ecological, 11, 12, 14, 18, 20, 21; sustainable, 4, 6, 61, 64, 67, 72, 73, 75
climate change, 1, 11, 12, 13–14, 43, 45, 52, 55n5, 61
color, 30, 100, 103, 104, 106, 161, 162–163, 164
communication, 48, 49, 53, 127–128, 129, 133, 138, 156n6

conceptual, 4, 5, 29, 30, 41, 62, 63, 68, 88, 89, 92, 99, 100, 102–103, 104, 105, 110, 111–113, 114, 115n12–115n15, 116n16, 116n26, 124, 145, 159; pole, 33, 55n8, 103, 111, 159; reversion, 103–104, 115n14
concrescence, 16, 64, 70, 88, 89, 91, 111, 123, 124, 144, 156n7
Cone, James, 157n11
Connolly, William, 149, 150, 156n7, 157n10
consciousness, 14–15, 16, 17, 22n4, 23n15, 28–30, 32, 33, 44, 54n1, 62, 65, 93, 115n8, 124, 126, 159–160, 165, 173; stream of, 160, 166
contemplation, 101, 127, 170
contraction, 170
contradiction, 13, 48, 51, 67
Continental philosophy, 3, 159, 168–169, 176n1
cosmology, 78, 88, 89, 90, 94
cosmopolitanism, 64
creativity, 17, 20, 33, 62, 64, 89–90, 100, 131, 141; creative transformation, 41, 53
Critchley, Simon, 168
Cruz, Ted, 43, 81, 95n2

data collection, 28, 33, 35–37, 39
Debaise, Didier, 101
Deleuze, Gilles, 5–6, 61, 62, 63, 65–66, 69, 71, 74, 75n2, 92, 104, 109, 114, 116n23, 122, 123, 126, 127–129, 130, 131, 131–132, 132–133, 134n3–134n6, 134n8, 138, 139, 142, 145, 147–148, 149, 150–151, 151, 154–155, 156n6, 157n8, 169–174, 175–176, 176n1
democracy, 125, 134n5
Derrida, Jacques, 62, 168, 174
Descartes, René, 12, 14, 15, 20, 23n16. *See also* Cartesian
deterritorialization, 66, 74, 130
difference, 16, 49, 62, 64, 67, 78, 91, 94, 101, 110, 112, 113, 124, 130, 150, 151, 155, 157n8, 168, 169, 172, 173, 175
dipolar, 159
discord, 3, 70–71, 75
dislocations, 3, 4–5, 71, 74, 127
duration, 72, 148, 160, 166, 170

ecology, 64, 106; deep, 5, 12
economics, 1, 3–4, 5, 11, 18, 22n6, 33, 46, 47, 52, 62, 64, 66, 74, 82, 86–87, 131, 132
education, 37, 43, 44, 45, 133
effect mark, 107, 108–109, 110
Ellul, Jacques, 28
embedded, 43, 51, 55n5, 63, 64, 67, 68, 69, 74, 85
embodied, 63, 64, 65, 67, 68, 69, 74, 106, 141, 161
emergence, 44, 46, 62, 111, 122, 141, 143, 151, 155
emigration, 77–78, 79–80, 83, 86–87, 89
empiricism, 2, 122, 126, 127, 130, 131, 161, 173
endurance, 64, 68, 74
environment, 28–29, 29–30, 32–33, 38, 42, 43, 46, 49, 84, 105–106, 110, 113–114, 124–125, 139, 146, 164, 165; human and animal, 31–32, 67, 69, 99, 106–108, 109, 110; and sustainability, 12, 14, 55n5, 64, 176n1
epistemology, 138, 139
essence, 16, 17, 19, 65, 85, 88, 92, 127, 129, 140, 142, 145
eternal objects, 13, 30, 39, 100, 102–103, 104, 112
eternal return, 172, 175
ethical, 5, 32, 47, 55n5, 64, 71, 74, 78, 79, 83, 85–86, 86, 87, 88, 89, 90, 92, 126
European, 1–2, 3, 4, 5, 65, 129
Evans, Fred, 131
event, 4, 13–14, 29–30, 33, 35, 41, 44, 46, 47, 71, 82, 100, 101, 103, 138, 139, 141, 142, 146, 147–148, 155, 162, 164, 166, 170, 173
evil, 3, 13, 45, 72, 137, 152
experience, 2, 5–6, 13, 16, 18, 22, 27, 28, 29–30, 33, 35, 38, 41, 50, 69, 71, 88, 89, 91, 99, 100–104, 105–106, 107, 109, 110–112, 113, 114, 115n4, 115n7–115n8, 115n11–115n13, 116n16, 116n27, 121, 122, 123–124, 126, 127, 128, 139, 143, 144, 148, 151, 156n3, 157n9, 159, 159–161, 162, 163, 165, 168, 169, 170, 173–174, 174–175; past, 1, 33, 70, 88, 123, 126, 164, 166; sense, 29, 30, 100, 109, 110, 160, 161, 162–163, 163–164, 165, 174–175
extension, 28, 33, 34–35, 72, 109, 140, 151, 162, 163, 164, 166, 170

Faber, Roland, 100
Facebook, 44, 53
fact, 11, 13, 14, 16, 17, 44, 47, 115n8, 115n11, 121, 122, 162, 163–164
fake news, 52
Fairchild, Mark, 106
fascism, 131
feeling, 4, 12, 30, 66, 68, 70, 72, 88, 89, 90, 91, 99, 100, 101–102, 103, 111, 113, 115n9, 115n11, 123, 125, 127, 132, 141, 143, 144, 160, 162, 165; conceptual, 5, 29, 88, 102–103, 104, 112, 114, 115n12; conformal, 43, 53, 55n4; physical, 29, 30, 88, 102–104, 115n12, 156n1, 163
Fitbit, 30–32, 35–38, 38
fitness tracking, 31, 35, 36–37
flesh, 12, 14, 15–16, 17, 18, 20, 30
fold, 1, 74, 139, 146, 147, 148, 150, 151, 155, 157n8
force, 1, 11, 32, 35, 44, 53, 63, 65, 71, 74, 86, 91–92, 93, 96n11, 100, 103, 127, 138–139, 139, 141, 141–142, 143–144, 145–146, 147, 148, 149–151, 151, 152–153, 154, 156n6–157n8, 157n10
Ford, Lewis, 115n14
Foucault, Michel, 6, 71, 139, 140–142, 142, 143, 145, 146, 148, 149, 154, 156n1, 156n6, 157n8
Funtowicz, Silvio, 46, 48
Fury, David, 137
future, 3, 4, 5, 11, 33, 56n16, 61, 63, 70, 71–72, 74, 86, 92, 123, 124, 126, 140, 144, 160, 162, 164, 165, 166, 169–170, 171–172, 175

Gadamer, Hans Georg, 50, 53
Gaia hypothesis, 21
gambling, 27
game, 5, 27, 54n2, 63
Gasché, Rodolphe, 134n4
genealogy, 104, 125, 139, 139–141, 146
Gestell, 19, 20
Gibson, James J., 108
Ginn, Franklin, 109

Glendinning, Simon, 168
Glieck, James, 46
God, 14, 23n24, 41, 54n2, 114n2, 115n14, 140–141, 142, 146, 147, 150, 160; conceptual nature of, 41, 114n2, 115n14; primordial nature of, 42
Gramsci, Antonio, 43–44, 45, 49, 54, 54n1, 55n6, 55n8
Guattari, Felix, 6, 63, 65–66, 69, 71, 109, 114, 122, 127, 127–129, 130, 132, 134n3–134n6, 134n8, 157n8

Hall, Stewart, 50–51
Hansen, Mark, 28–31, 33
Haraway, Donna, 62, 65, 68
Hardt, Michael, 153, 156n6, 157n12
harmony, 70
health, 11, 19, 20, 22, 34–35, 35, 37
hegemony, 5, 43, 43–44, 44, 45–46, 46, 47, 48–49, 50, 51, 53, 54, 56n14–56n15
Heidegger, Martin, 14, 14–15, 18–19, 19–20, 161, 163, 168
Hegel, Georg Wilhelm Friedrich, 38
Heraclitus, 168, 175
hermeneutics, 50
Heuman, Linda, 113
history, 2, 17, 42, 74, 106, 139, 140, 156n1
Hossino, Omar, 81
Hume, David, 12, 30, 115n14, 160, 163–164

idealism, 13, 116n22, 161
image, 106, 128, 129, 172, 173
immanence, 3, 5, 72, 74, 78, 84, 85, 87, 89, 90, 91, 92, 93, 94, 127, 148, 175; doctrine of mutual, 78, 85, 88, 91, 93, 94, 159, 164; plane of, 74, 128
immigration, 80
Ineinander, 15
Infinite, 29, 100, 104, 128
interaction, 20, 49, 55n9, 56n12, 61, 106, 116n21–116n22, 138, 139, 141, 142, 145, 146, 148, 151, 170
interrelation, 2, 5, 69, 75, 88, 92
Islam, 77, 79, 80, 94

James, William, 160, 166, 170, 173

Kant, Immanuel, 2

Keller, Catherine, 157n8
knowledge, 15, 31–32, 93, 116n26, 137, 139, 140, 148, 156n1, 161, 163

language, 17, 42, 50, 51, 54, 82, 114, 121, 129, 130, 143, 151, 155, 160, 165
Latour, Bruno, 29, 55n3, 113
Lawlor, Len, 159, 168
Leclerc, Ivor, 88–89
Leibniz, G. W., 14, 100, 104, 147, 159
Levi, Primo, 132
life, 1, 14, 16, 17, 18, 20, 21, 24n28, 35, 38, 42, 56n15, 72, 73, 74–75, 79, 82, 84, 88, 89, 90, 91, 92, 96n8, 96n10–96n11, 116n19, 121, 127, 133, 138, 148, 149, 151, 154, 173; precarious, 39, 78, 83, 84, 85, 86, 90; production of, 82, 83, 91–92, 151, 156n6, 160, 174; Syrian, 77–78, 79, 81, 81–82, 83, 87, 89, 91, 93–94; value of, 78, 83, 84, 85, 87, 88, 89, 90, 93
Lightbody, Brian, 139
Locke, John, 143, 145
logos, 63, 175; *endiathetos*, 17–18, 20; *proforikos*, 17–18, 20
love, 73, 138, 152–154, 155
Lovelock, James, 21
Lowe, Victor, 90

Maduro, Otto, 157n11
materialism, 14–15, 16, 20, 62, 159
mathematics, 2, 46, 116n21, 163
Mays, Wolfe, 112, 116n18
McLuhan, Marshall, 28, 33
majority, 55n4, 80, 129–130, 134n6
Malcolm X, 155
Malik, Wajeeha, 155
Marcel, Gabriel, 21, 24n32
Marrati, Paola, 134n7
Martin, Trayvon, 155
Marx, Karl, 4, 43, 45, 50, 55n8, 62
matter, 16, 21, 147
McCumber, John, 159, 168
media, 5, 17, 28–31, 33, 35, 43, 43–44, 44, 45–46, 47, 48, 50–51, 52, 53, 54, 55n5, 79, 81, 82; theory of, 28, 29
Meillassoux, Quentin, 177
memory, 138, 164, 171–172, 175
Mengue, Philippe, 134n5

mental pole, 103, 159
mentality, 68, 78, 101, 124, 156n1, 161
mereology, 104
Merleau-Ponty, Maurice, 5, 11, 12, 12–14, 14–18, 20–21, 21, 22n2–22n3, 22n6, 23n15, 24n26, 116n23, 161
metaphysics, 2, 5, 13, 18, 20, 27, 28–29, 41, 42, 53, 55n4, 61, 68, 72, 75, 99, 100, 104, 110–111, 114, 115n9, 115n14, 116n22, 123, 140, 150, 163, 166, 168, 171, 173, 176n1
Meyer, Stephen, 134n1
microprocessors, 27, 28, 29, 32–33
mind, 14, 15, 16, 20, 29, 50, 69, 156n6, 159, 161, 162, 170
minoritarian, 130. *See also* becoming minoritarian
monad, 143, 147
morals, 11, 42, 47, 54, 78, 87, 121, 126, 146; codes of, 121; Moral Mondays, 155
Morse, Jay, 82, 95n7
Moss, Michael, 24n27
Muslim ban, 80, 82, 94–95

Naess, Arne, 12
nature, 5, 11, 11–12, 13, 14, 15, 16–17, 17–19, 19–21, 21–22, 23n12, 23n15, 23n19, 24n28, 29–30, 32, 42, 44, 56n14, 61, 64, 69, 72, 88, 89, 92, 93, 100, 101, 121, 122, 124, 129, 130, 132, 146, 148, 159, 161, 163, 169, 174; bifurcation of, 5, 6, 29, 127, 144, 159, 159–161, 169, 173, 174, 176, 176n1; *natura naturans*, 17, 18; *natura naturarata*, 17
Negri, Antonio, 153, 156n6, 157n12
neocapitalism, 66. *See also* capitalism
neoliberalism, 33, 38, 86, 91, 96n10
neo-materialism, 5, 61, 62, 73, 75
new, 1, 2–3, 3, 4–6, 12, 14, 20, 28–29, 33, 38, 39, 42, 44, 45–46, 48, 49, 51, 55n9, 56n17, 62, 68, 70, 71, 90, 100, 105, 122, 131, 145, 149, 155, 156n6, 170, 171, 176, 176n1
new materialism, 62. *See also* neo-materialism
Nietzsche, Friedrich, 99, 110, 115n8, 125, 133, 139, 140, 142, 146, 149–151, 154,
156n2, 156n7, 157n11, 175, 176n1
Nobo, Jorge Luis, 115n14
Noë, Alva, 99, 104, 112, 114, 116n26
nomadology, 66
nonhuman, 4, 5, 28, 74, 93, 94, 99, 114
norms of recognizability, 83
novelty, 3, 6, 41, 46, 48, 53, 64, 70–71, 75, 89–90, 91, 94, 100, 103, 122, 124, 130, 131, 148, 151, 157n9

objective immortality, 72, 74, 143, 156n7
objects, 13, 16, 30, 38, 39, 63, 69, 100, 102–103, 104, 110, 112, 115n11, 145, 163, 166; enduring, 69, 124; eternal (*see* eternal objects); subjects and, 63, 101, 129, 144
occasion. *See* actual occasion
Occupy Wall Street, 155
Offenheit, 15
ontology, 5–6, 12, 14, 15, 16, 18, 20, 41, 61, 62, 64, 65, 68, 75, 84, 85, 87, 87–88, 92; ontological principle, 139, 145, 156n7
opinion, 12, 44, 54n2, 122, 127, 128–130, 132, 134n4–134n5, 134n7
Oral Roberts University, 37
organism, 5, 22, 28, 48, 85, 88, 92, 99, 105–106, 108–109, 116n20, 142–143, 164, 170
origin, 52, 67, 80, 83, 95n5, 103, 140–141, 142, 143, 144, 157n9, 161, 166, 169, 170–171, 172, 173, 174, 175–176
orthodoxy, 100, 129

pain, 19, 70, 137–138, 152, 154
panpsychism, 159
paradox, 138, 166, 171, 174, 175
past, 2, 30, 33, 43, 45, 70, 72, 74, 92, 101, 125, 127, 160–161, 164, 169–172, 175; inherence of, 2–3, 4, 88, 123–124, 126, 141, 143, 164, 166, 170, 171–172; relation to, 1, 55n4, 115n3, 124, 144, 160, 162, 165, 166
pathological, 34–35
Patton, Paul, 134n5
peace, 3, 64, 74
perception, 5, 23n11, 24n26, 29–33, 38, 53, 64, 88, 100, 101, 104, 106, 109, 113, 114n1, 115n9, 129, 144, 147, 159,

159–161, 162, 163, 164, 165, 166, 169, 170, 173, 174; perception mark, 107–109, 110
perishing, 74, 78, 101, 123, 156n7, 160
perpetual, 143, 160, 170, 171
personal identity, 72
personal tracking device, 5, 27, 31, 35, 36, 37
phenomenology, 23n11, 100, 127–128, 129, 165, 170
phenomenon, 17, 27, 31, 33, 103, 109, 111, 161, 164
philosophy, 1, 3–4, 5–6, 11, 12, 12–13, 14, 15, 16, 17, 23n12, 23n15–23n16, 28, 29, 41, 62, 63, 84, 88, 90, 101, 121–122, 122, 127–129, 131, 132, 133, 134n4–134n5, 139, 142–143, 161, 163, 168, 169, 176n1; Continental, 3, 6, 159, 166–169, 169, 174, 175, 176n1; speculative, 2, 3, 4
physical pole, 159
pluralism, 48, 50, 56n15, 122, 131
political, 3, 5, 11, 18, 22n6, 45, 49, 62, 71, 75n1, 79, 82, 86–87, 91, 129, 132, 134n5, 148
politics, 5, 13, 17, 46, 49, 55n11, 83, 84, 87, 96n11
Pollan, Michael, 19
Popper, Karl, 23n7
Porter, Theodore, 33
possibility, 3, 6, 13–14, 49, 50, 52, 53, 100–101, 109, 121, 124, 140, 148, 150–151, 151
posthuman, 62, 68, 90, 91, 93, 94, 96n12–96n13
Postman, Neil, 45, 48
postmodern, 2
poststructuralist, 2, 67
potential, 19, 37, 39, 41, 71, 74, 89, 100, 102, 103, 108, 115n11, 127, 137, 156n6
power, 6, 13, 42, 43, 45, 47, 53, 56n20, 62, 79, 82, 83, 84, 92, 93, 94, 96n11, 137, 138–139, 139–140, 141–142, 142–146, 148–149, 149, 150–152, 152–154, 154, 155, 156n6, 157n11, 160; relations of, 62; use of,
precarity, 78, 83, 84, 84–85, 85–86, 86–87, 89, 90, 94, 138, 154
predicates, 90, 144, 156n2, 159, 175

prehension, 30, 64, 68, 69–70, 88, 89, 91, 94, 101–102, 104, 115n8–115n9, 123, 144, 147, 148, 150, 173; conceptual, 5, 68, 99, 102, 104, 112, 113, 115n15
present, 2, 6, 35, 53, 55n4, 70, 72, 74, 88, 89, 90, 92, 94, 114n2, 116n16, 131, 142, 144, 160–161, 162–163, 164, 165–166, 168–169, 169, 170–172, 176, 176n1; living, 170–172, 175; specious, 166, 170, 174–175
presentational immediacy, 29, 30, 32–33, 53, 160, 162–164, 165
private, 55n5, 137, 148, 161, 164
process, 15, 18, 20, 21, 23n7, 29–30, 32–33, 35, 41, 50, 56n15, 68, 70–71, 71–72, 74, 88, 89, 90, 91, 100–102, 103–104, 106, 110–112, 113, 115n14–115n15, 116n18, 116n22, 126, 130, 131, 132, 138, 139, 141, 143–144, 146, 150–151, 154–155, 160–161, 163, 165, 170, 171; of becoming, 66, 67, 68, 91, 124, 145, 173; ontology, 5–6, 61, 62, 64, 67, 68, 75; philosophy, 2, 3, 20, 41, 65, 139, 159, 168, 169, 175
progress, 13–14, 18, 23n7, 42, 44, 61, 74
public, 12, 37, 41, 43, 44, 45, 47–48, 50, 55n5, 79, 96n10, 133, 148
pure potentials, 100
pure succession, 164, 170–171

quantified self, 5, 27, 31–33, 35

rationality, 50, 82, 126
Ravetz, J.R., 46, 48
reality, 2, 15, 17, 29, 33, 39, 53, 62, 64, 65, 67, 69, 90, 93, 105, 110–112, 115n10, 115n14, 122, 123, 126, 127, 128, 130, 131, 143, 148, 164, 166, 173
reflection, 23n15, 127, 132, 134n5, 159, 166, 176n1
refugees, 5, 77, 78–79, 79–80, 80–81, 81–82, 83, 84, 86, 87, 90, 94–95, 95n2–95n4, 155
relationality, 85, 88, 93, 138, 139
repetition, 3, 70, 75n1, 100, 160, 169, 172, 175
reterritorialization, 66, 130
Reynolds, Jack, 159, 169

Index

Ricoeur, Paul, 5, 49, 50, 52–53, 53, 54, 55n3, 56n18
Robinson, John, 27
Rousseau, Jean-Jacques, 125

Santayana, George, 160, 164
satisfaction, 71–72, 101, 103, 109, 123, 144, 156n7
Schelling, F. W. J., 14–15, 16–17, 20, 21, 23n12, 23n15, 23n24, 24n28, 24n31–24n32
Schmidt, Samantha, 155
Schül, Natasha Dow, 5, 27, 30, 32, 33, 38
Sehgal, Melanie, 115n9
self-creation, 123–124
semiotics, 105, 109, 110, 114, 116n24
sense, 22n6, 29, 30, 32, 38, 100, 109, 110, 160, 161, 162, 163–164, 165, 174–175
sense data, 33, 160, 162–163, 165
sexuality, 55n11, 83, 85, 91, 141
Shaviro, Steven, 4, 101, 103, 115n5–115n7, 115n14, 123
Sheldrake, Rupert, 21
Sherburne, Donald, 102, 103
simple location, 16, 160
singular, 34, 46, 64, 92, 100, 102, 115n12, 138, 143, 148, 149, 151, 155
social, 5, 18, 33, 35, 37, 41, 44, 48, 51, 52, 54, 54n1, 55n6, 62, 68, 69, 74, 81, 84, 85, 86, 87, 121, 125, 130, 156n6; issues, 1, 48
society (of actual occasions), 68–69
solipsism, 116n22, 160, 164
soul, 12, 21, 24n31, 68
sovereignty, 78, 79, 87, 140, 141, 146
Spinoza, Baruch, 17, 23n16, 92
Stengers, Isabelle, 103, 104, 115n14, 125
Stewart, Jon, 48
Stoics, 17
subjective aim, 88, 123, 151, 156n3
subjectivity, 5, 29, 33, 62, 63–64, 68–69, 70, 72, 73, 78, 87, 88, 90, 91, 92, 101, 103, 142, 143, 145, 151, 155, 156n4, 157n10, 165; nomadic, 61, 63–64, 65, 67, 68, 70–71, 73, 75, 91; non-unitary, 63
subjects, 4, 5, 16, 34, 62, 63, 64, 65, 67, 68, 69, 74, 85, 88, 92–93, 94, 96n10, 99, 100, 103, 109, 110, 114, 115n12, 129, 144, 156n6
substance, 15, 16, 23n16, 41, 68, 88, 90, 139–140, 141, 142–143, 144, 145–146, 159, 168
subversion, 48, 50–51, 52, 53, 54, 64, 71, 73, 74, 75, 75n1
suffering, 51, 82, 85, 95n2, 127, 132, 157n11, 169
sustainable, 1, 3, 4, 5, 61, 62, 63–64, 67, 68, 73, 74, 83, 90; civilization, 4, 6, 61, 64, 67, 72, 73, 75
symbolic reference, 30, 32, 53, 160, 162, 165, 166, 174
symbolism, 30, 42, 43, 44, 49, 50, 51, 53, 161, 165, 172, 173, 174–175
synchronization, 71, 73
Syria, 77, 80, 81; See also refugees, Syrian
Syrian-American Council, 81
systems, 3, 5, 41, 42, 46, 47–49, 55n5, 55n11, 56n14, 56n16, 62, 64, 67, 71, 74, 75, 93, 110, 141, 156n6, 175; complex adaptive, 42, 46, 47, 50, 56n14

technology, 4, 5, 14, 18, 19, 21, 27, 29–32, 33, 35, 36, 38, 48, 63, 91, 92; wearable, 5, 28, 30, 36, 37, 38
temporality, 159, 160, 168, 176n1. *See also* time
time, 6, 16, 32, 33, 36, 44, 48, 56n13, 65, 69, 71, 88, 92, 149, 159, 160, 162, 164, 166, 168–169, 169–171, 172–174, 174–176, 176n1
transcendence, 55n8, 72, 74, 84, 123, 128–129, 130
transcendental, 101, 109, 110–111, 115n7, 138
transmutation, 104, 111, 116n18, 116n25
Trump, Donald, 52, 77, 80, 81, 94, 95n2, 95n4; administration, 82, 96n10
truth, 13, 14, 17, 64, 67, 74, 134n4, 140, 146, 155

Umwelt, 105–106, 109, 110–112, 114, 116n20
UN Refugee Agency, 77
United States, 13, 79–80
universals, 122, 127

vagueness, 49–50, 50, 52, 53, 54

Valenza, Robert J., 15
value, 13, 14, 20, 22n6, 27, 33, 42, 43, 72, 78, 82, 84, 87–88, 89–90, 91, 94, 96n10, 103, 125, 127, 139, 141, 146, 163, 166, 175
Varela, Francisco, 106, 116n21–116n22
vector, 46, 142, 148, 156n7, 165, 170
violence, 56n20, 77, 79, 81–82, 83, 141, 145, 176n1
Virilio, Paul, 28
von Uexküll, Jakob, 5, 99, 104, 105–109, 110–111, 114, 116n19–116n20, 116n24
Voss, Daniela, 104
vulnerability, 78, 79, 84, 85–86, 86, 94–95, 138

Wilson, E. O., 21
Wirth, Jason, 12, 14, 19, 20, 21, 23n12, 23n15, 23n24, 24n28–24n29
Wolfe, Cary, 106
Wood, David, 176n1
Wordsworth, William, 20
World Economic Forum, 77
World Vision, 81

Zarathustra, 140
Zeno, 166, 173, 175
zoe, 72, 78, 90, 91–92, 93, 94, 94–95

About the Editor

Jeremy D. Fackenthal is a teacher, non-profit director, and filmmaker living in San Diego, California. He holds a PhD in Philosophy of Religion and Theology from Claremont Graduate University. Jeremy currently works as managing director for the Institute for Ecological Civilization and serves as adjunct faculty in the humanities for Vincennes University. Jeremy researches and writes in the areas of process thought, theopoetics, and critical theory. He co-edited *Theopoetic Folds: Philosophizing Multifariousness* (2012) and has directed a short documentary on spoken word art as communal transformation.

About the Contributors

Carl Dyke teaches modern European history, world history, and sociological theory at Methodist University. His research interests include identity formation, and the history and theory of societies as complex adaptive systems. He also owns a farm with his wife and a bank, and spends a lot of time around pigs, goats, ducks, guinea fowl, other country folks, and heritage breed chickens.

Bo Eberle is a PhD candidate at UNC Chapel Hill studying religion and culture and holds a Masters of Divinity from Union Theological Seminary in the City of New York. Bo's research interests lie in philosophy of religion, science and technology studies, and critical theory. His dissertation project examines how Christian confessional practice implicitly influences forms of wearable technologies and big data collection and the political economic and biopolitical consequences of these phenomena.

William S. Hamrick is Professor Emeritus of Philosophy at Southern Illinois University Edwardsville. He earned doctorates in philosophy from Vanderbilt University (1971) and the Katholieke Universiteit Leuven (2008). He is the author of more than two dozen articles in philosophy journals and papers presented to national and international philosophy meetings in Australia, Canada, Europe, and the United States. He also published *An Existential Phenomenology of Law: Maurice Merleau-Ponty* (1987); *Kindness and the Good Society: Connections of the Heart* (2002); and *Nature and Logos, A Whiteheadian Key to Merleau-Ponty's Fundamental Thought* (2011), written with Jan Van der Veken. He is a contributor to and the co-editor with Suzanne L. Cataldi of *Merleau-Ponty and Ecology: Dwelling on the Land-*

scapes of Thought (2007) and, with Duane D. Davis, *Merleau-Ponty and the Art of Perception* (2016).

J. R. Hustwit is associate professor of philosophy and of religion at Methodist University in Fayetteville, NC. He earned his PhD (Religion) from Claremont Graduate University in 2007. His area of specialization is philosophical theology. His academic interests include transreligious theology, East and South Asian religions, philosophical hermeneutics, and process philosophy. He is the author of *Interreligious Hermeneutics and the Pursuit of Truth* (Lexington Books, 2014).

Kris Klotz is a PhD candidate in philosophy at Pennsylvania State University. His areas of specialization include social and political philosophy, critical theory, and continental philosophy. He is currently completing his dissertation, which develops a conception of reasonableness that can adequately respond to agonistic critiques of proponents of this concept.

Deena M. Lin is a lecturer in philosophy at California State University, East Bay and San Francisco State University, where she teaches courses in comparative religion and philosophy. She received her PhD in Philosophy of Religion and Theology from Claremont Graduate University in 2013. Her research interests are in philosophical theology, poststructuralist thought, mystical theology and identity politics.

Tano Posteraro is a PhD Candidate in the Department of Philosophy at Penn State University and Research Fellow at the Rock Ethics Institute. His current project involves the reconstruction of Henri Bergson's philosophy of evolution in order to update it for contemporary concerns. In addition to co-editing *Deleuze and Evolutionary Theory*, he has also published a number of articles on biological themes in Continental philosophy.

Elijah Prewitt-Davis received his PhD from Drew University in Theological and Philosophical Studies in Religion. He is currently a visiting assistant professor of theology at Xavier University. His research focuses on modern and contemporary Continental philosophy of religion. The working title of his current manuscript is "Of the World: The Immanent Faith of Gilles Deleuze."

Keith Robinson is professor of philosophy at The University of Arkansas at Little Rock. He has published widely on Continental philosophy and process philosophy. His most recent publication is "Becoming and Continuity in Bergson, Whitehead and Zeno," in *Bergson Live*, ed. F. Buongiorno, R.

Ronchi, and C. Zanfi (http://www.losguardo.net/en/homepage-english/), 26, 2018.

www.ingramcontent.com/pod-product-compliance
Lightning Source LLC
Chambersburg PA
CBHW050907300426
44111CB00010B/1413